Cultural Competency in Health, Social, and Human Services

Garland Reference Library of Social Science
Volume 1085

Cultural Competency in Health, Social, and Human Services

Directions for the Twenty-First Century

Pedro J. Lecca
Ivan Quervalú
João V. Nunes
Hector F. Gonzales

Garland Publishing, Inc.
A member of the Taylor & Francis Group
New York & London
1998

Library of Congress Cataloging-in-Publication Data

Cultural competency in health, social, and human services / Pedro
    J. Lecca, Ivan Quervalú, João V. Nunes, and Hector F. Gonzales.
            p.   cm. — (Garland reference library of social
    science ; vol. 1085)
        Includes bibliographical references and index.
        ISBN 0-8153-2205-4 (hardcover) (alk. paper)
        ISBN 0-8153-2206-2 (paperback)

CIP information is available.

Printed on acid-free, 250-year-life paper
Manufactured in the United States of America

To our patients from all cultural groups who are the final consumers of the culturally competent services that will add to the quality of care for all population groups.

CONTENTS

PART II
Organizational Issues

CHAPTER 9

Cultural Competency and Human Resources 219

PART III
Policy Imperatives

CHAPTER 10

Future Policy Directions for Cultural Competency 247

CHAPTER 11

Twenty-First–Century Perspectives on Cultural Competency 269

CHAPTER 12

Conclusion 283

PREFACE

Cultural competency is an issue that continues to become more important as thousands of people come to this country each year. Health professionals in all areas are finding it difficult to communicate effectively with the various racial and ethnic groups coming to their offices and clinics for help.

For several years many practitioners, professionals, and students have been calling for more information to facilitate a knowledge base about the many new and diverse groups of clients that come to them.

The authors have attempted to provide the reader with essential information about these groups, so that important assessments can be made about the diagnosis and treatment modalities to be utilized.

We have divided the book into three parts to provide the reader with a comprehensive insight on cultural competency at different levels of concern and with directions for the future. Part I provides the rationale for the provision of culturally relevant services, including the inherent biases of western health practices. The authors have also provided an overview of some sociodemographic indicators impinging on health, mental health, and social services. Part II focuses on organizational issues to illustrate the many dimensions of which health providers of the minority elderly need to be cognizant in order to improve service delivery in a culturally competent manner.

This section also discusses the importance of social values within an organizational context and how leadership plays a role in dealing with cultural competency. The final chapters in Part III present the future policy directions that cultural competency should take and their impact on our service system today. A perspective into the twenty-first century is presented, with recommendations.

ACKNOWLEDGMENTS

The authors would like to thank the many colleagues who have given their help in the development of this book.

PART I
Cultural Competency Framework

CHAPTER 1

Cultural Competency Services for Multicultural Populations

The health, social, and human service practitioners of today are no longer faced with patients of only one culture, but also with patients who are of different cultural backgrounds with different needs. Historically, many practitioners from a wide range of disciplines lack knowledge of the diverse backgrounds of their patients, thus fostering a gap in their ability to assist such a diverse group of patients. Practitioners are finally coming to the realization that they lack the training and knowledge to assist and understand diverse population patients.

The 1990 U.S. Census revealed some major demographic changes. By the year 2000 it is estimated that one third of the population will consist of racial and ethnic minorities. It is also predicted that in some states the minorities will outnumber the "majority" population. Not only is there an apparent shift in demographics, but there is also a shift in paradigms. Some scholars have argued that the assimilation paradigm and the melting pot ideology have not been manifested in American society; instead, one can observe the essence of a cultural pluralistic or bicultural society (Gonzales, 1993; Isaacs & Benjamin, 1991; Sue & Sue, 1990). Some writers define biculturalism as an "ethnic group maintaining the values, beliefs, and customs of their own culture, while adopting some of the traits of the host culture, such as language, dress, and food" (Sue & Sue, 1990, p. 21). Due to the changing demographics and shifting paradigms it is becoming crucial that practitioners, agencies, and institutions become more culturally competent so that they can meet the needs of the increasing minority population.

Cultural competency is defined as "a set of congruent behaviors, attitudes, and policies that come together in a system, agency, or profession that enables that system, agency, or profession to work effectively in cross-cultural situations" (Chung, 1992). To understand the importance of cultural competency one must begin to examine the inherent biases in western mental health practices. Some scholars have pointed out that western psychiatry is drawn from a "white middle-class" perspective (Marsella, 1993; Proctor & Davis, 1994; Robinson, 1993; Solomon, 1992; Sue & Sue, 1990; Torrey, 1972). Since each culture is unique in its ideologies, values, and attitudes, such a strict white middle-class form of treatment would not effectively assist the diverse ethnic populations in America. Torrey (1972) has coined the term "psychiatric imperialism," which refers to practitioners who impose their cultural mental health services on groups that are culturally different from that of the practitioner.

Furthermore, some scholars believe that psychiatric values are based on "verbal expressiveness," "openness," and a certain degree of "psychological mindedness." In a study by Isaacs and Benjamin (1991) in which they compared the values of Anglo-Americans with those of other ethnocultural groups, they found that other cultures valued stronger familial bonds and more restrained modes of expression, unlike Anglo-Americans who valued openness, directness, and individuality. If practitioners treated such ethnic groups with the same psychiatric values as those of Anglo-Americans, inaccurate diagnosis, assessment, and treatment would be inevitable (Sue & Sue, 1990). Researchers have used the term "culturally encapsulated" when referring to therapists who stereotype ethnic minority groups rather than taking into account their cultural differences (Mokuaa & Matucka, 1992). By culturally encapsulating their patients, therapists tend to categorize any differences they do view during therapy as a form of resistance by the patients. Hence, the patients do not receive adequate counseling from their therapists, and many issues about their own culture and identities are left unresolved.

The results from such therapy on the diverse ethnic minority groups are very evident. Individuals from minority cultures have been more reluctant to seek mental health services than Anglo-Americans (Sue et al., 1977). Additionally, almost half of the minority patients who do seek therapy do not return after their first session. Furthermore, early terminations of therapy by the minority patients are common due to "a series of frustrations, misunderstandings, distortions, and defensive reactions [caused by] language problems, role ambiguities, misinterpretations of behavior, and differences in priorities of treatment" (Dana, 1993, p. 2).

In order to eradicate bias and stereotypes that practitioners may hold in respect to ethnic or racial minorities, Proctor and Davis (1994) state that culturally competent practitioners need to possess three characteristics. First, the practitioner needs to be aware of his or her own beliefs and attitudes about racial and ethnic minorities in order not to impose these feelings on his or her patient. Second, practitioners need to understand and be aware of the world views of the patient without judging them. The practitioner also needs to be aware of how race, culture, and ethnicity affects personality and personal choices, as well as life experiences. Third, the practitioners must be able to use culturally competent skills when interacting with a racially or ethnically minority patient.

Proctor and Davis's (1994) ideas on how to create a culturally competent therapist is quite similar to those of another author who conducted his study two decades earlier. Felix Biestek (1970) cited seven elements, rather than three, which would enhance the practitioner-patient relationship when cultural diversity plays a factor. The seven elements are individualization, purposeful expression of feelings, controlled emotional involvement, acceptance, nonjudgmental attitude, patient's self-determination, and confidentiality.

By individualization, Biestek means that the therapist must consider the patient's unique culture and adjust the therapy to fit the qualities and needs of that culture. Language, for instance, is a huge barrier that therapists must overcome with many of their minority patients. The proper use of translators is one of the most effective methods to overcome such barriers (Marsella, 1993). Furthermore, in some cultures, the family is an important part of an individual's identity (Sue & Sue, 1990). Therefore, utilizing family therapy as well as individual therapy in many cases is a more effective form of treatment for minority patients (Ross-Sheriff, 1992).

The purposeful expression of feelings is also an important element of therapy. This involves:

> . . . the recognition of the [patient's] needs to express his feelings freely, especially his negative feelings. The [therapist] listens purposefully, neither discouraging nor condemning the expression of these feelings, sometimes even actively stimulating and encouraging them when therapeutically useful. (Biestek, 1970)

Another example of the use of individualization by a therapist is the evaluation of body language. Because many cultures value discretion of expression rather than openness, nonverbal communication can also be noted by the therapist, as emotions which the patient is sometimes reluctant to express verbally may be evident in the patient's physical posture and expressions (Marsella, 1993).

Biestek's third element is that of controlled emotional involvements: that is, the practitioner should understand the minority individual but remain objective during therapy. Understanding the patient means that the communications between therapist and patient are clear and comprehensive: If need be, translators are utilized to ensure comprehensibility of the communication. Furthermore, therapists must be careful not to stereotype or overgeneralize similarities between minority groups, nor should they overidentify with their patients. Instead, the goal should be to work toward a level in which they can maintain both distance and closeness with the patient (Dean, 1979).

Acceptance is the fourth element in Biestek's list. The therapist's approach is one that accepts the patient and welcomes the patient's values, putting aside any stereotypes he or she may have about the particular patient. Along with this acceptance comes another element, a nonjudgmental attitude. Therapists must be careful not to assign guilt to a patient for his behavior (Dean, 1979). For example, in some cultures faith healers are thought to be very important (McQuaide, 1989). When treating individuals with such beliefs, practitioners need to recognize the importance of the faith healer to that person and try to evaluate the "healer's" role and meaning in the patient's life (Dean, 1979).

Patient self-determination is the sixth element in Biestek's list. Patient self-determination means that therapists respect the rights of the patient and allow him or her the freedom to make some of the decisions in the treatment process. In other words, the establishment of goals and the treatment plan should be performed together; otherwise unnecessary problems may arise. One such way to prevent problems between the patient and therapist is also Biestek's final element—confidentiality. Mental health professionals need to realize that minority patients may be uncomfortable discussing their problems. Therefore "the sense of betrayal is especially acute [for them] when information privately shared with one professional is known by many" (Dean, 1979). Such a betrayal could destroy the patient's trust in the therapist and make him reluctant to proceed with treatment.

Regardless of whether therapists follow the Proctor and Davis (1994) characteristics or the elements outlined by Biestek (1970), one thing is clear—practitioners need to build cultural competency within themselves. They need to learn about other cultures and to be able to empathize with their patients. Therapists should not be afraid to ask questions of the patient pertaining to the patient's own culture. The patient's own self-identification and self-description are sometimes the most important clinical data for the therapist (McGill, 1992). By asking questions the therapist acknowledges differences between the two cultures and helps to establish a middle ground (McGill, 1983).

Current literature stresses the importance of cultural competency, urging practitioners to utilize skills and knowledge that are culturally competent in order to prevent the underutilization and premature termination of services by minority individuals. If practitioners do not incorporate culturally competent skills and knowledge in their assessment, diagnosis, and treatment, many minority patients will fall victim to the "culturally encapsulated" practitioner.

Such encapsulating by the practitioner may even lead to misdiagnosis of the problem. For example, due to the racism many African Americans have encountered, they sometimes react in a manner commonly diagnosed as paranoia. Sue and Sue (1990) state that an African American's paranoia can be categorized as either cultural or functional. A culturally paranoid individual is someone who is distrustful of other cultures. These individuals are usually culturally paranoid due to their lack of interaction with other cultures or to the negative reactions they have received from individuals of different cultures (Sue & Sue, 1990). The second type of paranoia, functional paranoia, characterizes an individual who is distrustful of all individuals regardless of race. Both types of paranoia can be the direct result of racism for African Americans. However, both types of paranoia have often been misdiagnosed as schizophrenia by practitioners who have not considered the cause of the reactions (Sue & Sue, 1990). Therefore, in order to prevent such a mistake, practitioners may first need to acknowledge that the paranoia can be due to racism and then make a diagnosis (Sue & Sue, 1990). By understanding this basic concept the practitioner avoids misdiagnosing and encapsulating their African-American patients.

The importance of cultural competency cannot be overstated. The significant increase among minority populations has had, and will continue to have, an impact upon the workforce in the United States. During the 1990s, 75 percent of those entering the labor force were ethnic minorities and women. It is predicted that by the twenty-first century, whites will acquire minority status within certain states in the United States (Van Den Bergh, 1991), reducing the percentage of white American entrants into the labor force from 83 percent in 1985 to 58 percent by the year 2000 (Jackson, 1992).

Wright, Saleebey, Watts, and Lecca (1983) also indicate that many social programs fail to meet the needs and help solve the problems of ethnic

minorities because of ignorance of the reality and depth of culture difference. The programs are often designed with the dominant culture as the
primary clientele. Without the utilization of a cultural competency approach when examining the community and reassessing agency policies,
Asian Americans, African Americans, and Hispanic/Latinos will be overlooked.

Techniques and theories such as Total Quality Management and
Theory Y can also aid administrators in their development of culturally
competent organizations. Total Quality Management (TQM) has recently
been implemented in human service organizations and, like cultural
competent concepts, it emphasizes self-improvement, learning, and a
flexible, innovative management style and technique. In addition, it relies
on teamwork and cooperation. TQM stresses that if a human service organization fails, 85 percent of the failure is due to the system; it is the responsibility of management to create an organizational structure of quality. To accomplish this objective, management must be committed to
quality, empowerment, team building, training, and a long-term perspective. Total Quality Management complies with Theory Y, which assumes
that people are worthy, competent, honest, and can do a good job
(Weinbach & Dickerson, 1995). Brocka and Brocka (1992) maintain that
the TQM manager stresses the empowerment and involvement of all employees in both individual and group decision making.

Cultural competence is based on valuing differences and the belief
that differences are acceptable. Systems, agencies, and professionals do
not start as culturally competent entities: they develop through training,
experience, guidance, and self-evaluation (Isaacs & Benjamin, 1991). As
health and social service agencies enter into the twenty-first century, they
must change attitudes, initiate policies, and open up options to the vast
majority of individuals of ethnic origin who will be part of their future
workforce and clientele (Cross et al., 1989; Seck et al., 1993).

The Four Major Multicultural Populations in the United States

Background

There is no doubt that the ethnic profile of the United States has changed
over the last several decades. Census data have revealed these changes

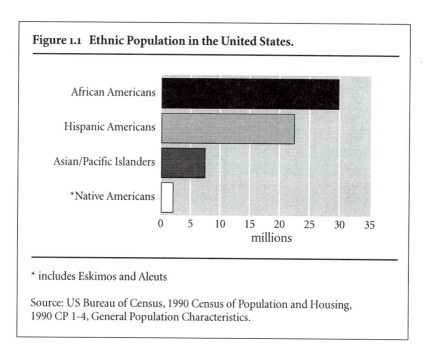

Figure 1.1 Ethnic Population in the United States.

* includes Eskimos and Aleuts

Source: US Bureau of Census, 1990 Census of Population and Housing, 1990 CP 1-4, General Population Characteristics.

particularly in immigration and migration patterns, and overall changes in ethnic group population characteristics. The Hispanic/Latino and Asian/Pacific Islander populations have been increasing more rapidly than the total U.S. population. Between 1980 and 1992 the Hispanic/Latino population doubled (National Center for Health Statistics, 1995).

Figure 1.1 presents the 1990 Bureau of Census statistics according to racial background. It shows that there are 29,986,060 blacks, 22,354,059 persons of Hispanic/Latino origin, 7,273,662 Asian and Pacific Islanders, and 1,959,234 Americans Indians (including Eskimos and Aleuts). According to the census data almost 10 million people refused to describe themselves as white, black, Asian, or American Indian and opted to check "other race" (Aponte & Crouch, 1995); the majority of these are of Hispanic origin, based on the ethnicity question (Betancourt, 1996). Of the U.S. population of 248,709,873, 25.1 percent is of the major ethnic groups described above.

Figure 1.2 presents the percentages of each group compared to the total population. It shows that African Americans comprise 12.3 percent of the U.S. population, followed by Hispanic/Latino Americans, 9 percent; Asian/Pacific Islanders, 3 percent; and Native Americans (including Eskimos and Aleuts) with .8 percent.

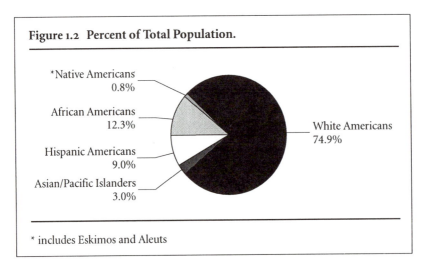

Figure 1.2 Percent of Total Population.

*Native Americans
0.8%

African Americans
12.3%

Hispanic Americans
9.0%

Asian/Pacific Islanders
3.0%

White Americans
74.9%

* includes Eskimos and Aleuts

Figure 1.3 presents the breakdown of Hispanic/Latino variations in the United States. Those of Mexican ancestry account for 61.4 percent of Hispanic Americans, followed by Puerto Ricans, 12.9 percent; Central and South Americans, 11.9 percent; Cubans, 5 percent. Other Hispanics/Latinos account for 8.9 percent (U.S. Bureau of the Census, 1990a). The majority of the Hispanics/Latinos, 67 percent, were born in the United States and are heavily concentrated in the four states of California, Texas, New York, and Florida, with most of the population living in urban areas

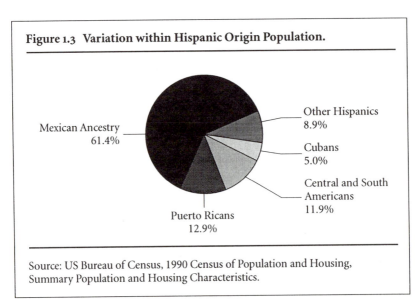

Figure 1.3 Variation within Hispanic Origin Population.

Mexican Ancestry
61.4%

Other Hispanics
8.9%

Cubans
5.0%

Central and South
Americans
11.9%

Puerto Ricans
12.9%

Source: US Bureau of Census, 1990 Census of Population and Housing, Summary Population and Housing Characteristics.

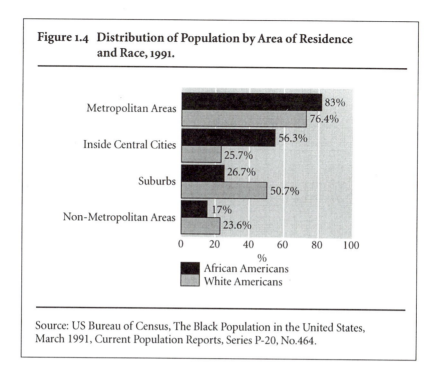

Figure 1.4   Distribution of Population by Area of Residence and Race, 1991.

Source: US Bureau of Census, The Black Population in the United States, March 1991, Current Population Reports, Series P-20, No.464.

(U.S. Dept. of Health and Human Services, 1993). The majority of African Americans, 83 percent, live in metropolitan areas, with 56.3 percent living inside central areas within the metropolitan areas and 26.7 percent living in the suburbs.

Figure 1.4 presents the distribution of black and white Americans by areas of residence for 1991. It shows an inverse relationship for place of residency (inside central area versus suburbs) between black and white Americans.

Figure 1.5 presents the breakdown of Asian Americans and Pacific Islanders in the United States: 23.8 percent are of Chinese origin, followed by Filipinos, 20.4 percent; Japanese, 12.3 percent; Asian Indians, 11.8 percent; Koreans, 11.6 percent; Vietnamese, 8.9 percent, and other Asian Americans, 11.2 percent (U.S. Bureau of the Census, 1990a). In the United States it is estimated that there are thirty or more different Asian ethnic groups (Chan, 1994).

Immigration accounted for almost half of the Hispanic/Latino and nearly three quarters of the Asian American growth in the United States during the last three decades (Passel & Edmonston, 1992). Table 1.1 pre-

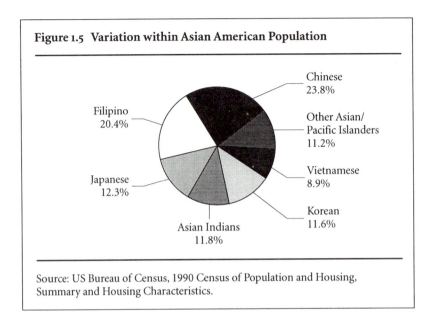

Figure 1.5 Variation within Asian American Population

Chinese
23.8%

Filipino
20.4%

Other Asian/
Pacific Islanders
11.2%

Japanese
12.3%

Vietnamese
8.9%

Korean
11.6%

Asian Indians
11.8%

Source: US Bureau of Census, 1990 Census of Population and Housing, Summary and Housing Characteristics.

sents immigration figures from 1984 to 1989 by selected country of birth and selected metropolitan cities within the United States.

Table 1.1 shows that within the United States, New York is the city with the most immigrants between 1984 and 1989, 566,299; followed by Los Angeles, 400,896; Miami, 136,580; Chicago, 133,406; and Washington, 103,785.

Table 1.2 presents the number of Native American populations for the top ten states as broken down by the Bureau of the Census. The Native American population comprises an estimated 400 tribal nations, speaking about 200 languages or dialects. Approximately 55 percent of Native Americans reside in urban areas, while the remainder live on reservations throughout the United States. Twenty-two percent of the American Indians/Eskimos and Aleuts live on 314 reservations and trust lands (Patterson, 1996).

Sociodemographics

Table 1.3 presents basic sociodemographics for the major ethnic minority populations in the United States. It shows that Hispanic/Latino Americans are the youngest of all the groups, with a median age of 26. They are

TABLE 1.1

Immigrants by Top Five Source Countries (Country of Birth) for United States and Selected U.S. Metropolitan Cities*

United States		New York		Los Angeles	
All Immigrants	3,572,271	All Immigrants	566,299	All Immigrants	400,896
Top 5 Source Countries	38.5%	*Top 5 Source Countries*	50.2%	*Top 5 Source Countries*	57.9%
Mexico	419,002	Dominican Republic	93,567	Mexico	92,796
Philippines	293,810	Jamaica	59,352	Philippines	43,313
China	267,741	China	56,108	China	37,310
Korea	206,841	Guyana	40,893	Korea	31,786
Vietnam	186,716	Haiti	34,606	Iran	27,026

Miami		Chicago		Washington	
All Immigrants	136,580	All Immigrants	133,406	All Immigrants	103,785
Top 5 Source Countries	74.4%	*Top 5 Source Countries*	56.1%	*Top 5 Source Countries*	36.2%
Cuba	63,697	Mexico	25,222	Korea	10,219
Haiti	18,888	India	14,971	El Salvador	7,582
Jamaica	7,837	Philippines	13,833	China	6,715
Colombia	7,242	Poland	12,599	Vietnam	6,714
Nicaragua	4,000	Korea	8,209	India	6,334

Boston	
All Immigrants	69,915
Top 5 Source Countries	37.5%
China	7,456
Haiti	5,367
Vietnam	5,081
Cambodia	4,063
Dominican Republic	3,891

*For 1984–1989. U.S. Immigration and Naturalization Service (unpublished).

TABLE 1.2

Number of Native Americans in Top Ten States in the United States

State	Numbers
Oklahoma	252,420
California	242,164
Arizona	203,527
New Mexico	134,355
Alaska	85,698
Washington	81,483
North Carolina	80,155
Texas	65,877
New York	62,651
Michigan	55,638

followed by Native Americans, with a median age of 26.3; Asian/Pacific Islanders, 29.9; and African Americans, 28.4 years. All of the ethnic minority groups are younger than white Americans, who have a median age of 34.4 years. White Americans have the lowest household size in terms of persons per household, with 2.5 persons. Hispanic/Latino Americans have the highest number of persons per household, with 3.6, followed by Asian/Pacific Islanders, 3.4; Native Americans, 3.1; and African Americans, with 2.9 persons per household. In terms of households headed by females, African Americans have the highest percentage, 47 percent, followed by Native Americans, with 28.7 percent.

Asian/Pacific Islanders, with 10.1 percent, have the lowest number of female headed households. Table 1.3 also shows that 82.6 percent of African Americans aged 25–29 attained a high school diploma or more, while Hispanics/Latinos lagged behind with only 60.8 percent. White Americans attained a high school diploma or more at the rate of 87.2 percent. However, this figure does not reflect the number of high school dropouts, which is quite high among Puerto Ricans and other Hispanics/Latinos in general (O'Hare, 1992). The mean per capita income for white Americans is $15,687, followed by Asian Americans with $13,638. Native Americans have the lowest per capita income of all the groups, $8,328, followed very closely by Hispanic/Latino Americans with $8,400 and African Americans with $8,859. African Americans have the highest percentage of persons and families below the poverty line, with 31.9 percent, followed by Native Americans with 30.9 percent and Hispanic/Latino Americans with 28.1

TABLE 1.3

Sociodemographics of the Major Ethnic Groups in the United States

	African Americans	Hispanic/Latino Americans	Asian/ Pacific Americans	Native Americans	White Americans
[1]Median Age	28.4	26.0	29.9	26.3	34.4
[2]Household Size (Persons Per Household)	2.9	3.6	3.4	3.1	2.5
[3]Percentage of Households Headed by Females	47	22.2	10.1	28.7	14.0
[4]Percentage of People with High School Diploma (or More) for Ages 25–29	82.6	60.8	—	—	87.2
[5]Mean Per Capita Income	$8,859	$8,400	$13,638	$8,328	$15,687
[6]Percentage Below Poverty	31.9	28.1[6]	14.1[7,8]	30.9[7,8]	10.7
Percentage of Persons under 18 Years Old	44.2	37.7[6]	17.1[7,8]	38.8[7,8]	15.1
[9]Percentage of Low Birth Weight (Live Births) by Race of Mother	13.3	6.1[10]	6.6[11]	6.2	5.8
[12]Percentage of Very Low	2.96	1.04[13]	.91	.95	.96

(continued on next page)

Table 3 (*Continued*) Sociodemographics of the Major Ethnic Groups in the United States

	African Americans	Hispanic/Latino Americans	Asian/ Pacific Americans	Native Americans	White Americans
Birth Weight (Live Births) by Race of Mother					
[14]Percentage of Mothers under 18 Years Old (Live Births) by Race	10.3	7.1[15]	2.0[16]	8.0	3.9
[17]Percentage of Unmarried Mothers (Live Births) by Race	68.1	39.1[18]	14.7[19]	55.3	22.6
[20]Infant Mortality Rate (Deaths) per 1,000 Live Births from Mothers with Less than 12 Years Education	20.7	10.6[21]	9.1	16.2	12.5
[22]Male Life Expectancy	65.0	NA	NA	NA	73.2
[22]Female Life Expectancy	73.9	NA	NA	NA	79.8
Both Sexes	69.6	NA	NA	NA	76.5

1. U.S. Bureau of the Census (1992). 1990 Census of Population, CP 1–4, General population characteristics. Washington, DC: U.S. Government Printing Office.

2. O'Hare, W.P. (1992). America's minorities—The demographics of diversity. *Population Bulletin, 47*(4), 1–47.

3. U.S. Bureau of the Census (1990). *1990 Census of population and housing—Summary tape file 3. Summary social, economic and housing characteristics.* Washington, DC: U.S. Government Printing Office.

4. Children's Defense Fund (1996). *The State of America's Children—Yearbook 1996.* Washington, DC: Children's Defense Fund. (Data from the Bureau of the Census, 1993).

5. *Op. cit.,* O'Hare, W.P.

6. National Center for Health Statistics [NCHS] (1995). *Health United States 1994.* (Table 2). Persons and families below poverty level, according to selected characteristics, race and Hispanic origin: United States, selected years 1973–93 (1990 data). The percentage for Puerto Ricans is highest of all groups, with 40.6 percent and 56.7 percent for persons under 18 years old.

7. *Op. cit.,* O'Hare, W.P.

8. Bianchi, S.M. (1990). America's children: Mixed prospects. *Population Bulletin, 45,* 1–43.

9. *Op. cit.,* NCHS (1995). *Health United States 1994.* (Table 7). Low-birthweight live births, according to mother's detailed race, Hispanic origin, and smoking status: United States, selected years, 1970–92 (less than 2,500 grams for 1992). U.S. Health and Human Services, NCHS. Washington, DC: U.S. Government Printing Office.

10. Percentage of low birthweight for Puerto Ricans is 9.1.

11. Percentage for Japanese and Filipino is 7.00 and 7.45, respectively.

12. *Op. cit.,* NCHS (1995). (Table 7). (Very low birthweight is less than 1,500 grams for 1992).

13. Percentage of very low birthweight for Puerto Ricans is 1.70.

14. *Op. cit.,* NCHS (1995). (Table 11). Maternal age and marital status for live births, according to detailed race of mother and Hispanic origin of mother: United States, selected years, 1970–92 (1992 data).

15. Percentage of live births for Puerto Ricans is 9.6.

16. Percentage of live births for Filipinos is 1.9.

17. *Op. cit.,* NCHS (1995). (Table 11).

18. Percentage of live births for Puerto Ricans is 57.5.

19. Percentage of live births for Hawaiians is 45.

20. *Op. cit.,* NCHS (1995). (Table 21). Infant mortality rates for mothers twenty years of age and over, according to educational attainment, detailed race of mother, and Hispanic origin: Selected States, 1983–88 birth cohorts (1986–88 and less than twelve years of education data).

21. The rate for Puerto Ricans is 13.2 per 1,000 live births.

22. *Op. cit.,* NCHS (1995). (Table 30). Life expectancy at birth, at 65 years of age, and at 75 years of age, according to race and sex: United States, selected years 1900–93 (1992 data).

percent. However, the percentage for Puerto Ricans is highest of all the ethnic groups, with 40.6 percent (See no. 6 in notes) (not illustrated). The percentages are even higher for persons less than eighteen years of age, particularly for African Americans (44.2 percent) and Puerto Ricans (56.7 percent).

Table 1.3 also illustrates some of the more important maternal health indicators which have implications for health care policy. It shows that African Americans have the highest percent of low birth weights (less than 2,500 grams), with 13.3 percent of live births falling in that category. African Americans have more than double the low birth rate of the next highest group, Asian/Pacific Islanders (6.6 percent), with Japanese and Filipinos having the highest percentage within the group, 7 percent and 7.45 percent respectively (see notes to Table 1.3). Puerto Ricans have the highest percentage of low birth weights within the Hispanic/Latino American group, 9.1 percent. Similar ethnic patterns are indicated for very low birth weights (less than 1,500 grams). African-American females at the rate of 10.3 percent, are less than eighteen years of age when they give birth. African Americans also have the highest percentage of unmarried mothers, 68.1 percent, followed by Native Americans with 55.3 percent and Hispanic/Latino Americans with 39.1 percent, compared with 22.6 percent for white Americans.

Table 1.3 shows that among those with less than twelve years of education, African Americans have the highest infant mortality rate, with 20.7 deaths per 1,000 live births (for 1986–88). Native Americans have an infant mortality rate of 16.2, and Puerto Ricans have a rate of 13.2 per 1,000 live births (see notes to Table 1.3). The life expectancy for African Americans is 69.6 years for both sexes, lower than the 76.5 years life expectancy for white Americans. The life expectancy for females for both African and white Americans is higher than that of males, 73.9 and 79.8 years, respectively.

Mortality Data

The following set of figures presents an overview of some of the leading causes of death for the ethnic minority groups in the United States compared with those for white Americans. Figure 1.6 presents the death rates for all causes according to race and gender for 1992. It shows that African-American males have the highest death rate with 1026.9 deaths per 100,000 resident population, in comparison to white American males with 620.9 deaths per 100,000. Native Americans are third highest with 579.6 deaths, followed by Hispanic/Latino Americans and Asian/Pacific

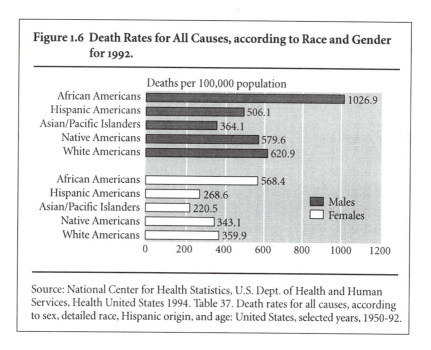

Figure 1.6 Death Rates for All Causes, according to Race and Gender for 1992.

Deaths per 100,000 population

African Americans	1026.9
Hispanic Americans	506.1
Asian/Pacific Islanders	364.1
Native Americans	579.6
White Americans	620.9
African Americans	568.4
Hispanic Americans	268.6
Asian/Pacific Islanders	220.5
Native Americans	343.1
White Americans	359.9

■ Males
□ Females

Source: National Center for Health Statistics, U.S. Dept. of Health and Human Services, Health United States 1994. Table 37. Death rates for all causes, according to sex, detailed race, Hispanic origin, and age: United States, selected years, 1950-92.

Islanders with 506.1 and 364.1 deaths, respectively. The African-American female death rate, 568.4, which is the highest among the females, is higher than that of Hispanic/Latino males, and almost as high as the male death rate of Native Americans, 579.6, and white Americans, 620.9.

Figure 1.7 shows that the death rate for diseases of the heart is highest among African-American males, with 264.1 deaths per 100,000 resident population, in comparison to that of white American males, with 190.3 deaths. Among females, African Americans have the highest rate, with 162.4 deaths. Native Americans follow with the second highest rate for both males and females, with 146.6 and 74.5 respectively.

Figure 1.8 presents the death rates from malignant neoplasms for the same ethnic groups. It shows that African-American males have the highest death rates from malignant neoplasms, with 238.1, followed by white American males with 157.3 deaths per 100,000 population. The rates for Asian/Pacific Islanders, Hispanic/Latino Americans, and Native Americans are fairly similar, with 97.7, 95.1, and 94 deaths per 100,000, respectively. Among females the rate for African Americans, 136.6 deaths per 100,000, almost equals that of white American males at 157.3 deaths. White American females also have a high rate, 110.3, which surpasses the rates for Hispanic/Latino, Asian/Pacific Islanders, and Native American males.

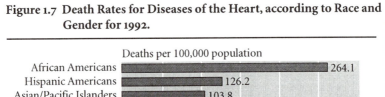

Figure 1.7 Death Rates for Diseases of the Heart, according to Race and Gender for 1992.

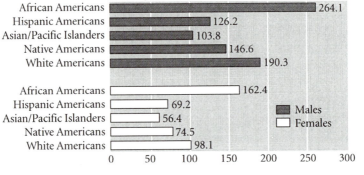

Source: National Center for Health Statistics, U.S. Dept. of Health and Human Services, Health United States 1994. Table 38. Death rates for disease of heart according to sex, detailed race, Hispanic origin, and age: United States, selected years, 1950-92.

Figure 1.8 Death Rates for Malignant Neoplasms, according to Race and Gender for 1992.

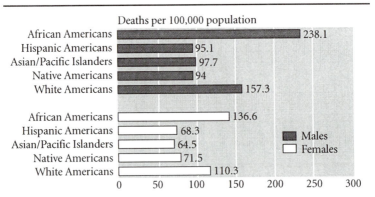

Source: National Center for Health Statistics, U.S. Dept. of Health and Human Services, Health United States 1994. Table 40. Death rates for malignant neoplasms, according to sex, detailed race, Hispanic origin, and age: United States, selected years, 1950-92.

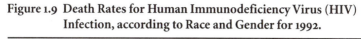

Figure 1.9 Death Rates for Human Immunodeficiency Virus (HIV) Infection, according to Race and Gender for 1992.

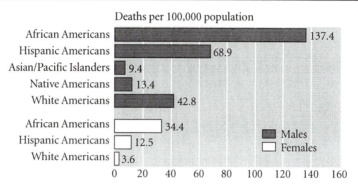

Source: National Center for Health Statistics, U.S. Dept. of Health and Human Services, Health United States 1994. Table 44. Death rates for Human Immunodeficiency Virus (HIV) Infection, according to sex, detailed race, Hispanic origin, and age: United States, selected years, 1987-92.

Figure 1.10 Death Rates for Respiratory Cancer, according to Race and Gender for 1992.

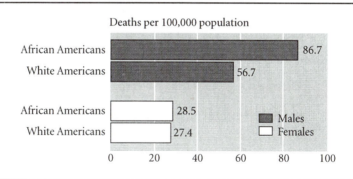

Source: National Center for Health Statistics, U.S. Dept. of Health and Human Services, Health United States 1994. Table 41. Death rates for malignant neoplasms for respiratory system, according to sex, detailed race, Hispanic origin, and age: United States, selected years, 1950-92.

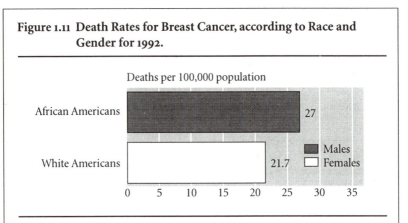

Figure 1.11 Death Rates for Breast Cancer, according to Race and Gender for 1992.

Deaths per 100,000 population

African Americans — 27

■ Males
□ Females

White Americans — 21.7

0   5   10   15   20   25   30   35

Source: National Center for Health Statistics, U.S. Dept. of Health and Human Services, Health United States 1994. Table 42. Death rates for malignant neoplasms of breast, according to sex, detailed race, Hispanic origin, and age: United States, selected years, 1950-92.

Figure 1.9 shows the death rates for Human Immunodeficiency Virus (HIV) infection for 1992. It shows that African-American males have the highest number of deaths per 100,000 resident population, 137.4, compared to Hispanic/Latino Americans, with the next highest rate, 68.9 deaths. White American males have the third highest rate, 42.8 deaths per 100,000 resident population.

The rate for African-American females, 34.4 deaths, is the highest among females and almost triples that of the next highest rate of 12.5 deaths per 100,000 resident population for Hispanic/Latino American females.

Figure 1.10 presents the death rates from respiratory cancer for 1992. It shows that African-American males have a death rate of 86.7 per 100,000 resident population, in comparison to that of white American males with 56.7. The female rates are fairly similar, 28.5 and 27.4 for African and white Americans, respectively.

Figure 1.11 presents the death rates from breast cancer. It shows that African-American females have 27 deaths per 100,000 resident population, in comparison to white Americans with 21.7 deaths.

Figure 1.12 shows the death rates from suicide for 1990–1992 among all the ethnic minority groups. It shows that white American males have the highest suicide rate, 19.9 deaths per 100,000 population, followed by Native Americans with 19.4 deaths, and African- and

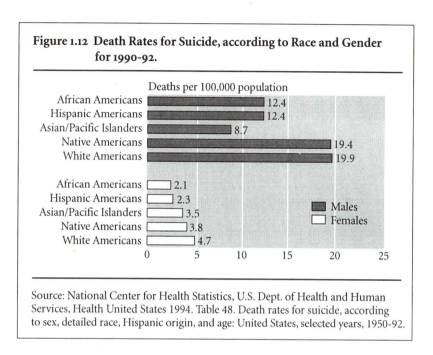

Figure 1.12 Death Rates for Suicide, according to Race and Gender for 1990-92.

Deaths per 100,000 population

	Males
African Americans	12.4
Hispanic Americans	12.4
Asian/Pacific Islanders	8.7
Native Americans	19.4
White Americans	19.9

	Females
African Americans	2.1
Hispanic Americans	2.3
Asian/Pacific Islanders	3.5
Native Americans	3.8
White Americans	4.7

Source: National Center for Health Statistics, U.S. Dept. of Health and Human Services, Health United States 1994. Table 48. Death rates for suicide, according to sex, detailed race, Hispanic origin, and age: United States, selected years, 1950-92.

Hispanic/Latino -American males each with the same death rate of 12.4 per 100,000 resident population. Asian/Pacific Islanders have the lowest suicide death rate among the males. Among females, white Americans have the highest rate, 4.7, followed by Native Americans, 3.8, and Asian/Pacific Islanders, 3.5.

Figure 1.13 presents the data for homicide and legal intervention for 1990–92. It shows that African-American males have a death rate of 69.7 per 100,000 resident population, followed by Hispanic/Latino Americans, Native Americans, white Americans, and Asian/Pacific Islanders with 29.9, 17.5, 9.2, and 8.4, respectively.

Figure 1.14 presents data for cocaine-related emergency room episodes for 1993. It shows that African-American males had 46,497 episodes, more than double that of the next highest number of episodes for white Americans, 21,418; Hispanic/Latino Americans had 8,693 episodes. Females in general had less than half the number of episodes as males.

Figure 1.15 shows that 37.4 percent of African-American males over twenty years of age have hypertension (1988–91). Hypertension among Mexican Americans is at 26.9 percent, while among white Americans it is 25.1 percent. The figures are about 5 to 6 percent lower for females across the three groups.

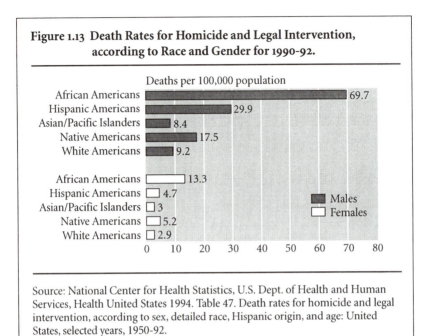

Figure 1.13 Death Rates for Homicide and Legal Intervention, according to Race and Gender for 1990-92.

Source: National Center for Health Statistics, U.S. Dept. of Health and Human Services, Health United States 1994. Table 47. Death rates for homicide and legal intervention, according to sex, detailed race, Hispanic origin, and age: United States, selected years, 1950-92.

Figure 1.14 Cocaine-related Emergency Room Episodes according to Race and Gender for 1993.

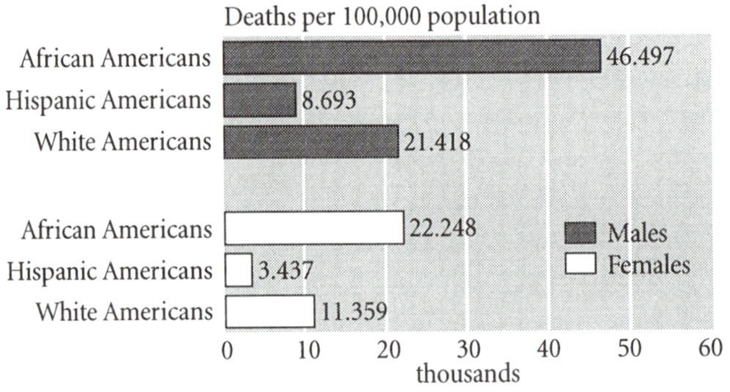

Source: National Center for Health Statistics, U.S. Dept. of Health and Human Services, Health United States 1994. Table 68. Cocaine-related emergency room episodes, according to age, sex, race, and Hispanic origin: United States, selected years, 1985-93.

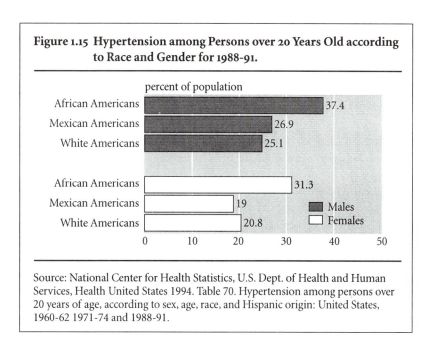

Figure 1.15 Hypertension among Persons over 20 Years Old according to Race and Gender for 1988-91.

Source: National Center for Health Statistics, U.S. Dept. of Health and Human Services, Health United States 1994. Table 70. Hypertension among persons over 20 years of age, according to sex, age, race, and Hispanic origin: United States, 1960-62 1971-74 and 1988-91.

Health Issues for Women

Recently, the first national conference on Cultural Competence and Women's Health Curricula in Medical Education (USPHS, 1995) convened in Washington, D.C. The conference illustrated the importance of women's health services not only from a cultural competency perspective, but also from the attitude of mainstream institutions, which have traditionally ignored many women's issues, just as they have historically ignored ethnic and minority concerns, not to mention domestic violence (Warshaw, 1993). Domestic violence accounts for 20 percent of all medical visits and 30 percent of all emergency room visits (Williams & Dickerson, 1995).

Only within the past twenty years has research on women's health risen steadily. Prior to this period, women were excluded from clinical studies (LaRosa & Pinn, 1993), as were minorities. Most of the biomedical knowledge about the causes and treatment of the three major diseases—heart disease, cancer, and stroke—derived from studies of men and is applied to women on the supposition that there are no differences. As statistics on death and disease specific to women were gathered, the following issues were identified:

1. Women will constitute the larger population and will be the most susceptible to disease in the future.
2. Overall, women have worse health than men.
3. Certain health problems are more prevalent in women than in men.
4. Certain health problems are unique to women or affect women differently than they do men (NIH, 1991).

The conditions worsen when the focus is turned to women of color (Adams, 1995). Studies have found that women of color are at highest risk for certain health conditions such as cancer, violence, systemic lupus, sexually transmitted diseases, HIV/AIDS, and depression (Giachello, 1995). Among African-American women, the death rate from HIV infections is ten times that of Caucasian women, with the death rate disproportionately higher in younger women (Council on Graduate Medical Education, 1995). In terms of stroke mortality, the death rate for African-American women is almost twice that for Caucasian women. Diabetes mellitus affects one in seven women over the age of 45 in general, but the prevalence rate is even higher among African-American, Hispanic, and Native-American women (Council on Graduate Medical Education, 1995). Cancer mortality rates are 15 percent higher among African-American women than Caucasian women, although the breast cancer incidence rate is 20 percent lower in African-American women. Hispanic women have a high risk of cervical and stomach cancer. In addition, ethnic minority women have the highest infant and maternal mortality rates, with African-American women having the highest rate, which is 3.5 times greater than for Caucasian women

Among the ethnic minority women, Hispanic women receive the least amount of preventive care. Figure 1.16 shows that Hispanic-American women have the highest percentage for not getting blood pressure readings, PAP smears, complete physical exams, clinical breast exams, and pelvic exams. Approximately 57 percent of African-American women do not get mammograms (Council on Graduate Medical Education, 1995).

In conclusion, the data presented above shows a fairly dismal picture of some of the problems faced by ethnic minority clients in the United States. This is the background in which human service providers, physicians, and other professionals find themselves every day when working with ethnic and racial minority groups. Furthermore, there are

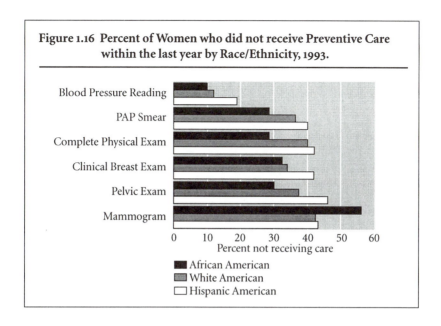

Figure 1.16 Percent of Women who did not receive Preventive Care within the last year by Race/Ethnicity, 1993.

other ethnic groups—for example, Haitians, Russians, and Middle Eastern groups—which have not been included within the statistics above, but which are additional populations to be cared for within the health and social service settings throughout the metropolitan and rural areas of the United States.

References

Adams, D.L. (1995). *Health issues for women of color–A cultural diversity perspective.* Thousand Oaks, CA: Sage.

Aponte, J.F., & Crouch, R.T. (1995). In J.F. Aponte, R.Y. Rivers, & J. Wohl (Eds.), *Psychological interventions and cultural diversity.* Boston: Allyn and Bacon.

Betancourt, I. (1996). Hispanic Americans. In A. Boyd (Ed.), *Guides to multicultural resources, 1995–1996.* Fort Atkinson, WI: Highsmith Press.

Biestek, F.P. (1970). *The casework relationship* (p. 57). Chicago, IL: Loyola University Press.

Brocka, K.B., & Brocka, M.S. (1992). *Quality management: Implementing the ideas of the masters.* Homewood, IL: Richard D. Irwin, Inc.

Chan, S. (1994). *Asian American curriculum for mental health service delivery: The Chinese curriculum.* New York: Multicultural Education, Research and Training Institute, Dept. of Psychiatry, Metropolitan Hospital Center.

Chung, D. (1992). Asian cultural commonalties. In S.M. Furuto, R. Biswa, D.K. Chung, K. Murase, & F. Ross-Sheriff (Eds.), *Social work practice with Asian Americans* (pp. 274–275). Newbury, CA: Sage.

Council of Graduate Medical Education (1995). *Fifth report: Women and medicine.* Rockville, MD: U.S. Dept. of Health and Human Services.

Cross, T., Bazron, B., Dennis, E., & Isaacs, M. (1989). *Toward a culturally competent system of care* (Vol. 1). Washington, DC: CASSP, Georgetown University.

Dana, R.H. (1993). *Multicultural assessment perspectives for professional psychology.* Boston: Allyn and Bacon.

Dean, R.G. (1979). Understanding health beliefs and behavior: Some theoretical principles of practice. In *Removing cultural and ethnic barriers to health care* (pp. 49–67). Chapel Hill, NC: University of North Carolina Press.

Giachello, A.L. (1995). Cultural diversity and institutional inequality. In D.L. Adams (Ed.), *Health issues for women of color: A cultural diversity perspective.* Thousand Oaks, CA: Sage.

Gonzales, Jr. (1993). *Racial and ethnic groups in America.* Dubuque, IA: Kendell/Hunt Publishing Company.

Isaacs, M.R., & Benjamin, M.P. (1991). Toward a culturally competent system of care. *Monographs of programs which utilize culturally competent principles.* Washington, DC: CASSP, Georgetown University.

Jackson, S.E. (1992). *Diversity in the workplace: Human resource initiatives.* New York: Guilford Press.

LaRosa, J.H., & Pinn, V.W. (1993). Gender bias in biomedical research. *Journal of the American Medical Women's Association, 48*(5), 145–151.

Marsella, A.J. (1993). Counseling and psychotherapy with Japanese Americans: Cross cultural considerations. *American Journal of Orthopsychiatry, 63*(2), 200–207.

McGill, David, W. (1992). The cultural story in multicultural family therapy. *The Journal of Contemporary Human Service.* Family Service of America, Inc. *73*(6).

McQuaide, S. (1989). Working with Southeast Asian Refugees. *Clinical Social Work Journal, 17*(2), 165–175.

Mokuaa, S., & Matucka, R. (1992). The appropriateness of personality theories for social work with Asian Americans. In S.M. Furuto, R. Biswas, D. Chung, D. Murase, & F. Ross-Sheriff (Eds.), *Social work practice with Asian Americans* (pp. 67–85). Newbury, CA: Sage.

National Center for Health Statistics (1995). *Health United States, 1994.* Washington, DC: Dept. of Health and Human Services, Government Printing Office.

National Institute of Health (1991). *Executive summary. Report of the National Institute of Health: Opportunities for research on women's health.* Pittsburgh, PA: Superintendent of Documents.

O'Hare, W.P. (1992). America's minorities—The demographics of diversity. *Population's Bulletin, 47*(4), 1–47.

Passel, J.I., & Edmonston, B. (1992). *Immigration and race: Trends in Immigration to the United States.* Washington, DC: Urban Institute.

Patterson, L. (1996). Native Americans. In A. Boyd (Ed.), *Guide to multicultural resources, 1995–1996.* Fort Atkinson, WI: Highsmith Press.

Proctor, E.K., & Davis, L.E. (1994). The challenge of racial differences: Skills for clinical practice. *Journal of the National Association of Social Workers, 39*(3), 314–323.

Robinson, T. (1993). The intersection of gender, class, race, and culture: On seeing clients whole. *Journal of Multicultural Counseling and Development, 21,* 249–259.

Ross-Sheriff, F. (1992). In S.M. Furuto, R. Biswas, D. Chung, D. Murase, & F. Ross-Sheriff (Eds.), *Social work practice with Asian Americans* (pp. 67–85). Newbury, CA: Sage.

Seck, E.T., Finch, W.A., Jr., Mor-Barak, M.E., & Poverny, L.M. (1993). Managing a diverse workforce. *Administration in Social Work, 17*(2), 67–79.

Solomon, A. (1992). Clinical diagnosis among diverse populations: A multi-cultural perspective. *Families in Society: The Journal of Contemporary Human Service, 73,* 371–377.

Spector, R.E. (1991). *Cultural diversity in health and illness.* (3rd ed.). Norwalk, CT: Appleton and Lange.

Sue, D.W., Arredondo, P., & McDavis, R. (1977). Multicultural counseling competencies and standards: A call to the profession. *The Journal of Counseling and Development, 70,* 356–363.

Sue, D.W., and Sue, D. (1990). *Counseling the culturally different.* New York: Wiley-Interservice Publication.

Torrey, E.F. (1972). *The mind game: Witch doctors and psychiatrists.* New York: Independent Publishers Group/David White.

U.S. Bureau of the Census (1992). *1990 Census of population, CP 1–4, general population characteristics.* Washington, DC: U.S. Government Printing Office.

U.S. Bureau of the Census (1991). The Black population in the United States: March, 1991. *Current Population Reports,* (Series P 20, No. 464, Table 3). Washington, DC: United States Government Printing Office.

U.S. Bureau of the Census (1990a). *1990 Census of population and housing—Summary tape file 1: Summary population and housing characteristics.* Washington, DC: United States Government Printing Office.

U.S. Bureau of the Census (1990b). *1990 Census of population and housing—Summary tape file 3: Summary social, economic and housing characteristics.* Washington, D.C.: U.S. Government Printing Office.

U.S. Department of Health and Human Services (1993). *Surgeon General's national Hispanic/Latino health initiatives. One voice-one vision-Recommendations to the Surgeon General to improve Hispanic/Latino health.* Washington, DC: USDHHD, Government Printing Office.

U.S. Immigration and Naturalization Service (unpublished INS data 1984–1989). *In the newest New Yorkers: An analysis of immigration into New York City during the 1980's.* New York, NY: Dept of City Planning, June 1992.

U.S. Public Health Service Office of Women's Health and the Office of Minority Health (1995). *First national conference on cultural competence and women's health curricula in medical education,* October 26–28, 1995. Rockville, MD: Department of Health and Human Services.

Van Den Bergh, N. (1991). Managing biculturalism at the workplace: A group approach. *Social Work with Groups, 13*(4), 71–84.

Weinbach, D.R., & Dickerson, N. (1995). The social worker as manager: Theory and practice. Boston: Allyn and Bacon.

Williams, D.R., & Dickerson, N. (1995). Conclusion. In D.L. Adams (Ed.), *Health issues for women of color: A cultural diversity perspective.* Thousand Oaks, CA: Sage.

Wright, R., Jr., Saleebey, D., Watts, T.D., & Lecca, P.J. (1983). *Transcultural persepectives in the human services.* Springfield, Ill. Charles C. Thomas.

CHAPTER 2

Cultural Values of the Major Ethnic Groups

Throughout this book you will read about the many diverse views exhibited by people from different ethnic backgrounds. You have learned about various health and mental health beliefs but may still ask yourself about other areas of human behavior. As a provider you might ask yourself, what are the client's beliefs about death and dying, about child care, about his or her support systems, or about his or her view of strangers or the therapist.

Ethnic Identification

Sue and Sue (1990) have pointed out that while commonalities exist among cultural groups, there are differences that seem significantly correlated with cultural values. These differences stem from ethnic group background, historical experiences in the United States, and the treatment and stereotyping of the minority group. These factors are very important and must be considered during the process of assessment so that the practitioner can understand his or her own perception of the client's ethnic identification and his or her own position within the Minority Identity Development Model as presented by Atkinson, Morten, and Sue (1989).

That model presents five stages of development that oppressed people experience as they struggle to understand themselves in terms of their own culture, the dominant culture, and the oppressive relationship between the two cultures. The model then continues with the need to discover the attitude and beliefs of the individual in terms of self, others of the same minority group, others of different minority groups, and attitude toward the dominant group. The five stages are:

1. *Conformity.* In this stage, the minority individual shows an absolute preference for dominant cultural values over his own.

2. *Dissonance.* The individual has personal experiences or encounters successful people of his own minority group that seem to contradict his belief of the inadequacies of his own culture. Generally speaking, an individual moves into this stage gradually and is in a period of conflict, but may be propelled into the next stage by a traumatic public event such as the killing of Dr. Martin Luther King, Jr., or a personal racist attack.

3. *Resistance and Immersion.* The individual tends to completely approve minority held views and to reject the values of the dominant society. There is a deep desire to eliminate oppression of the individual's minority group by the dominant group or society. If the person has undergone the previous two stages, there are active feelings of guilt (having "sold out"), shame, and anger at the dominant white society.

4. *Introspection.* The individual realizes that to be angry as in the resistance and immersion stage can be psychologically draining and misdirected, as energy should be focused on understanding of self, one's own racial group, and the dominant group.

5. *Integrative Awareness.* The minority individual has developed an inner sense of security and can appreciate his own culture as well as that of the dominant society. Conflicts from previous stages are resolved and there is the belief that there are acceptable and unacceptable aspects in all cultures. The individual strives to eliminate all forms of oppression.

Sue and Sue (1990) caution that counselors should use this model as a conceptual framework, as cultural identity development is a dynamic process: certain clients may exhibit dominant characteristics of one stage and others may exhibit a mixture of the various stages. Sue and Sue also present the same model and stages for white counselors in terms of their own identity and development. They caution the reader that this model should not be viewed as a global personality theory, and that cultural identity development is a dynamic process depending on the individual.

Acculturation

Beyond the ethnic identity of clients, the practitioner may also be faced with determining the acculturation level of the minority client, depending on the type of acculturation group to which the individual belongs (Aponte & Crouch 1995). There are immigrants, who are voluntary migrants; refugees, who are essentially involuntary; native people, who are indigenous, nonmigratory, and involuntary; ethnic groups, who are nonmigratory and less willing to interact with the larger society; and sojourners, who have temporary contact with the society (e.g., foreign students, diplomats, etc.).

After determining the acculturation group the individual comes from, the practitioner can assess which of the following acculturation levels or modes of adaptation fits the patient:

1. *Traditional.* Retention of his or her original or traditional culture,
2. *Assimilation.* Identification with the dominant Anglo-American culture,
3. *Bicultural.* Identification with both the original and the adopted culture,
4. *Marginality.* Rejection of both original and Anglo-American identities,
5. *Transitional.* A transitional orientation in which individuals are bilingual, but question traditional values and religion.

Once a practitioner assesses where the individual stands in terms of acculturation, then he or she can begin to understand which cultural values and beliefs that particular individual holds in high esteem, what that person's world view or cultural characteristics are, and finally, individual characteristics. The presumption is that the practitioner is aware both of his or her own cultural values and beliefs and those of the other major ethnic groups in making the cultural assessment and treatment plan.

Cultural Values Among the Major Ethnic Groups

The Value Orientation Model advanced by Kluckhohn and Strodtbeck (1961) gives us a framework in which to begin to understand the differences and similarities between individuals and groups (Table 2.1). The value orientation theory promotes three basic functions of the human individual: the directional (selection between alternative behaviors), cognitive (view of the world), and effective function (degree of emotion or commitment). There are five core dimensions addressed in the Value Orientation Model: time, human activity, social relations, and human nature. The model also provides three possible responses or solutions to each dimension. Although there is variability within this model, it renders a schema of responses common to most people.

1. *How is time perceived?* There are three common responses; past, present, and future. Some people believe the past is most important because you learn from history, while others believe the present moment is everything and do not worry about tomorrow. Others plan for the future by sacrificing today for a better tomorrow.

2. *What measures human activity?* The three value-orientation responses are being, being and becoming, and doing. Being means it is enough to just be; being and becoming emphasizes that our purpose is to develop our inner selves. Doing means to be active; by working hard your efforts will be rewarded.

3. *Social relations focus on how human relationships are defined.* The three responses are lineal, collateral, and individualistic. Lineal relationships are vertical, with leaders and followers. Collateral relationships emphasize that we should consult with friends and families when problems are presented. An individualistic orientation promotes the importance of individual autonomy and the belief that we control our own destiny.

4. *The people-to-nature relationship asks what is the relationship of human beings to nature.* The responses can be: subjugation to nature, harmony with nature, or mastery over nature. The subjugation to nature response is that life is dependent on external forces such as God, fate, or genetics. The harmony with nature response is that people and nature coexist in harmony. The third response, mastery of nature, is the belief that our challenge is to conquer and control nature.

5. *Is human nature good or evil?* Possible answers are good, evil, neutral, or mixed good and evil.

TABLE 2.1

Value Dimensions of the Five Major Cultural Groups

		Dimensions*			
Group	Human Nature	Person-to-Nature Relationship	Time Focus	Relationships	Activity
Anglo-American	Evil	Mastery of nature	Future	Individual	Doing
African American	Good/ Evil	Harmony with nature	Future	Individual	Doing
Asian American	Good	Subjugation to nature	Past	Lineal	Being-in-becoming
Hispanic American	Good/ Evil.	Subjugation to nature	Present	Lineal	Being
Native American	Good/ Evil	Harmony with nature	Present	Collateral	Being/ doing

*Subject to preferences within-group variations

In an attempt to understand different world views of culturally different families, Kluckhohn and Strodtbeck's model (1961) compares differences in value preferences among Anglo-Americans, African Americans, Asian Americans, Hispanic Americans, and Native Americans. Table 2.1 presents these differences.

In 1985 Dr. Jaime Inclan introduced a value orientation chart for lower-class immigrant Puerto Ricans that illustrates another value orientation model in action. Table 2.2 presents the value orientation model for first-generation poor Puerto Ricans in comparison to middle-class Anglo-Americans. As illustrated in Table 2.2, time is perceived differently by ethnic and racial groups. As compared to Anglo middle-class norms and expectations, poor Puerto Ricans are concerned more with a present time value orientation than with future or past time references. Dr. Inclan presents a therapist-patient scenario that illustrates the point. The therapist informs Mrs. Rivera that her next appointment for the whole family is at 3:00 P.M. next Wednesday. Mrs. Rivera responds, "Very good, after the kids return from school we can come right in." Consequently, Mrs. Rivera may get there late (since school ends at the same time as the appointment), thus upsetting the therapist, who then speculates about the client's motivation for treatment. Whereas the therapist is clock-time conscious, especially with managed care caseloads, the patient operates from a view-

TABLE 2.2.

Comparison of Value-Orientation Profiles for First-Generation Poor Puerto Ricans and Middle-Class Anglo-Americans.

Dimension	First-Generation Poor Puerto Rican	Middle-Class Anglo-American
Time	Present>Future>Past	Future>Present>Past
Activity	Being>Doing>Being-in-Becoming	Doing>Being>Being-in-Becoming
Relational	Lineal>Collateral>Individual	Individual>Collateral>Lineal
Person-Nature	Subjugated>Harmony>Dominant over	Dominant over>subjugated>Harmony
Basic human nature	Mixed>Evil>Good	Neutral>Evil>Good

point of practicality or with a concept of time as a sequence of events. Many Hispanics/Latinos, particularly recently migrated Hispanics, initially operate within this ingrained time concept as well.

In terms of the activity dimension, the Puerto Rican is more concerned with being with his family and enjoying the moment, whereas the Anglo mentality focuses on doing something. For example, on weekends many Puerto Rican families may just go to the park with their families (since it costs nothing), while Anglos may place importance on an activity or event for which they pay, because they are "doing something." Puerto Ricans are very family oriented; in the relational dimension, family is first. If a Puerto Rican is in a position to hire someone for his firm, it is expected that a relative will be hired, whereas among middle-class Americans the individual is the most important. In the person-nature dimension, Puerto Ricans believe that human life is controlled by nature and that people are not able to change events, which occur by God's will, whereas the white middle-class view is that nature can and should be controlled or dominated (i.e., science or space travel). In terms of basic human nature, the Puerto Rican feels that human nature is mixed, and that whether an individual is good or bad is dependent on supernatural forces. Middle-class Americans see basic human nature as neutral and able to be changed.

Although there are some differences between the Puerto Rican's value orientation (shown in Table 2.2) compared to that of Hispanic/Latino Americans (*see* Table 2.1), there are some similarities as well. However, the

TABLE 2.3

Value Orientations of Three Major Ethnic Groups.

Modality	Black American	Asian American	Anglo-American
Activity	Being	Being-in-Becoming	Doing
Relational	Collateral	Lineal	Individualistic
Time	Present	Past	Future
Human-to-Nature	Subjugation to nature	Harmony with nature	Mastery over nature
Human nature	Basically good but corruptible	Basically good, imperfection understandable	1) Neutral 2) Mixed-Evil perfectible

overall difference is that the four major ethnic minorities in general have different value orientation from middle-class white Americans. Additional examination of the value orientation model shows that the dimensions are subject to extreme variations within groups due to age, generation, educational status, social class, residence, and cultural orientation. For example, the groups used in Kluckhohn and Strodtbeck's original comparison are Zuni, Navajo, Mormon, Spanish American, and Texan (Anglo-American) samples. In a study by Sjostrom (1988) of mainland- and island-living Puerto Rican college students, mainland students retained the original person-nature pattern of subjugation to nature, whereas islanders preferred harmony with nature (Dana, 1993). In another sample of Mexican American teachers and custodians (Jackson, 1973), the custodians displayed the typical traditional Hispanic pattern, while the teachers exhibited a value portrait including future or present time mastery over nature, "doing" activity, and individualistic relationship orientations consistent with the dominant society (Dana, 1993)

Table 2.3 presents a more recent value orientation model that shows the same pattern of differences and similarities as the preceding two tables. Kendrick, MacMillan, and Pinderhughes (1983) have pointed out that within their framework, adapted from Papajohn and Spiegel (1975) and MacMillan (1979), black Americans are generally experienced as having a "being orientation" in a "present" time orientation, that they follow the "collateral" relationship mode, that they see humankind as basically "good but corruptible," and that blacks tend to feel more "subjugation to nature," yielding to "God's will." They further state that these values are understandable when viewed from a philosophical base that includes a history of racism and discrimination, which lends itself to feelings of subjugation to nature, a sense of powerlessness, and existential fearfulness. However, in 1987, based on a sample consisting of black college students, Carter and Helms reported a "future" time focus, "harmony" in man-nature relationships, an "individualized" relational stance, and a "doing" activity orientation. They state that their findings are identical to those reported by the dominant culture and ". . . reiterate the expectation for extreme within-group differences" (Carter & Helms, 1987).

Dana (1993) reports that many African Americans have opted for identification with the dominant Anglo-American culture and will be more egocentric in lifestyle and less communal in orientation. However, to the extent that they become Afrocentric, middle-class persons will deal with their individual life experience in a collective manner, with a strong emphasis on sharing, flexibility, and concern for the welfare of other persons within their immediate environment or sphere of responsibility and influence. This is clearly illustrated in the informal adoption process that had its origins in African tribal traditions, by which the "taking in" of children by other slave families occurred when the parents were sold or killed (Boyd-Franklin, 1989; Hill, 1977). Nobles (1976) reported that the values of group centeredness, sensitivity to interpersonal matters, and cooperation are results of African heritage, which stresses group identity, community, cooperation, and interdependence and being one with nature. Nevertheless, because of racism in the United States, African Americans are often more guarded, formal, and less verbal with white Americans than with other African Americans with whom they are often more open, responsive, playful, and expressive (Gibbs, 1980).

Religion and spirituality also have had a significant role in the cultural value formation of African Americans. The black church in particular has been a crucial part of the support system on which many African Americans have come to rely. The black church also has become one of the most important pillars for leadership, role modeling for young black families, and for development of African-American communities. Practitioners need to be aware of the importance of the church as it relates to African-American families. It functions essentially as another extended family beyond the nuclear and the extended family members.

Regarding Native Americans, various authors have written that because of their diversity and variation (there are approximately 400 tribal nations), it is difficult to describe one set of values that encompasses them all (Dana, 1993; Sue & Sue, 1990). Sue has provided us with the works of Everett, Proctor, and Cartmell (1983) and Wise and Miller (1983), which provide some generalizations regarding Native American values. They are

1. *Sharing.* Shared responsibility includes shelter, food, child care, automobiles, etc. There is a practice of tribal consensus for decisions regarding the community. In the dominant American culture, status is gained by the accumulation of wealth or material goods; Native Americans gain honor and respect by sharing and giving.

2. *Cooperation.* Whereas in the dominant culture "winning is everything" and individualism is highly valued, cooperation by Native Americans is seen as a harmonious act enacted with other tribal members. In a counseling session they often agree with the counselor's suggestions, but may not necessarily follow through with them, particularly if it puts the client outside of the tribal group's normal functioning.

3. *Noninterference.* Native Americans are taught to observe rather than react impulsively and interfere with others.

4. *Time Orientation.* Native Americans are more conscious of the present than the future. Things are accomplished in a rational and natural harmonic order; that is, they are more concerned with whether the environment is favorable for an activity than with meeting a deadline.

5. *Extended Family Orientation.* There is a strong respect for elders and their wisdom and knowledge.

6. *Harmony with Nature.* Native Americans coexist with nature and do not try to control and master it, as does the majority culture.

Since there are many within-group differences among Native Americans, the above value orientation may not apply to all Native Americans. About 55 percent live in urban areas of the United States and may be more likely to be assimilated into the main society, retaining few traditional beliefs. As stated above, it is necessary for the practitioner to make an assessment of each individual client regarding his or her acculturation level. This is a crucial step if the practitioner is to have a successful counseling relationship with his or her clients.

Zitzo and Estes (1981) point out other counseling issues that are common areas for discussion with Native Americans:

1. Alcoholism

2. Substance abuse

3. Feelings of distrust toward non-Indian mental health professionals

4. Prejudice and discrimination

5. Lack of self-identity

6. Fear of failure and ridicule

7. Lack of exposure to Native American role models

8. Frustration about being responded to as a stereotype rather than as an individual

9. Conflicts about higher education and its time commitment, which often causes feelings of alienation from tribal and extended family and customs.

Among Asian Americans there are differences similar to those found within other ethnic racial groups. Some Asian-American individuals may hold on to their traditional values, while others may have grown up in the United States assuming "American" values. As mentioned above, there are value differences among Asian-American individuals, depending on the sample group surveyed, social class, gender, and regional location. Laura Uba (1994) presents an inventory of values which are based on clinical observations and historical analyses. These values are but an attempt to begin to understand the differences between Asian-American values and European-American values, and the implications of these differences in the assessment of the behavioral and attitudinal activities of Asian-American clients. They are the following:

1. Emphasis on maintaining harmony in relationships, based on the religious teachings of Confucianism and Buddhism

2. Group interests over individual interests

3. Duties over rights, and the importance of fulfilling obligations, particularly regarding the family

4. Being patient, gentle, well-mannered, and cooperative

5. Being accommodating, conciliatory, and receptive rather than confrontational

6. Blending in with the group rather than differentiating oneself with either good or bad behavior

7. Avoiding aggressive behavior by talking about one's achievements or expressing one's opinion

8. Being humble and modest

9. Withholding the free expression of feelings

10. Suppression of conflict by avoiding divisive arguments or discussions, or keeping discussion on a superficial, nonthreatening level

11. Reliance on nonverbal communication

12. Social sensitivity, referring to subtle verbal and nonverbal cues

13. Emphasis on reciprocating the kindness of others

14. Respect for people of status including parents, people with authority, and the elderly

15. Academic and occupational achievement, which elevates the individual as fulfilling a family obligation. (It can also bring shame if not accomplished.) Associated values are:

    a. Self-control, self-discipline

    b. Education, hard work, delayed gratification

    c. Suppression of both positive and negative emotions

    d. Silent forbearance and perseverance, particularly in difficult or unpleasant situations.

Uba (1994) points out that most of the value literature has focused on Chinese Americans and Japanese Americans, and that although there is significant overlap between the different Asian groups, their values are not identical. For example, although most Asian Americans are Buddhist, Filipinos are Catholic, and Koreans are most often Protestant. As discussed above, there will be differences within the groups as well as across the groups.

Laura Uba also lists the most important cultural values, based on the work of Matsushima and Tashima (1982), for therapists to take into consideration:

1. Importance of family

2. Shame and guilt

3. Respect for people based on their status and roles

4. Styles of interpersonal behavior

5. Stigma associated with mental illness

6. Restraint of self-expression

7. Orientation toward group

8. Achievement

9. Sense of duty and obligation

10. Expectations that follow from different roles

Uba (1994) also lists important ethnic-specific problems therapists need to know about (based on Matsushima and Tashima):

1. Immigration experiences (see the impact of migration on families in chapter 4)

2. Cultural conflicts in lifestyles and values

3. Importance of family issues

4. Racism

5. Conceptualizations of mental health and attitudes toward mental health services

6. Behavioral styles and norms

7. Language

8. Ethnic identity

9. Intergenerational problems

American Values and Beliefs

Now that some basic parameters have been presented about the value systems of the four major government-protected ethnic groups, the reader is faced with making comparisons as to how these groups differ from the Anglo-American culture and how to interact in a given situation. This is usually accomplished not only by reading about a particular group, but by participating in training workshops or courses designed specifically to address multicultural issues within a particular setting (i.e., hospital, mental health centers, educational institution, etc.).

At this point it is necessary to know more about the Anglo-American value system to begin making comparisons. Robin M. Williams (1970) has identified Anglo-Saxon cultural themes which Locke (1992) has listed as follows:

1. *Achievement and success.* Both are goals with great significance, exemplified by the rags-to-riches success story.

2. *Activity and work.* A strong work ethic is emphasized.

3. *Humanitarian mores.* People spontaneously come to the aid of others and usually favor the "underdog."

4. *Moral orientation.* Life events and situations are judged in terms of right and wrong.

5. *Efficiency and practicality.* There is a strong focus on getting things done.

6. *Progress.* A positive view is held that things will get better.

7. *Material comfort.* People aspire to the "good life." Many are conspicuous consumers.

8. *Equality.* There is a consistent declaration of the commitment to equality.

9. *Freedom.* There is a strong belief in individual freedom.

10. *External Conformity.* There is great uniformity in dress, housing, recreation, manners, and political ideas.

11. *Science and secular rationality.* A strong belief exists that science will help master the environment.

12. *Nationalism-patriotism.* There is a strong sense of loyalty to that which is "American."

13. *Democracy.* There is a belief that every person should have a voice in the political destiny of the country.

14. *Individual personality.* There is a strong belief that the individual has precedence over the group and that every individual should be independent, responsible, and self-respecting.

15. *Racism and related group superiority.* There is an emphasis on differential evaluation of racial, religious, and ethnic groups, that is seen as a cultural conflict.

Based on the work by Stewart, Danielian, and Festes (1969), and Stewart (1971), who described five American patterns of cultural assumptions and values, Katz (1985) identified similar cultural themes as R.M. Williams and utilized them as components for counseling. Listed as the components of the values and beliefs of white culture, they are:

1. *Rugged individualism.* The individual is the primary unit, has primary responsibility, is independent and autonomous, is highly valued and rewarded, and can control the environment.

2. *Competition.* The premise is that winning is everything, and that situations fall into a win/lose dichotomy.

3. *Action orientation.* Man must master and control nature, must always do something about a situation, is pragmatic, and maintains a utilitarian way of life.

4. *Communication.* Language is standard English and has a written tradition; people have limited physical contact, use direct eye contact, and control their emotions.

5. *Time.* It is strictly followed and viewed as a commodity.

6. *Holidays.* They are based on the Christian religion, white history, and male leaders.

7. *History.* It is based on European immigrants' experience in the United States and focused on romanticizing war.

8. *Protestant work ethic.* This is the belief that working hard brings success.

9. *Progress and future orientation.* People plan for the future, delay gratification, and value continued improvement and progress.

10. *Emphasis on scientific method.* There is an emphasis on objective, rational, linear thinking, cause and effect relationships, and quantitative emphasis.

11. *Status and power.* These are measured by economic possessions, credentials, titles and positions; belief in superiority of "own" system, and that it is better than other systems.

12. *Family structure.* The nuclear family is the ideal social unit; a patriarchal structure, with the male as the breadwinner and the head of the household, and the female as the homemaker, subordinate to the husband.

13. *Esthetics.* Music and art are based on European cultures; women's beauty ideal is blond, blue-eyed, thin, and young; men's attractiveness is based on athletic ability, power, and economic status.

14. *Religion.* There is a belief in Christianity, and no tolerance for deviation from the single God concept.

Training Directions

American corporations have recognized the importance of cultural differences, and since the 1980s have been moving toward training employees about cultural diversity in the work force. This training, sometimes known as "bias busting," aims not only at understanding cultural differences, but at self-acceptance and flexibility within one's own cultural background (Harris & Moran, 1991). U.S. companies also provide cross-cultural training for employees going overseas either for short- or long-term visits. Some areas covered are the following (Harris & Moran, 1991):

1. *Cognitive:* focuses on knowledge of other peoples and their culture, including customs, values, and social institutions.

2. *Awareness:* involves both self-awareness and cultural awareness outside of one's cultural group.

3. *Behavioral:* accentuates specific cultural behavior and expectations in the host culture. The teaching approach is to simulate the host culture environment and provide experiential exercises.

4. *Interaction:* uses interactive techniques with representatives of the host country (i.e., students and foreign visitors), or host environment of a minority community.

5. *Area simulation:* mimics the host country in many areas, including physical climates and conditions (The Peace Corps and military personnel utilize this technique).

6. *Relationship systems:* emphasis is on intercultural relations or human relations in terms of a systematic approach applicable across cultures.

7. *Language studies:* focus is on specific foreign languages and the cultures associated with people who speak that language.

8. *Cross-cultural communication:* includes the study of communication theory in general and intercultural communications in particular; includes verbal and nonverbal behaviors and customs.

9. *Confrontation/Contrast:* a role-play approach by which a cross-cultural encounter is played out around a confrontational issue or situation. Behaviors and communications are observed, discussed, and evaluated for improving future encounters.

In a similar training program developed for Metropolitan Hospital Center in New York City, which serves a large multicultural community, APAC, Inc. (Pernell-Arnold, 1995) designed a twelve-week course (three hours a week) with key staff who could then return to their units or wards and conduct mini-training sessions. After an initial introductory "awareness of self" session in which participants presented their own cultural background, as well as that of their parents and ancestors, the sessions covered the following topics:

1. *Cultural history:* includes migration history, relationship of motherland and group, history of the ethnic group in the United States (regarding racism and discrimination), values, beliefs, gestures, religion, and acculturation.

2. *Language:* the client's preference for English or other language, the role of the translator if needed, and the translator's clinical knowledge. The client's length of time in the United States.

3. *Communication styles:* includes description of different types such as stoic, expressive (with feelings), factual (direct or metaphor, indirect or analogy), verbal, nonverbal, psychic.

4. *Cognitive styles:* involves the group's approach to knowledge: for example, abstract and scientific reasoning requiring documentation of facts; sharing of common experiences of what works or does not work; relationships between the individual (human) and other animate and inanimate objects; or knowledge based on conclusions and assumptions of a master or group of masters from the past.

5. *Organizational culture:* an understanding of the hierarchy and structure of the setting in which one works; access to authority; the relationship and interaction between ethnicity, staff, and the setting; rules and procedures; managing diversity in the work place.

6. *Cultural psychosocial assessment:* identification of potential barriers that influence a good assessment; reviews of the cultural assessment process; identification of cross-cultural issues in critical incidents.

7. *Medical and psychiatric assessment and diagnosis:* identification of cultural psychosomatic symptoms, ethno-cultural diseases and syndromes, help-seeking behaviors.

This chapter has attempted to describe the value orientation models of the major ethnic racial groups and those of the Euro-Anglo Americans in the United States. It has been pointed out that although these are generalizations, many of these values are seen to be common among the respective groups. We have cautioned, however, that there are variations within and between the groups, and that the health and social service practitioner should treat each patient or client as an individual with his or her own characteristics in addition to the cultural-background value orientation. The common thread seems to be that Americans have been historically unwilling to accept ethnic immigrant groups, primarily due to an inherited European historical and capitalist background, as well as a U.S. history of slavery, racism, domination, and discrimination. It is only since the 1954 desegregation law that Americans have begun to accept blacks, and other people of color, as well as Jews, as people entitled to live a normal life.

Although there have been many changes for the better in the way society treats minority groups, there is still a long way to go.

Cultural diversity training helps one understand why people behave the way they do. Training staff about cultural diversity issues within the institutional setting and community is but the first step toward assuring that appropriate services are rendered and that quality of service is not sacrificed in the process of maintaining a sound fiscal organization.

With today's emphasis on managed care it behooves an administrator or director of a program to know marketing and the population base that his or her agency/institution is most likely to be servicing. Studies have shown that many ethnic clients terminate treatment prematurely, sometimes after only one initial assessment session, mainly because of language difficulties and other cultural beliefs. These include suspicion of the therapist or authority figures (who may expose them as illegal immigrants), ignorance of available services, lack of evening hours, shortage of culturally sensitive staff, or inhibitions about seeking mental health services because of its associated stigma within their immediate community (Uba, 1994). If the client does not return because of dissatisfaction, exit interviews that are critical in order to evaluate and implement corrective action plans will be lost. Given the budget cuts due to downsizing that are affecting the nation's business and health and social services fields, there is no doubt that health and human service organizations have to retain their clients, as well as maintain and improve services to their community patient population base as they look for new clients in a highly competitive atmosphere.

References

Aponte, J.F., & Crouch, R.T. (1995). In J.F. Aponte, R.Y. Rivers, & J. Wohl (Eds.), *Psychological interventions and cultural diversity.* Boston: Allyn and Bacon.

Atkinson, D.R., Morten, G., & Sue, D.W. (1989). *Counseling American minorities: A Cross-cultural perspective.* Dubuque, IA: W.C. Brown.

Boyd-Franklin, N. (1989). *Black families in therapy: A multi-systems approach.* New York: Guilford.

Carter, R.T., & Helms, J.E. (1987). The relationship between black value-orientations and racial identity attitudes. Special issue: Assessments for minority populations: Traditional and nontraditional approaches. *Measurement and Evaluation in Counseling and Development, 19*(4), 185–195.

Dana, R.H. (1993). *Multicultural assessment perspectives for professional psychology.* Boston: Allyn and Bacon.

Everett, F., Proctor, N., & Cartmell, B. (1983). Providing psychological services to American Indian children and families. *Professional Psychology: Research and Practice, 14,* 588–601.

Gibbs, J.T. (1980). The interpersonal orientation in mental health consultation: Toward a model of ethnic variations in consultation. *Journal of Applied Behavioral Science, 21,* 445–458.

Harris, P.R., & Moran, R.T. (1991). *Managing cultural difference.* Houston: Gulf.

Hill, R.B. (1977). *Informal adoption among black families.* Washington, DC: National Urban League Research Department.

Inclan, J. (1985). Variations in value orientations in mental health work with Puerto Ricans. *Psychotherapy, 22,* 324–334.

Jackson, R.G. (1973). Preliminary bicultural studies of value orientations and leisure activities. *Journal of Leisure Research, 5,* 10–22.

Katz, J. (1985). The sociopolitical nature of counseling. *The Counseling Psychologist, 13,* 615–624.

Kendrick, E.A., MacMillan, M.F., & Pinderhughes, C.A. (1983). A racial minority: Black Americans and mental health care. *The American Journal of Social Psychiatry, III* (2), 11–18.

Kluckholm, F.R., & Strodtbeck, F.L. (1961). *Variations in value orientations.* Homewood, IL: Dorsey.

Locke, D.C. (1992). A model of multicultural understanding. In D.C. Locke, *Increasing multicultural understanding—A comprehensive model.* Newbury Park, CA: Sage.

MacMillan, M. (1979). *Evaluation and treatment of patients from nonwhite ethnic groups.* Presented at the 132nd annual meeting of the American Psychiatric Association, Chicago.

Matsushima, N.M., & Tashima, N. (1982). *Mental health treatment modalities of Pacific/Asian-American practitioners.* San Francisco: Pacifica Asian Mental Health Research Project.

Nobles, W.W. (1976). Black peoples in white insanity: An issue for black community mental health. *The Journal of Afro-American Issues, 4,* 21–27.

Papajohn, J., & Spiegel, J.P. (1975). *Transactions in families: A modern approach for resolving cultural and generational conflict.* San Francisco: Jossey-Bass.

Pernell-Arnold, A. (1995). Diversity and health care training. *Training Curriculums.* Philadelphia: APAC.

Sjostrom, B.R. (1988). Culture contact and value orientations: The Puerto Rican experience. In E. Acosta-Belen & B.R. Sjostrom (Eds.), *The Hispanic experiences in the United States: Contemporary issues and perspectives.* New York: Praeger.

Stewart, E.C. (1971). *American cultural patterns: A cross-cultural perspective.* Pittsburgh: Regional Council for International Understanding.

Stewart, E.C., Danielian, J., & Festes, R.J. (1969). *Stimulating intercultural communication through role playing.* Alexandria, VA: Human Resources Research Organization.

Sue, D. W., & Sue, D. (1990). *Counseling the culturally different: Theory and practice.* New York: Wiley.

Uba, L. (1994). *Asian Americans: Personality patterns, identity and mental health.* New York: Guilford.

Williams, R.M. (1970). *American society: A sociological interpretation.* New York: Knopf.

Wise, F. & Miller, N. (1983). The mental health of American Indian children. In G.J. Powell, J. Yamamoto, A. Romero, & A. Morales, (Eds.), *The psychosocial development of minority group children.* New York: Brunner/Mazel.

Zitzo, D., & Estes, G. (1981). The heritage consistency continuum in counseling Native American children. In *Contemporary American Issues: American Indian issues in higher education,* 133–139.

CHAPTER 3

Cultural Competency and Its Role in Health Services

When asked to define the role of culture within health and social services, a wide range of possible responses or interpretations comes to mind. The literature reflects both articles from the ancient historical perspectives of the cultural healing practices of the Chinese, Egyptians, Native Americans, and Greeks, describing the use of shamans and medicine men, to articles by present-day human service providers explaining the use of espiritistas, santeros(as), and curanderos(as) among ethnic and racial populations in need of general health and mental health services.

Although there have been many articles recently on ethnic and cultural issues within the professional health, social, and human services delivery system, few have focused on cultural competency per se. A review of the literature on cultural competency provides us with a model developed by the CASSP (Child and Adolescent Service System Program) Technical Assistance Center (Cross et al., 1989) based at Georgetown

Figure 3.1 Cultural Competence Continuum Scale

University. It is a continuum scale—the Cultural Competence Continuum—which ranges from cultural destructiveness to cultural proficiency (Figure 3.1). The six points along the continuum and the characteristics for each position are as follows (Cross et al., 1989):

1. *Cultural destructiveness.* This is the most negative end of the
   continuum and is represented by attitudes, policies, and practices
   that are destructive to cultures and consequently to the individuals within the cultures. Besides legislation that in the past was
   geared to cultural genocide, there is the process of dehumanizing
   or subhumanizing minority clients; such as agencies that risk the
   well-being of minority individuals in social or medical experiments without their knowledge or consent. One study, the
   Tuskegee Syphilis Experiment (Roy, 1995), did research on the
   effects of syphilis on African Americans without their consent or
   knowledge of having syphilis. Another example is the Indian
   Child Welfare Act, which removed Native American children
   from their families and land and placed them in non-Indian
   foster and adoptive homes (Deitrich, 1982). Over a hundred years
   ago, Native American children were forcibly removed from their
   reservations and placed in boarding schools.

2. *Cultural incapacity.* This occurs when the system or agency does
   not intentionally seek cultural destructiveness, but lacks the
   capacity to help minority clients or communities. It is a position
   wherein the agency or system believes in its racial superiority as a
   dominant group. Such agencies may support segregation or
   enforce racist policies and maintain stereotypes. Basically, the
   agency does not believe in, understand, or respect the religion
   and beliefs of the group being served. It believes that its own
   culture is the best. Some characteristics may include discriminatory hiring practices and lower expectations of minority clients.

3. *Cultural blindness.* This is the belief that color or cultures make
   no difference and that all people are the same. Culturally blind
   agencies believe that the helping approaches traditionally used by
   the dominant culture are universally applicable. If the system
   worked as it should, all people, regardless of race or culture,
   would be served with equal effectiveness. Agencies with this
   position on the continuum suffer from a lack of information
   about the community, and may also lack the avenues through

which they can obtain needed information. They view themselves as unbiased and responsive to minority needs; however, in reality they are very ethnocentric. They ignore cultural strengths, encourage assimilation, and blame the victim for his or her problems. Institutional racism also restricts minority access to professional training, better staff positions, and equal services.

4. *Cultural pre-competence.* This is the first step toward the positive end of the continuum. The agency realizes its weakness in serving minorities and attempts to improve some aspect of its services to a specific population. At this point in the scale the agency tries to reach people of color in its catchment (service) area. The agency hires minority staff and an effort is made to initiate training for its workers in cultural sensitivity. There is a desire to deliver quality services and a commitment to civil rights. However, the person or agency feels that they have done enough, and does not try for more—there is a false sense of accomplishment from one goal or activity, which can lead, for example, to tokenism (hiring one black for show purposes). If the effort fails, the agency's reluctant to try again.

5. *Cultural competence.* Agencies at this point on the continuum are characterized by acceptance and respect for difference, continuing self-assessment of staff and policies regarding culture, careful attention to the dynamics of difference, continuous expansion of cultural knowledge and resources, and a variety of adaptations to service models in order to better meet the needs of minority populations. These types of agencies seek minority staffs that are committed to their community and capable of negotiating a bicultural world. They provide support for staff members to help them be comfortable in working in cross-cultural situations. They seek advice from and consult with the minority community.

6. *Cultural proficiency.* This is the most positive end of the spectrum. Culturally proficient agencies hold culture in high esteem. Culturally competent practice is enhanced by research, by therapeutic approaches based on culture, and by publishing and disseminating the results of demonstration projects. These agencies hire staff who are specialists in culturally competent practice. The agency respects different cultures and can work with community agencies and clergy even if they do not agree with their practices. The proficient agency builds cultural knowledge,

institutes self-assessment procedures, and understands dynamics. Policies are flexible and culturally impartial and board members as well as administrators and line workers are part of the process.

For some time now there has been a growing desire among social service practitioners to enhance their cultural competency skills; and among policy planners to develop guidelines for the implementation of cultural competence standards. More and more states (California and New York, among others) now mandate and regularly monitor psychiatric facilities which treat multicultural populations to insure that they have culturally competent staff and provide appropriate services. These states have developed clear regulations and guidelines which are mandatory in order to avoid citations and be fully accredited. As a result, many departments of psychiatry in hospital-affiliated universities have established ethnic cultural training programs for their psychiatry residents in the form of workshops, grand round presentations, and twelve-week courses.

Among medical schools, however, this movement is slow. A recent survey (Lum & Korenman, 1994) found that of 126 medical schools in the United States, only thirteen offered cultural sensitivity courses to their students (78 percent of the schools responded). All but one of these courses was optional, despite a great perceived likelihood by students that they would have contact with African-American patients ($p < .05\%$) in the near future, and felt only "somewhat prepared" to provide culturally sensitive services.

Fortunately there is genuine interest among social service professionals as to how an individual or facility becomes culturally competent. Although there are a number of recent books to address the need for cultural competency, as well as an increase of literature on minorities, there are few which bring all of their findings under one cover. The focus of this chapter is on how a practitioner can become culturally competent and upgrade his or her cultural competency skills in order to strengthen practitioner-patient relationships.

How Health Providers Can Become Culturally Competent

Once practitioners have adjusted their own attitudes and accepted their position within the cultural competence continuum, they can begin to learn and comprehend the beliefs and attitudes of the various groups under their treatment. This knowledge base can then be funneled into the skills development phase of their education and applied to clinical practice.

Communication

One of the first steps toward cultural competency is improving communication skills. At times it may seem that a practitioner hasn't communicated well with a patient; for example:

> The health of a middle-aged Asian patient had not improved after weeks when the physician had given him a prescription for the particular problem. The physician asked the patient if he had taken the medicine; the patient assured the doctor he had taken the medicine regularly. The physician asked the patient, "show me exactly how you take the medicine." To the amazement of the physician, the patient reaches for his pocket and takes out the original prescription which is barely legible; the writing is blurred and runny as if it were left in the rain. The patient then proceeded to demonstrate how he took his medicine. Twice a day, he would take a piece of paper from within another wax paper containing the prescription and place it into a glass of water and then drink the water. He then refolded the paper and carefully placed it back into the waxed paper. He had done exactly as the physician had told him: "Here, take this with a glass of water twice a day." (Desmond, 1994)

In this scenario, the patient took the doctor's words literally. In reality, in many Chinese communities acupuncturists treat patients and frequently write prescriptions which are then taken to a local herbal store. There the prescribed herbs are selected and placed onto a large sheet of white paper which is folded and taken home to be prepared as a tea for the particular ailment or problem.

Clearly specific and open communication between the physician and the patient is an essential clinical skill for medical compliance. Today's medical institutions have barely begun to assimilate communication skills with ethnic and cultural groups as an integral part of the medical training curriculum. The above example is just one of many cases where lack of clear communication does make the difference. The following example further underscores the point.

> A Mexican-American couple was being seen in an examining room. The husband asked the doctor why the pills aren't working. The

woman has had one baby since their last visit to the clinic and is now pregnant again. There are five other children at home. The doctor asks, "Is the pill taken on schedule?" "Yes," he says, taking out a small calendar from his pocket: Every day right on schedule, he takes the pill. (Desmond, 1984)

Desmond offers us a framework which provides the human services worker or practitioner with some essential approaches toward improving relationships with and the delivery of services to culturally diverse clients.

Gain the patient's trust by making small talk, perhaps showing interest in the patient's country and culture.

Avoid any political or controversial issues. This can be done in English or, if the practitioner's language skills are sufficient, in the patient's native tongue. Be aware of social distance values of certain ethnic groups, particularly recent immigrants. Although a well-intended formality, tapping a child on the head is not a welcome gesture among recently migrated Asian families, because they believe the head holds the essence of life. Touching it may cause the soul to leave or an evil spirit to enter the body (Sherer, 1993).

Show respect for differences among your patients with regard to their cultural beliefs about illness and health care.

Many third-world people with low, moderate, or even high educational levels believe in spiritual causes as the root of their illness. They may or may not tell you about this unless you ask. Kleinman et al. (1978) suggest the following questions be asked in determining the patient/family explanatory model of sickness:

1. What do you think has caused your problem?
2. Why do you think it started when it did?
3. What do you think your sickness does to you?
4. How does it work?
5. Will it have a short or long course?
6. What kind of treatment do you think you need?
7. What are the most important results you hope to receive from this treatment?
8. What are the chief problems your sickness has caused for you? What do you fear most about your sickness?

These questions are derived from Kleinman's five major explanatory model questions: (1) etiology or cause of the problem, (2) timing and onset of symptoms, (3) description of the problem as a pathophysiological process, (4) course of illness in terms of severity, acuteness, or chronicity, and (5) length and type of treatment. Kleinman proposes that the provider first ask general open-ended questions, preferably in the home setting. This will allow the patient or client to explain his or her reason for the illness in a more comfortable setting than an alien office.

Keep in mind that many people have different conceptualizations of illness and curing. Health providers should understand the "world view" which determines what people from other countries believe regarding the cause of illness and appropriate cures. Essentially there are three categories to keep in mind (Pernell-Arnold, 1995):

1. *Natural.* These causes can be a series of things: illness caused by damp cold; among the Chinese, the yin and yang being out of balance; or eating things that are poisonous or out of season.

2. *Supernatural.* The illness is caused by someone/thing/spirit that is angry with you and puts (hexes, curses, fixes) something on you. It can be caused by breaking or violating a taboo.

3. *Religious/spiritual.* The illness is caused by thinking or doing evil, not praying enough, not having faith, lying, cheating, or not respecting your elders, the shaman, minister, other religious leaders, or God.

There are certain groups of people that hospital staff may need to learn more about. For instance, among Muslim patients pork products are strictly forbidden and fasting is practiced during Ramadan (a religious holy period). If a patient is dying, there are certain practices which are observed, such as confessing one's sins while the family prepares the body and turns it to face Mecca. Only family members may touch the body. In addition, there are other ethnic groups which have rigid beliefs about organ transplants, death, and burial practices. Jehovah's Witnesses are forbidden to have blood transfers, and many Orthodox Jews cannot travel on the day of the Sabbath, which starts on Friday at dusk (Shelby, 1996). In Togo, a republic in West Africa, and throughout the Middle East, part of the initiation into womanhood is the practice of genital mutilation. It would be very difficult to observe that practice in the United States, but physicians need to be aware that recent female immigrants from Togo and several other countries may suffer psychologically from this painful ritual.

Don't assume the patient dislikes you, mistrusts you, or isn't listening to you because he or she avoids eye contact.

It is usual for Asian and Hispanic/Latino clients, particularly recent nonacculturated first generational clients, to avoid eye contact. It is part of their upbringing to show respect for a professional or a person in a powerful position by not looking him or her directly in the eye (Gaw, 1993). In the United States, white Americans tend to make eye contact with a speaker about 80 percent of the time. This is in contrast to black Americans, who tend to make greater eye contact when speaking and less frequent eye contact when listening (Sue & Sue, 1990).

Proxemics, which refers to the perception and use of personal and interpersonal space, can also play an influential role in the patient-physician relationship. In the United States, individuals seem more uncomfortable when others stand too close rather than far away (Goldman, 1980). The opposite is true among Hispanics, black Americans, Arabs, and French. If a counselor backs away from a Latino client when he gets closer, the client may interpret this as coldness or a desire not to communicate (Sue & Sue, 1990).

Determine other health care resources and methods the patient has used or continues to use while under your care.

Among Puerto Ricans, South Americans, and Caribbean blacks, many herbal remedies are utilized for arthritis, ulcers, colds, asthma, etc. Consequently, it is important for the health provider to know that this practice may influence compliance to a medical prescription. Understanding the Hot/Cold theory of disease (Harwood, 1971) is a good first step toward this goal. The Hot/Cold theory is the system whereby food, herbs, and other medications are classified as hot or cold, wet or dry, and used to restore the body to its natural balance. Under this system illness is classified as resulting from an imbalance of the bodily humors,causing the body to become excessively dry, cold, hot, wet, or a combination of these states. In the Puerto Rican's modification of this system, diseases are grouped into hot and cold classes, while medications and foods belong to hot, cold, or intermediate (cool) categories (Harwood, 1981). For arthritis, a cold illness, for instance, one might take castor oil, a hot medicine, or a hot food such as anise in tea form (Harwood & Kleinman, 1981).

A number of folk or herbal remedies currently in use by Puerto Ricans have been documented in personal interviews by Benedetti (1992). For example, massages and ginger-root teas are used to improve circulation. Tea made from cabbage mixed with a half-teaspoonful of anise is used to treat colic. Table 3.1 presents a number of herbal remedies that have been collected during the last thirty years by Dr. Joseph Suarez from the Multicultural Education, Research, and Training Institute (MERTI), mostly by personal interviews.

TABLE 3.1

Collected Herbal Remedies Utilized by Puerto Rican and Hispanic People

Indication	Herb Spanish	English	Preparation
Abdominal pain	Cascara de china	Orange peel	Boil dried peel in water.
	Guanabana	Sour sop	
	Manzanilla	Chamomile	Prepare as tea.
	Yerba Buena	Peppermint	Prepare as tea.
Agitation	Azahar water	Orange flower water	Drink to calm down; for everyone above the age of eight.
Anorexia	Yerba Buena	Peppermint	Boil leaves in milk.
Asthma	Achiote		Decoction drunk in place of water to prevent asthmatic attack.
	Ajo	Garlic	Grind three cloves in cooking oil, take every morning to prevent asthmatic attack.
Attack	Azahar water	Orange flower water	Drink one cup immediately after attack.
	Berro	Watercress	Boil in milk; drink to stop attack.
Back pain	Hoja de tuna	Prickly pear leaf	Char the leaf, mix with camphor oil and apply to back.
Baldness	Romero	Rosemary	Used in shampoo to arrest baldness.
Burns	Papa	Potato	Grate, apply to burn.
Colds	Clara de huevo	Egg whites	Whip one egg white until stiff, drain off

(continued on next page)

Table 3.1—*Continued*

Indication	Herb Spanish	English	Preparation
Colds *(cont.)*	Clara de huevo	Egg whites	remaining fluid and add to fluid one tsp. almond oil and two tsp. castor oil; shake; dose is ¹/₂ tsp.
Constipation	Pasa	Raisins	
Diarrhea	Guanabana	Sour sop	
Earache	Aceite de camphor	Camphor oil	Mix camphor leaf with cooking oil and apply to ear to relieve pain.
Heart condition	Flor de tilo	Linden	Prepare as tea to reduce pain.
Hemorrhage, excessive menstruation	Flor de malva	Mallow	Prepare as tea.
Insomnia	Flor de tilo	Linden	Prepare as tea for sedative.
Infant colds	Oregano chiquito	Little oregano	Prepare as tea.
Infant colics	Manzanilla	Chamomile	Prepare as tea.
Infant diarrhea	Naranjo	Orange	Decoction given to infant when changing formula to prevent diarrhea.
Kidney disorders	Ajonjoli	Sesame seed	Drink decoction to refresh kidney.
	Barba de maiz	Corn silk	Drink decoction to reduce pain.
	Hoja de tuna	Prickly pear leaf	Make decoction of leaves.
Labor	Nuez moscada	Nutmeg	Prepare as tea; drink before birth of baby.
Lactation	Horchata de ajonjoli	Orgeat of sesame seed	Crush sesame seeds, add water, shake and strain; drink to stimulate lactation.

(continued on next page)

Table 3.1—*Continued*

Indication	Herb Spanish	English	Preparation
Measles	Pasa	Raisins	Boil in milk to bring out measles quickly and reduce fever.
Menstruation	Ruda	Rue	Prepare as tea to regulate menstrual period.
Nervous Tension	Flor de tilo	Linden	Prepare as tea.
Neuralgia	Tabaco	Tobacco	Mix with olive oil, apply to face for pain of neuralgia.
Oral lesions	Miel rosada	Pink honey	Apply to sores in the mouth.
Parasites	Guanabana Pasote	Sour sop Saltward	Prepare as tea; drink early in the morning to kill worms and induce catharsis.
Post partum	Nuez moscada	Nutmeg	Decoction of 1 nut in 2 quarts of water; drink for 40 days after delivery to prevent complications and to keep air out of womb.
	Ruda	Rue	Boil in chocolate milk to regulate womb after childbirth.
Rheumatism	Pepa de aguacate	Avocado pit	Grate and mix in alcohol with balsamo de apodeldo and balsamo seramento and apply as a rub.
Tonsillitis	Flor de malva	Mallow	Boil milk, then strain through cotton; drink as gargle. Crush and use as plaster on the throat.
Vomiting	Yerba Buena	Peppermint	Boil leaves in milk.

Source: Collected by Dr. Joseph Suarez, Multicultural Education, Research, and Training Institute.

Haitians also use a number of home remedies which can either be self-administered or applied by a traditional healing person. There are four basic types of traditional healers in Haiti (JSDHG, 1982):

1. *Docteur-feuilles* or *bocars*: leaf doctors that treat patients with medicinal plants, herbs, and roots, occasionally along with mystical ritual.

2. *Houngans/Mambos*: voodoo priests/priestesses who practice a combination of magic and religion.

3. *Sages-femmes/Matrones/Famsaj*: lay midwives, wise women, women without medical training who perform deliveries and other work.

4. *Piquristes*: assistants with some technical experience who give shots and apply dressings.

Some traditional home remedies are presented in Table 3.2.

TABLE 3.2

Plants, Leaves, Roots, Bark and Flowers Considered Therapeutic in Traditional Haitian Culture

Haitian	English Name	Botanical Name	Efficacy
Acajou	Mahogany	Swietemia Mahogani	Bark, enriches blood.
Bambou	Bamboo	Bambussa vulgaris, vel Arundian	An infusion of the leaves is used to control coughs and to cure cold.
Bois de Chene	Oak tree	Catapa longissimue	An infusion of the leaves is used to cure cramps and fever.
Callebasse Marron	Wild calabash	Cressentia Cujete	A syrup made of the calabash pulp is used to melt the "deposits" in "foulaille." After a contusion to prevent "foulaille."
Avocat Marron	Wild avocado		An infusion of the leaves relieves hypertension.
Cresson Marron	Wild watercress	Lepidian Virginium	A tea made from these along with the leaves of

(continued on next page)

Table 3.2—*Continued*

Haitian	English Name	Botanical Name	Efficacy
Cresson Marron	Wild watercress	Lepidian Virginium	eayemite and papaya stimulate breast milk of a nursing mother.
Graine de Cotonnier Violet	Cotton seed	Gosypium	Roasted cotton seeds prepared like coffee stimulate breast milk.
Pistache Marron	Wild peanut	Polygala forniculata	An infusion made of the leaves combined with those of laiteron is used to treat grippe. Alone it is said to prevent hypertension.
Citronelle	Citronnella	Cymbopoyam nardus	Infusions of these leaves are taken to cure gas or stomach cramps. Also used in soothing baths.
Thyme Grandes Feuilles	Thyme	Thymus vulgaria	An infusion made from 2–3 thyme leaves is good for all sorts of pain, fever, chills, grippe or cramps. To relieve a headache, several leaves are inhaled.
Safran	Saffron	Curcuma longa	A small piece of the root soaked in a glass of cold water is used in cases of fever, particularly when accompanied by jaundice.

Source: John Snow Public Health Group, Inc., 1982.

Asian medical practices are based primarily on ancient Chinese medicine and practices which are more than 4,700 years old. The Chinese view their body as a gift given to them by their forebearers. It is not one's personal property and must be cared for properly. This view is based on a Confucian teaching that states, " Only those will be truly revered who at the end of their lives will return their physical bodies whole and sound" (Spector, 1991). The Chinese physician therefore approaches the treatment of the body from a preventive scheme or philosophy. Disease is diagnosed by palpation and inspection. The physician looks at the tongue for color and texture (glossoscopy), listens, and smells. The tongue is divided into two portions, the *She* (the body of the tongue) and the *Tai* (the coating or "fur" of the tongue). A number of illnesses can be preliminarily identified from examination of the tongue. The following are but a few examples (Shen, 1990):

Appearance	Indication
if *Tai* is white	indicates a cold
if *Tai* is thick	digestive system not functioning properly
if *Tai* is thin, small, and white	the internal organs are not functioning well
if there is cleavage down the middle of the tongue	indication of a weak heart, the deeper the cleavage, the more serious it is

During palpation the physician feels the pulses of both the right and left wrist (sphygmo palpation) with the goal of determining if there are any weaknesses or impediments in the flow of blood from one organ to another (Shen, 1990).

Asians also utilize acupuncture, another Chinese medical procedure wherein the body is slightly punctured with special thin metal needles along certain meridian points. Dr. Shen (1990) reports a case where acupuncture helped enormously

> . . . a woman in her twenties came to me five months pregnant and complained that both her abdomen and her lower back hurt. The hospital found that she had a kidney infection, and she was advised to have an abortion in order to save the kidney. The woman was unwilling to give up her baby, so she came to me. I found that her heart and kidney pulses (on the left) were weak. Only her right pulse was a little more normal. Her eyes did not show signs of infection, and her tongue and *Tai* was clean. She told me that she had been ill for three weeks but had not noticed anything abnormal about her urination. She also said she felt better if she was lying down. I diagnosed that it was not a true case of kidney infection, but that her *Qi* [Yin-Yang] was too weak (her body was weak), an infection took place. This was a reactionary illness that required the fetus to be raised away from the kidney; the infection then disappeared.
>
> Reasons for diagnosis and treatment: If it was a true kidney infection, there would be these three indications - the left *chi* pulse should be small, tight, and rapid; the eyes would be red; the urine would be

hot, and there would be frequent urination. Also, there should be no difference in the pain felt in different postures. Instead, the patient's symptoms were indicative of a *xu* illness. Her pain lessened when she lay down. This was evidence that the strain of carrying the fetus aggravated the condition of the kidney. . . . As there was a great lack of *Jing* and blood, I asked if she and her husband had frequent sexual intercourse. Her husband confirmed it. I told them to stop. I made the patient lie down, and applied acupuncture to her *ren zhong* point (GV–26). In a few seconds, she felt better. However, she returned the next day, complaining of the pain again. I realized that the acupuncture had made the *Qi* go upward, raising the fetus, but the trip home had brought the *Qi* down again, so the pain recurred. I showed her husband how to apply the needle; he could then do it at home. In the meantime, the patient had to stay in bed for a week and take the medicine, to nourish the fetus. A week later, she was feeling much better.

This is an example of the effectiveness of the diagnosis and acupuncture technique by a Chinese doctor, as well as a treatment approach contrary to the recommended abortion. Similarly, the author (Dr. Quervalú) received acupuncture treatment for lower back problems which repeated visits to doctors and hospitals could not cure.

Another common practice among Asians is moxibustion, which can be seen at clinics where recent migrants or refugees are treated (Buchwald, et al., 1992). Moxibustion is based on the therapeutic value of heat, whereas acupuncture is a cold treatment. Moxibustion is performed by heating pulverized wormwood and applying it directly to the skin over specific meridians. Among other purposes, it is helpful for women during the labor and delivery periods.

Ginseng is one of the oldest and most famous of the Chinese herbs. It is recommended for more than two dozen ailments including anemia, colic, depression, indigestion, impotence, and rheumatism. Some other remedies derived from ginseng are the following (Spector, 1991):

Purpose	Preparation
to stimulate digestion	rub ginseng to a powder, mix with white of egg, and take three times a day
as a sedative	prepare a light broth of ginseng and bamboo leaves
for faintness after	administer a strong brew of

Purpose	Preparation
childbirth	ginseng several times a day
as restorative for frail children	give a dash of raw, minced ginseng several times per day

Other popular Chinese remedies are (adapted from Spector, 1991)

Ingredient	Purpose
Deer antlers	to strengthen bones, increase a man's potency, and dispel nightmares
Lime calcium	to clear excessive mucus
Quicksilver	used externally to treat venereal disease
Rhinoceros horns	highly effective when applied to boils, also antitoxins for snakebites
Turtle shells	to stimulate weak kidneys and remove gallstones
Snake fish	to keep eyes healthy and vision clear
Seahorses	pulverized and used to treat gout

Asians have a different concept of illness and its treatment, and generally believe that herbal drugs, which are produced from natural plants, are not as harmful or toxic as western medicines are. Consequently, Asian patients may combine herbs with western drugs and not inform their physician or psychiatrist. Since there are few studies which have documented the interactive effects of herbal drugs and medication, it is difficult for the psychiatrist or physician to know the interaction between them. In general, herbal drugs are likely to cause side effects if they contain an atropine-like substance that is known to produce anticholinergic effects (Chien, 1993). A soon-to-be published article by Crone and Wise (in press) provides a seminal foundation for helping physicians understand the use of herbal medicines, their risks, interactions, and efficacy.

Among Native Americans the traditional healer is the medicine man, although he is known by various names, such as Grandfather or Medicine Priest. The Hopi medicine man uses meditation or sometimes a crystal ball to determine the cause of a person's illness. He chews on the root of jimsonweed, which enables him to go into a trance, and envisions the evil that has caused the illness. Once the evil is identified, the medicine man prescribes a particular herbal treatment. Sweats, which may also be part of the treatment, are used for spiritual cleansing or healing, particularly of fevers. The ceremony is usually held in a tepee with steam provided by pouring water over very hot rocks. Among the Sioux medicine men there are specialists; some treat wounds and snake bites, while others treat internal ailments alone (White & Maccabe, 1996).

Specific rituals are followed in gathering herbs. Only specific plants are picked, and care is taken not to disturb other plants or animals in their natural environment. Some of the more common ailments using herbal treatments are presented in Table 3.3.

Native Americans also utilize western as well as traditional medicine. Unfortunately, many western physicians do not collaborate with traditional Indian medicine practitioners; nor are they aware that their Indian patients are seeing them (White & Maccabe, 1996). Herbal medicines are used exclusively by Indian healers, and are used for laxative, diuretic, emetic, and fever-reducing purposes. Some remedies used by the Oneida Indians are (Spector, 1991):

Illness	Remedy
Colds	Witch hazel, sweet flag
Sore throat	Comfrey
Diarrhea	Elderberry flowers
Headache	Tansy and sage
Ear infection	Skunk oil
Mouth sores	Dried raspberry leaves

Some additional remedies used among the Micmac Indians from Canada are (Spector, 1991):

Illness	Remedy
Warts	Juice from milkweed plant
Obesity	Spruce bark and water
Rheumatism	Juniper berries
Diabetes	Combination of blueberries and huckleberries
Sleep help	Eat a head of lettuce a day
Diarrhea	Tea from wild strawberry

TABLE 3.3

Common Herbal Treatments Used by the Hopi Indians

Ingredient	Purpose	Preparation
Globe mallow	for cuts and wounds for broken bones	applied and the root is chewed
Pinon gum	to keep air from cuts	applied to the wound
Cliff rose	to wash wounds	
Sand sagebrush	for boils	boils are brought to a head
Sunflowers	for spider bites	person bathes in water in which flowers have been soaked
Bladder pods	for snakebites	the root is chewed and then placed on the bite
Lichens	to treat gums	ground to a powder and then rubbed on the affected areas
Fleabane	to treat headaches	the entire herb is tied to the head or drunk as a tea
Blue gillia	for digestive disorders	leaves are boiled in water and drunk
Yucca	as a laxative	using the stem
Thistle flower	to expel worms	
Blanket flower	as a diuretic for painful urination	as a tea
Painted cups	to relieve the pain of menstruation	drunk as a tea
Winter fat	if the uterus fails to contract properly during labor	tea from the leaves

Source: Adapted from Spector, 1991.

African Americans also have a rich tradition of folk medicine reflecting their ancestral knowledge of plants and herbs from Africa and applied in the Americas when they were uprooted and subjected to slavery. The use of willow leaves in tea to treat fever, dampened mullen leaves to heal skin lacerations, or the use of spring tonics which were used to "flush the system" of children to prevent and cure infestations of worms during the 1800s and 1900s (Gaw, 1993) are examples of practices that have been handed down primarily by older African Americans. The use of cod liver oil, which is given to children to prevent colds, is also quite common. An-

TABLE 3.4

Reported Successful African American Home Remedies

Ingredient	Purpose	Preparation
Sugar and turpentine	to get rid of worms	mixed and taken orally
	to cure a backache	rubbed on skin from the navel to the back
Potatoes	to fight inflammation, infection or disease	potatoes are sliced or grated and placed in a bag which is placed on the affected area of the body. Potato turns black and draws out disease (penicillin mold is produced).
Goldenrod roots	to treat pain and reduce fevers	boiled
Sassafras	to treat colds	boiled
Bluestone (mineral)	for open wounds, prevents inflamma-tion, also poison ivy	stone is crushed into a powder and sprinkled on the affected area
Two pieces of silverware	to treat a "crick" in in the neck	over the painful area in the form of an X
Nine drops of turpentine	as a contraceptive	after intercourse
Sour or spoiled milk	for cuts and wounds	placed on stale bread, wrapped in a cloth, and placed on the wound
Salt and pork (salt pork)	to treat cuts and wounds	placed on a rag
Clay	for sprained ankle	place clay in a dark leaf and wrap it around the ankle
Lemon water with honey	for cold	boil and drink while hot
camphorated oil	for congestion in the chest and coughing	rub chest with hot oil and wrap the person with warm flannel
Garlic, onion, fresh parsley	as expectorant for colds	mix chopped ingredients with a little water in the blender
Raw onions	to break a fever	place raw onions on feet and wrap with warm blankets
Garlic	to remove evil spirits	place on the ill person or in their room

Source: Adapted from Spector, 1991.

other example is a massage concoction of sulfur and molasses which is prepared and given in the spring because it is believed that people are more
susceptible to illness at the start of the new season. Wearing a copper or
silver bracelet around the wrist can indicate when the wearer is about to
become ill—the skin around the bracelet becomes black (Spector, 1991).
Some of the more successful home remedies reported are presented in
Table 3.4.

Part of folk healing or doctoring is the practice of "working of roots,"
which involves the use of plants in the preparation of potions to bring
about good or evil. Among Puerto Ricans, it is called "Espiritismo,"
among Cubans it is "Santeria," and among South Americans and Latinos
it is "Curanderismo" (see Cultural Concepts in chapter 4). The health
care provider or physician needs to probe for home remedy usage and for
any interactive side effects between a prescribed medication and the
home remedy, and should discuss these effects with the patient (perhaps
curtailing the home remedy for few days, if necessary).

Verify how the patient will take the medication or follow the treatment plan.

As our case vignettes illustrate, patients, particularly recent first generation immigrants, may have a completely different view of taking medication from that of the provider, who should therefore speak slowly and
then repeat the instructions.

Many Asian Americans are skeptical of western medicine because
they believe physicians overprescribe medications, and consequently they
do not comply with the physicians' instructions. They may take half of
the medicine or none at all. Several cultural groups believe that drawing
too much blood can make a person weak and upset their balance (*chi*).
Sometimes enlisting the help of a family member or significant other may
help the patient understand that a particular medicine will effectively
treat the illness.

Don't assume that the patient understands you and will follow your medical advice simply on the basis of his or her nod and a verbal "yes, yes." If in doubt, use an interpreter.

Many times limited-English-speaking people understand certain
parts of a question but not its totality. Clients may also provide a gesture
or vocal tone which can be a clue for the provider to probe for a deeper
understanding. Interpreters should have a good understanding of com-

mon health problems and diseases experienced by patients in a given culture, and should have a solid grasp of their folk traditions and health care beliefs. When using an interpreter, there are three general types of interaction which affect the triadic relationship between the provider, interpreter, and patient (Bloom, 1966):

1. The interpreter becomes the interviewer. The interpreter has gained control of the meeting when the interviewer allows the interpreter to ask original questions not originally designated or asked by the provider. The interpreter has in the process gained the trust of the client, as well as eliciting the client's cooperation.

2. The interpreter is a tool. The interpreter translates literally; adding no nuances or meaning within the cultural context of responses. In this scenario the provider may have a rigid control and not allow the interpreter to explain or express the cultural beliefs of the client.

3. Both the interpreter and interviewer are partners. This allows both to work as an effective team, allowing full communication between them and the client. The interpreter is allowed to interpret as well as translate all responses and to explain any cultural health beliefs the client may have expressed.

Be aware of the basic beliefs, values, and mores of various cultures.

This is probably the most extensive area of information simply because of the number of different cultural groups that have settled in both urban and suburban areas throughout the United States. As stated above, the provider should first be grounded in understanding his or her own cultural background and heritage, and then proceed to learn about other groups' cultural values and beliefs. Although there will be some social service providers who know more than others, depending on their experiences with different populations, no one person can know all there is to know about all the ethnic cultural groups.

Physicians should become familiar with diseases and illnesses which are endemic to countries around the world. Children of recent immigrants may have been exposed to malaria or tuberculosis and may not have had a full complement of immunizations (Christenson & Fischer, 1993). Children are also susceptible to hepatitis A (HAV), which is highly endemic in the developing countries of Central and South America, Africa, and Asia. Typhoid fever, a serious systemic illness, is also common in developing countries such as Mexico, Peru, India, Pakistan, Chile, and Haiti. The problem of infectious disease is not necessarily restricted to when immigrants arrive, but also arises when they return to their homeland for visits and come back to the host country (Cook, 1992).

Religion and Folk Beliefs

People in all cultures seem to have a common ground in their belief in the supernatural, which is manifested primarily in religion and religious practices. Western culture is largely influenced by the Judeo-Christian and Islamic traditions, while Eastern culture is dominated more by Buddhism, Confucianism, Taoism, and Hinduism. Religion influences culture and vice versa. Prayer has often been a resource for people with chronic problems. Despite the paucity of literature on the role of prayer in medicine, more and more articles and books are being published about the healing power of prayer (Bearon & Koenig, 1990; Hufford, 1993). Dr. Larry Dorsey, after practicing medicine for many years, was amazed to discover scientific evidence of the healing power of prayer. In his research, he writes about the way prayer can be assessed in laboratory experiments, and examines which methods of prayer show the greatest potential for healing and how one's innate temperament and personality affect prayer style (Jacobs, 1995).

Among African Americans, health beliefs may vary from community to community and from family to family. The etiology of illness can be divided into three categories:

1. Those which have natural causes; for example, failure to cure one's own body or sinful behavior,
2. Illnesses caused by extraordinary powers that are used for personal gain or for good or bad intentions (such as hexing), and
3. Religious causes.

A person may believe he or she has been "fixed," "mojoed," "hoodooed," "hexed," or "rooted." People may believe they are "spirited" because another person may be jealous of them, may want something they have, or is seeking revenge (Snow, 1974). A person may pay someone to do a "fix" that results in another person suffering from an illness which often is accompanied by a strong sense of fear. The rituals can include candles, potions, beads, prayers, incantations, and rituals which are performed at specific times and places; such as under a full moon by the river. If an individual's beliefs are strong enough, the rituals may result in a cure or hex. Although these beliefs are practiced predominately by low-income, poorly educated African Americans, moderate and higher income families may have experiences with either "roots" or folk medicine. Home remedies have been utilized for many generations by members of the black community (Spector, 1991) in conjunction with prayer.

Prayer is the most common method of treating illness. Many blacks believe in the power of some persons to heal and help others, and there are numerous reports of many healers among the African-American communities. The reliance on healers reflects the deep religious faith of the people and is described in Maya Angelou's book, *I Know Why the Caged Bird Sings* (Spector, 1991).

Many blacks have followed the Pentecostal movement long before its tent meetings became popular. Ezra Griffith has written numerous articles on the impact of religion and culture on psychiatric care (Griffith, 1982; Griffith et al., 1984). Griffith and his colleagues (1984) isolated three elements of the church service which can be considered directly therapeutic for the participants: Holy Ghost possession, prayer, and testimony. One of the religious phenomenons experienced by some in the group was "speaking in tongues." They described specific benefits such as receiving help, gaining strength, and group closeness. When church participants were interviewed, they said:

"Everybody needs prayer. People are burdened and they go there and leave it at the altar. It's like a service station. You go there and get filled up."
"You gain strength. Prayer changes things."

In this study of the healing ministry in a West Indian Church which uses both orthodox medicine and prayer, Griffith found that of thirty-nine adults who used the clinic, 10 percent felt the doctor alone made them feel better, and 69 percent felt that the doctor plus prayer had contributed to their improvement (Griffith, 1982).

The three main religions of China are Confucianism, Taoism, and Buddhism: however, the ancestral cult of the Chinese is the oldest and most pervasive of its religions (Gaw, 1993). It is based on the belief that the living can communicate with the dead, thus forming the basis for the veneration of ancestral spirits. A typical Asian home may therefore have a

shelf for ancestral tablets on which incense is burned and offerings to the
ancestors are made. This is very similar to espiritismo and other cult religions in which offerings are made to different saints. The person who
deals with the spirit world is the shaman. He is usually called upon to
help treat a sick person either by herbal medications in combination with
acupuncture, or by working out a malevolent spirit when the patient believes he is possessed.

In general the Southeast Asian has been strongly influenced by Chinese philosophy, believes in the Yin-Yang concept of disease, and follows the hot and cold theory of illness. Consequently clients may speak
of letting out spirits which have invaded the body (Gaw, 1993). Spirits
or forces can be let in and out of the body by cupping or coining (see
Cultural Concepts in the next chapter). Since both of these procedures
cause abrasions, physicians should be aware of this treatment application and not confuse it with physical abuse, particularly when practiced
on children. For Buddhists, which include the majority of Cambodians,
emphasis is placed on the life cycle and rebirth. Buddists believe that
this life is painful because of possible misdeeds in a previous life. Buddhist monks and traditional healers may be seen by patients before or in
conjunction with a western physician. However, in many isolated communities in the United States there are few Buddhist monks or traditional healers whom Asian believers can turn to for help, even when
western medical professionals respect the traditional healers and their
techniques.

In the white American community, Edgar Cayce was probably one of
the most famous nontraditional healers during the late 1930s. When in a
self-induced hypnotic trance state, he had the gifts of a psychic: clairvoy-
ance and precognition. In this trance state, he could diagnose individuals
with difficult illnesses and suggest treatments for them (Bolton, 1969).
Dozens of his treatments which were initially scorned by the medical institutions are now accepted as practice (McGarey, 1985). Edgar Cayce believed he had received his gift to do good from God. He believed in the
power of prayer as well.

At the Association of Research and Enlightenment, which Cayce
founded, prayer groups were formed and the members were given a list of
names of people who asked to be healed. The list was reworked every
month. According to their reports there have been many people healed.
One group used the "laying on of hands," which worked well for a woman
who had been told after an examination by her doctor that she had prob-
able cancer of the breast. The go-between to the group was asked to be

the "channel" of the healing energy from the group to the woman. The following is a summary of that encounter:

> I felt the creative energies passing through, (had placed my right hand on her forehead and the left hand on the neck at approximately the thyroid gland). There was much heat, not only in the hands but throughout the whole body. She felt the energies enter and felt the heat. Each member of the group said they felt the flow of energy . . . when she went for another examination at the hospital on Monday (the next day), she was examined by four doctors. The lump had decreased in size to about the size of a very small pea, and it was decided that there was no reason to perform the biopsy at all. They were somewhat puzzled and asked what had happened. She told them about the laying on of hands. You can imagine the consternation. One, a woman doctor, followed our friend out of the examination room of the hospital and said that she had always been able to "see" a patient's illness before there was a physical examination but had never told anyone because she thought they'd think she had flipped her lid. (McGarey, 1985)

Native Americans also have a number of ceremonies, as well as different conceptualizations of the origin or creation of the world and its people (Mann et al., 1995). Within the many tribes there are unique individuals who possess special and sacred skills which are used when things are out of balance with an individual. They are known by different names, but generally they may be referred to as ceremonial or medicine people. These medicine people integrate spiritual ways and tribal values into their ways of living. It is the medicine man who provides not only resolution of spiritual issues, but also treatment and care for health problems.

The importance of culture in medicine is slowly becoming recognized and integrated into the fabric of the educational curricula of medical schools. In 1977, for the very first time, Native-American medicine men moved into the Rough Rock Community Health Center in Arizona and began working side by side with the health center's licensed medical personnel, creating a bicultural and holistic approach in treating the medical problems of the community (*Rough Rock News*, 1977). More recently, the University of Washington School of Medicine, in conjunction with the Seattle Indian Health Board, developed and implemented a program wherein medical residents could practice alongside medicine men in various designated communities throughout their region. Besides understanding the traditional Indian perception of health and illness, one of the goals is to understand the role of religions such as the Native American Church and the Indian Shaker Church within health-related practices. Their educational experience includes learning about sweat lodges, and the use of traditional Indian medicine, as well as the extent (and, presumably, the interactive effect) of their simultaneous use with western medicine.

In 1995 New York Medical College, in conjunction with the Multicultural Education Research and Training Institute, conducted a symposium in which selected faculty members and invited guests were asked to make recommendations, prior to the symposium date, on how to integrate culture into their medical curricula (MERTI, 1996). Recommendations from the symposium included a framework for knowledge of basic cultural tenets in order to strengthen baseline information, including sociodemographics of the patient community as well as the contributions of multicultural groups to their respective communities. Other recommendations focused on learning skills in several areas, for example: cultural communication skills, including the proper use of a translator, history taking, and the patient-physician relationship; culture and its impact on gender issues, death and dying, medical compliance, child-rearing, herbal and alternative healing and herbal/medicine combinations and their side effects, pain management, cadaver procurement, physiological differences among ethnic groups, mental health, and right to die issues.

The above mentioned are some of the few schools of medicine which are actively reviewing their curricula and addressing the issues of the cultural beliefs and health practices of the population they service. As stated earlier (Lum & Korenman, 1994), few medical schools have fully integrated cultural changes and cultural sensitivity into their training programs. However, there are several schools which have workshops or lectures in which ethnic and cultural concerns relevant to health services are addressed. Stanford University School of Medicine has such a series of lectures, which covers a wide range of issues, including the coexistence of indigenous medicine and allopathic medicine, case conferences with ethnic and racial populations, and ethnic considerations in transplant medicine.

Understand the value of the family presence and role in the illness and recovery process.

Most ethnic and cultural groups are extended-family oriented whereas individuals from a white European-American background are essentially nuclear-family oriented. In America an individual is expected to become independent of the family of origin. Among Puerto Ricans and Hispanics, intimate relationships with the kinship family are a highly valued source of pride and security (Badillo-Ghali, 1982). The families on the island of Puerto Rico, as well as on the mainland, use the extended-family system in times of crisis. Within the concept of familism, which stresses family loyalty and interdependence among its members (by cooperation rather than competition), the needs of the individual are subordinate to the needs of the family.

The other major extended-family system is "compadrazgo" or godfatherism. This system stresses the relationships between godparent and godchildren, and godparent and the natural parents. Consequently, when a Hispanic client presents symptoms to a physician, more than likely there will be family members worried about the patient and involved in his or her outcome. These family members may seek folk remedies, if appropriate, either prior to or in conjunction with medication. The same can be said for Asian Americans who turn to the acupuncturist, as well as to the shaman, for herbal treatment, while also keeping in mind the physician's medication.

Medical Compliance

Up to this point there has been an attempt to emphasize that people from various ethnic and cultural groups have different views about illness and culturally based approaches to their treatment. The task of the physician or health care provider is first to establish "where the patient is coming from" in order to be able to determine what kinds of intervention will be needed.

Along with the process of knowing the patient, the provider needs to determine that there is a good fit between the provider and the patient. The focus of this fit would be on a relationship in which there is mutual respect and trust. Thus, it is important for the provider to know that people from different ethnic and cultural groups have different concepts about control, and about where the locus of control might be for things that are happening to them (MERTI, 1995).

Some people may feel that the control rests entirely within them, whereas others, from a different ethnic cultural group, may see the locus of control as entirely outside of themselves (such as in their family, in God, in spirit, or in some other factor that may influence what happens to them). People with different points of view have different expectations of physicians and of themselves, and may require a different type of interaction from the physician. Dr. Richard Dudley in his presentation (MERTI, 1995) to an audience of medical students, states that:

1. People who see all the locus of control within themselves would work best with the physician who could have a more cooperative interaction with them and work with the patient as a partner in the decision-making process.
2. People who believe the locus of control is somewhere else, because of their belief system, might do better with the physician who could be a little bit more directive with them and teach them about taking responsibility of their own care.

Dr. Dudley also states that physicians need to be knowledgeable and concerned about side effects of medications with different ethnic cultural groups. A small but growing literature within the mental health services area has demonstrated that for years patients from ethnic cultural backgrounds have essentially been overmedicated (Chou et al., 1991; Rosenblat & Tang, 1987; Lin & Finder, 1983; Yamamoto et al., 1979). Subsequently, studies found that low dosages are effective and preferred by patients because of lesser side effects. Dr. Dudley states that when one prescribes, one has to take into consideration the individual's experiences with medication and the adverse side effects as which will influence their compliance. Other factors also influence compliance, such as whether the physician or health care provider is trying to get people to alter their lifestyles, diets, or other habits that are valuable to them. Consequently, all of these factors need to be taken into consideration when developing a treatment plan for the patient.

Use an interpreter whenever appropriate.

Because of changing demographics, more and more health providers are faced with limited-English-speaking patients. In too many instances the health provider is faced with using hand signals if he or she can't find an interpreter. Sometimes the provider is faced with an embarrassing situation. For example, sitz baths were prescribed for a poor working thirty-year-old woman who was seven months pregnant and suffered from diabetes and swelling and pain in her hands. The sitz baths were prescribed to provide immersion therapy for her arms and hands. On a subsequent visit the physician and dietician were concerned because of the patient's unexpected weight loss. They decided to call an interpreter to help find the cause. The patient told them that her hands still hurt, but that she's been very faithful about doing her sitz baths. She said that "they are very tiring, but I have been doing them for twenty minutes twice a day." Feeling very concerned, the physician asked her to show him how she does them. She explained that she fills the tub with water and gets in and sits down, then she stands up, sits down, stands up, sits down for twenty minutes at a time (Haffner, 1992).

Had the interpreter been present on the first visit the scenario would never have happened. When using an interpreter to obtain information, the health care provider must be aware of certain fundamental principles. Here are some basic rules to keep in mind:

1. Get to know the client's language ability.

2. Have a pre-interview meeting with the interpreter and advise him or her of the following:

   a. Don't normalize the interpretation. Whenever possible the interpreter should convey the same or similar emotional intent of the client.

   b. The interpreter needs to give a verbatim—word-for-word— translation of the client's account.

   c. The interpreter should concentrate on how things are said, as well as on what is said.

3. Have a post-interview meeting with the interpreter to get additional information and clarity.

The health care provider should also be aware of certain problems that could arise during the interview (Marcos, 1979; Ruiz, 1992):

1. The patient will give you two to three minutes of response, but the interpreter gives you twenty-five seconds, consequently leaving out information.

2. The patient may have an ambivalent attitude. The patient will say "yes," then "no." The interpreter may reply with a no, thus losing subtle interactions particularly vital in psychotherapy.

3. The patient may give circumstantial or loosely associated answers. Interpreters may tend to make sense of things or normalize the answers. As stated above, the interpreter should give a verbatim translation.

4. The depth of quality of affect or feelings is lost. Interpreters need to concentrate not only on what is said, but on how the patient is saying it.

5. If a family member serves as the interpreter, the patient may feel inhibited. He or she may be hesitant to reveal sexual issues or personal family matters. Many times family members will answer for the patient, giving their impressions before the patient can respond (Hardt, 1991). The health care provider will need to instruct the family member about basic interpretation rules, as stated above.

6. Reliance on the bilingual staff member. A staff member may be resistant to being the unit's interpreter in addition to already assigned tasks.

Here are some additional problem areas and issues:

1. Patients' emotional suffering and despair are underestimated.

2. Interpreters tend to overidentify with patients.

3. The use of interpreters creates a great deal of tension during the interviewing process for all involved.

4. Interpreters may become embarrassed when having to translate sexual and suicidal questions.

5. Paralinguistics and vocal cues are not translated.

6. Cultural behavior is difficult to translate.

7. Certain patients alter their responses when interpreters are used, due to the extra attention they get.

References

Angelou, M. (1970). *I know why the caged bird sings.* New
York: Random House.

Badillo-Ghali, S. (1982). Understanding Puerto Rican traditions. *Social Casework* (October 1977) 459–468.

Bearon, L.B., & Koenig, H.G. (1990, April 30). Religious cognition and use of prayer in health and illness. *Gerontologist*, (2), 249–253.

Benedetti, M. (1992). *Hasta los banos te curan! Remedios caseros y mucho mas de Puerto Rico.* Also entitled *Earth and spirit: Healing, lore and more from Puerto Rico.* (2nd ed.). Saline, MI: McNaughton and Gunn.

Bloom, M. (1966). The use of interpreters in interviewing: Characteristics, conceptualizations and cautions. *Mental Hygiene, 50*(2), 214–217.

Bolton, B. (Ed.). (1969). *Edgar Cayce speaks.* New York: Avon.

Buchwald, D., Panwala, S., & Hooton, T.M. (1992). Use of traditional health practices by southeast Asian refugees in a primary care clinic. *Western Journal of Medicine, 156*(5), 507–511.

Chien, C.P. (1993). Ethnopsychopharmacology. In A.C. Gaw (Ed.), *Culture, ethnicity and mental illness.* Washington, DC: American Psychiatric Press.

Chou, J.C.Y., Douyon, R., Czobar, P., & Volavka, J. (1991, May). Paper presented at the annual meeting of the American Psychiatric Association, New Orleans, New Research Presentation # 205.

Christenson, J.C., & Fischer, P.R. (1993). Health risks of travel: Back in the USA. *Contemporary Pediatrics, 10*(7), 39–56.

Cook, G.C. (1992). Some medical problems affecting the ethnic minorities of the United Kingdom. *Journal of Research in Social Health, 112*(3), 137–142.

Crone, C.C., & Wise, Thomas (Eds.) (in press). Use of herbal medicine among C-L populations: A review of current information regarding risks, interactions, and efficacy. *Psychosomatics.* Washington, DC: American Psychiatric Press, Inc.

Cross, T.L., Bazron, B.J., Dennis, K.W., & Isaacs, M.R. (1989). *Towards a culturally competent system of care.* Washington, DC: Georgetown University Child Development Center, Technical Assistance Center.

Deitrich, G. (1982). Indian child welfare act: Ideas for implementation. *Child Abuse and Neglect, 6*(2), 125–128.

Desmond, J. (1994). Communicating with multicultural patients. *Life in Medicine, 7–25.*

First time in history . . . Hati move into clinic (1977, Nov. 29). *Rough Rock News,* Vol. XIII, No. 3. Rough Rock, AZ.

Gaw, A.C. (1993). Psychiatric care of Chinese Americans. In A.C. Gaw (Ed.), *Culture, ethnicity and mental illness.* Washington, DC: American Psychiatric Press.

Goldman, (1980). Effect of eye contact and distance on the verbal reinforcement of attitude. *The Journal of Social Psychology, 111,* 73–78.

Griffith, E.H. (1982). The impact of culture and religion on psychiatric care. *Journal of the National Medical Association, 74*(12).

Griffith, E.H., Young, J.L., & Smith, D.L. (1984). An analysis of the therapeutic elements in a black church service. *Hospital and Community Psychiatry, 35*(5), 464–469.

Haffner, L. (1992, Sept.). Translation is not enough—Interpretation in a medical setting. *Western Journal of Medicine, 157,* 255–259.

Hardt, E.J. (1991). *Discussion leader's guide for the bilingual medical interview I and the bilingual medical interview II: The geriatric interview,* Edited by B. Harrington, L.A. McElaney, M. Nash, & S. Simon. Boston: Boston Department of Health and Hospitals.

Harwood, A. (1971). The hot and cold theory of disease: Implications for treatment of Puerto Rican patients. *Journal of the American Medical Association, 216*(7), 1153–1158.

Harwood, A. (1981). *Ethnicity and medical care.* Cambridge, MA: Harvard University Press.

Harwood, A., & Kleinman, A. (1981). Ethnicity and clinical care: Selected issues in treating Puerto Rican patients. *Hospital Physician, 17*(9), 113–118.

Hufford, D.J. (1993, April). Epistemologies in religious healing. *Journal of Medical Philosophy, 18*(2), 175–194.

Jacobs, P.D. (1995). *500 tips for coping with chronic illness.* San Francisco: Robert D. Reed Publishers and PDJ Publishing.

JSPHG. (1982). *Common health care beliefs and practices of Puerto Ricans, Haitians and low income blacks living in the New York, New Jersey area.* Under contract with NHSC/DHHS/Region II, Contract No. 120–83–0011, Washington, DC: John Snow Public Health Group, Inc.

Kleinman, A., Eisenberg, L., & Good, B. (1978). Culture, illness and care: Clinical lessons from anthropologic and cross-cultural research. *Annals of Internal Medicine, 88,* 251–258.

Lin, K.M., & Finder, E. (1983). Neuroleptic dosage for Asians. *American Journal of Psychiatry, 140,* 490–491.

Lum, C.K., & Korenman, S.G. (1994). Cultural-sensitivity training in U.S. medical schools. *Academic Medicine, 69*(3), 239–241.

Mann, H., Sadler, J., & Blanchard, E. (1995). In K.R. Argrette and J. Suarez (Eds.), *An introduction to Indian life: A Native American curriculum.* New York: Multicultural Education, Research and Training Institute, Dept. of Psychiatry and CMHC, Metropolitan Hospital Center.

Marcos, L.R. (1979). Effects of interpreters on the evaluation of psychopathology in non-English speaking patients. *American Journal of Psychiatry, 136*(2), 171–174.

McGarey, W.A. (1985). *The Edgar Cayce remedies.* New York: Bantam Books.

MERTI. (1996). *Recommendations from the culture and medical education action plan round table symposium* (April, 1995). New York: Multicultural Education, Research and Training Institute, Department of Psychiatry, Metropolitan Hospital Center.

MERTI. (1995). Seminar presentation by Dr. R. Dudley in I. Quervalú (Ed.), *Culture in medicine* (Sept., 1994). New York: Multicultural Education, Research and Training Institute, Department of Psychiatry, Metropolitan Hospital Center.

Pernell-Arnold, A. (1995). *Diversity and health care training. Training curriculums.* Philadelphia: APAC, Inc.

Rosenblat, R., & Tang, S.W. (1987). Do Oriental psychiatric patients receive different dosages of psychotropic medication when compared with Occidentals? *Canadian Journal of Psychiatry, 32,* 270–273.

Rough Rock News. (1977). Rough Rock, AZ.

Roy, B. (1995). Tuskegee syphilis experiment: Biotechnology and the administrative state. *Journal of National Medical Association, 87,* 56–67.

Ruiz, P. (1992). In J. Suarez (Ed.), *Keynote addresses: New York State forums.* New York: Multicultural Education, Research and Training Institute, Dept. of Psychiatry and CMHC, Metropolitan Hospital Center.

Shelby, J. (1996, April 3). A patient approach to cultural change. *Daily News,* p. 3.

Shen, J.F. (1990). *Chinese medicine.* (2nd ed.). Shanghai, China: Chinese Medicine Research Foundation of Dr. John Shen, 381 Fifth Avenue, New York, NY.

Sherer, J. (1993). New waves: Hospitals struggle to meet the challenge of multiculturalism now—and in the next generation. *Hospitals,* May 20, 29–31.

Snow, L.F. (1974). Folk medical beliefs and the implications for care of patients: A review based on studies among black Americans. *Annals of International Medicine, 81,* 82–96.

Spector, R.E. (1991). *Cultural diversity in health and illness.* (3rd ed.). Norwalk, CT: Appleton and Lange.

Sue, S., & Sue, D. (1990). *Counseling the culturally different: Theory and practice.* (2nd ed.). New York: Wiley.

White, K., & Maccabe, T. (1996, March). Native healing: An ancient art. *The Medical Herald, 6*(2), South Florida, FL: The Medical Herald Publishing Co.

Yamamoto, J., Fung, D., Lo, S., & Reece, S. (1979). Psychopharmacology for Asian Americans and Pacific Islanders. *Psychopharmacology Bulletin, 15*(4), 29–31.

CHAPTER 4

Cultural Competency and Mental Health Services

In 1960 Gurin, Veroff, and Feld reported on their seminal nationwide survey (circa 1957) on how Americans view their mental health. They were interested in two broad areas of concern: (1) feelings of adjustment, which explored some of the satisfactions and dissatisfactions people were deriving from life, and (2) methods of handling emotional problems, which explored the general approach that people were taking in handling tensions and problems.

They were also interested in studying the particular sources of help to which people turn when faced with emotional and adjustment problems: do they go to a psychiatrist, a social agency, a minister, their physician, family, or friends? They included an anxiety and psychosomatic "symptom" list which is similar to Langner's twenty-two-item psychiatric screening instrument.

In analyzing their data they were concerned with questions of whether psychological and emotional stresses are experienced more in some groups than in others, and whether different subgroups in their "normal" population experience stress differently. The primary concern in their analysis was to view their measurements not on a continuum of mental illness, but rather as indices of "subjective need." Because they were interested in studying a sampling of the "normal" population, their approach was appropriate to their survey design, as well as acceptable to the Joint Commission on Mental Illness and Health, which sponsored the project.

Data of this nature, mental health resources or help-patterns in the

Hispanic/Latino community, had been sporadic throughout this period. Some studies were available on Puerto Ricans, not on mental health resources per se, but rather on psychological illnesses. The studies indicated the overrepresentation of Puerto Ricans in treatment facilities (in New York State) ranging from the chronically mentally disabled, to those involuntarily committed to mental institutions, to other emergency cases treated as mental illnesses (Dohrenwend, 1966; Malzberg, 1956; Srole et al., 1962). However, studies of the utilization of outpatient mental health services by the Mexican-American population in the southwestern United States revealed that Mexican Americans were underrepresented as clientele of mental health service facilities (Abad et al., 1974; Jaco, 1959; Padilla & Ruiz, 1973). Among Chinese-American women the prevalence of mental health problems was found to be high, particularly depression, anxiety, and psychosomatic disorders, yet the service utilization was low (Loo, 1982).

In general, there is an underrepresentation of minority clients in mental health settings. Not only are the statistics low but when minority clients present themselves to the clinics, a large percentage terminate after their first visit in comparison to Anglo clients (Sue et al., 1975, 1974; Sue & McKinney, 1975). When they finally get therapy, their disorders tend to be more severe than those of other clients, or they require hospitalization as a consequence of not receiving culturally appropriate services early, during the developmental stages of their problems (Uba, 1994).

Consequently, many researchers have argued that minority ethnic groups do not utilize these services because the available facilities are inadequate due to certain socio-cultural variables such as: (a) geographic isolation, (b) language barriers, (c) class-bound values, and (d) culture values (Torrey, 1969, 1973).

Whatever the reasons for this underutilization by ethnic cultural groups from low socioeconomic environments, be they the above variables or other stress indicators, there is substantial evidence that there is a demonstrable need for mental health resources based on indices of high drug abuse, alcoholism, high school dropout rates, juvenile delinquency, and the rising number of children going to foster placements. The major ethnic cultural groups are also exposed to other variables which have been shown to correlate with mental illness; such as lower income, lower social status, deteriorated housing, problems associated with acculturation (Rogler & Hollingshead, 1965), and forced mobility due to housing relocation or being new arrivals (Dohrenwend, 1966; Gorbea, C., 1975;

Hollingshead & Redlich, 1958; Rogler, 1978; Taeuber & Taeuber, 1976; Torrey, 1969).

A recent study of Hispanics/Latinos and mental health services utilization was conducted by Rodriguez (1987). In this study of South Bronx (New York City) residents of the Fordham-Tremont Community Mental Health Center catchment area, he found that Hispanics had a higher symptom rate than both blacks and whites and that the majority of blacks and Hispanics do not report emotional problems and do not use mental health services. Reluctance to acknowledge such problems is the main source of underutilization among Hispanics/Latinos (and other ethnic groups) with a high number of demoralization symptoms. In conclusion, he states that the data suggests that social networks are instrumental in a person's decision to seek services, that service agencies need to be cognizant that social networks function as both outreach and treatment resources, and that intake personnel need to learn about members of the client's social network.

Help-Seeking Behavior

If the mental illness incidence rates are high in Puerto Rican and Hispanic groups, then what about the majority of families in other minority groups who live in similar environments and face similar or equivalent problems and stresses? What do they do if they are faced with an emotional or behavioral problem? Where do they go for help? If they do not reach out, then what else do they do? Do they have the same problems as those who have used public mental health centers or facilities?

Since the early 1970s several researchers have hypothesized that an individual's social support system may help moderate or buffer the effects of life events upon his or her well-being (Antonovsky, 1974; Cobb, 1976; Liem & Liem, 1978). In addition to loss (of a spouse or one's health, for example), Moriwaki (1973) also found that the number of confidants as reported by respondents correlated with emotional well-being. McKinlay (1973) examined numbers of friends, proximity, frequency of interaction, duration of friendship, age of friends, as well as family support, and found that underutilizers of health and welfare services relied on their social networks for advice prior to using services. Mitchell and Moos (1984) stated that individuals who reported more severe depression also reported more negative events and strains, fewer positive events and number of close friends, and lower levels of family support.

In a longitudinal study, Warheit (1979) found that the availability of friends (or a spouse) was significantly correlated with lower depression scores for the high-loss (life events) groups. Lin and Ensel (1984) in their study of 1,091 adults in New York State found that improvement of the recovered (depressed at Time 1 but not at Time 2) and deteriorating groups (depressed at Time 2 only) were related to changes in undesirable life events and in social support provided by strong ties of companions and friends. Brown et al. (1975) similarly pointed out that an intimate, confiding relationship with a husband or boyfriend was the most powerful mediator between adverse events and psychiatric disturbance for women.

In their study of Chinese Americans in Washington, D.C., Lin and associates (1979) reported that community support can best be assessed by measuring (1) community—neighborhood interaction and satisfaction, (2) participation in voluntary organizations, and (3) use of organized services. Lin et al. (1986) also pulled together the various definitions and methodologies and subsequently presented a clear definition for social support, as well as for the dominant existing hypothesis-testing models for future research direction. Besides addressing some theoretical research issues, they applied their twelve models to a study sample (in Albany, New York). They found that "social support has a strong and independent (compensating) effect on depression and its change both contemporaneously and over time," and that social support serves as a mediating factor between prior undesirable life events and change in depression.

In summary, they not only presented hypothesis-testing models, but also identified three clearly distinct levels of social support which link the individual to his or her social environment: (1) the community, (2) the social network, and (3) the intimate and confiding relationships. These levels of support are extremely important to understand and to identify when working with multi-cultural groups, particularly individuals and their families migrating from the southern United States, the Caribbean, or southeast Asia.

The Family

Upon review of the mental health literature regarding the four major ethnic minority groups, it becomes clear that they all share one dominant characteristic—a very strong family orientation (Billingsley, 1968; Boyd-Franklin, 1989; Hill, 1972; Ramos-Mckay et al., 1988). This cultural value for the importance of family differs both among cultural groups and from the typical middle-class, Eurocentric American family (Attneave, 1982; Isaacs & Benjamin, 1991). For example, whereas Anglo-American families encourage their sons and daughters to become independent by age eighteen, and to leave home and get their own place of residence, traditional and marginally assimilated Hispanic/Latino families usually discourage independence until a much later age. Among Asian families it is also discouraged, as it is in direct opposition to the cultural priority that places the family over individual rights (Ho, 1992; Sue & Sue, 1990).

Several studies have shown that the family (including the extended family) is usually the first place to which individuals turn when faced with emotional or stressful life events (Ortiz & Vazquez-Nuttral, 1987; Quervalú, 1990; Rogler, 1978; Rogler & Santana-Cooney, 1985; Sussman & Burchinal, 1962; Veroff et al., 1981). In fact, the family is not only seen as the referral source, but also as a source for intervention, particularly in the therapeutic process for the client. Often, one of the therapeutic goals set by the clinician and client is to rebuild and strengthen the family structure, including the extended family, which may have eroded as a result of migration or the acculturation/assimilation process. With blacks and Hispanic families that have been here for generations, the erosion of the family is due to various socioeconomic pressures such as poverty, unemployment, drug abuse, housing, and relocation from other states, as well as from racism and discrimination. Additionally, although informal adoptions have been carried on successfully for generations by black and Hispanic families and are one of their strengths, many minority children are overrepresented in foster care homes and institutions. During the past decade, however, kinship foster home placements have been institutionalized as a result of community pressure, but not without their share of problems; for example, in the kinship placement there are unsupervised visitations by the biological parents, who may be under the influence of drugs or alcohol. In addition many biological parents do not comply with treatment goals and objectives, yet request to have children discharged to them.

The Impact of Migration on Families

In working with migrant families, the clinician is faced not only with dealing with the erosion of the family, but with the additional tasks of assessing where the individual and his family currently are in the assimilation process, how the migratory process affected them, and how they dealt with the resulting problems. Sluzki (1979) provides a general framework of the migration stages which can be applied to all cultural groups. The migration stages are listed as: (1) preparatory stage, (2) act of migration, (3) period of overcompensation, (4) period of decompensation, and (5) transgenerational phenomena.

In the *preparatory stage* the individual begins to make the commitment to migrate, which is usually associated with a reason for the move. Reasons for migration are typically economic, political, educational, medical, family, or otherwise. This commitment takes form with an exchange of letters, phone calls, or the process of applying for visas and passports. The manner in which the family accepts this decision is critical, because it sets the stage for what is to follow after the actual migration to the host country. Does the husband make the final decision alone, while the wife and children (teenagers) grudgingly follow? Or is there a lengthy discussion with resulting negotiations and compromises between husband and wife? In most cultural groups children and teenagers are not part of the adult decision-making process, thus setting up potential family problems for the teenager in the host country. Other stresses leading to family feuds may begin to form, particularly among families that have been fairly stable in the home country. For families that are escaping for political reasons, migration is for the most part a positive experience. Many Mexican families migrate because of economic need and a chance for a better life.

The *act of migration,* or the actual voyage itself, may be one that takes four hours by plane (from Puerto Rico or other Caribbean countries), or it may take months, particularly for politically motivated migrants who may be detained in refugee camps upon arrival. Some voyages may be turbulent, such as those voyages taken by Cubans or Haitians fleeing military dictatorships. Other voyages may be both long and turbulent, such as those taken by Chinese migrants, whose voyage may entail leaving their place of origin in a rural area of China and traveling to a large coastal city in order to buy a fare on a ship that may travel throughout Southeast Asia making several stops, perhaps even including the western coast of Africa, with a final stop in Miami, Florida. From there the migrant may need to travel farther, by land, until he or she reaches New York City and eventually a suburban town in upstate New York. For women, the trip is especially dangerous, as females are vulnerable to sexual and physical abuse, in addition to the typical problems faced by migrant individuals on transcontinental ship voyages.

Some families migrate legally, while others, such as many Mexicans, migrate illegally. Consequently, Mexicans shun institutions and authority figures, such as social workers, and experience intense feelings of alienation and mistrust even when services are geared for them. Sluzki (1979) presents the importance of the style or mode of the migratory act. For example, some families "burn bridges," thus insuring that they will never return to their homelands, as with the Cubans, Vietnamese, or Central Americans who were forced to leave because of civil strife or totalitarian regimes in their countries. Other families may decide to try it "only for a while." Puerto Ricans and other Caribbeans in effect have an "air bridge" which allows them to fly back and forth if things don't work out (Inclan, 1990). Although the same is possible for South Americans, it is not used as frequently because the cost of traveling to and from South America is much higher. African Americans as well as European Americans have different travel restrictions. Although economics is one of them, most such voyages are not as expensive as those to other continents.

The manner in which family members decide to migrate is also critical to the decision-making process. For instance, among Hispanic families the husband is usually the trail blazer or the scout who prepares the way by obtaining employment and, eventually, housing for the rest of his family. It may take years for families to reunite because of the cost of travel for each individual family member. Difficult family decisions have to be made as to who comes next.

The *period of overcompensation* is one in which the individual is not totally aware of the stresses he and his family have undergone during the recent migration. In fact, it is a phase in which the family feels euphoric in its new surroundings, and the first few weeks are a period of "a heightened task oriented efficiency" in its effort to adapt. It is a period when for months migrant families maintain a relative moratorium on the process of acculturation. Thus, any conflicts and symptoms tend to remain dormant, but family rules and styles may appear slightly exaggerated. For example, if family members were close, physically or emotionally, they will seem even closer. Some families cling to their country's cultural norms and beliefs and refuse to adapt to the new environment. Eventually, they will fall to the pressures of their new reality and major crisis will have to be faced head-on.

The *period of decompensation* is the stormy period when all of the repressed conflicts and difficulties come to the surface. It is during this period that family treatment centers see many of the families. Typical problems presented may be that the money starts running out and employment does not materialize as predicted, or perhaps the main wage earner is laid off. Women may find a job more easily than men, thus creating a challenging situation within the family hierarchial structure, given the "macho" posture taken by many men. Children and adolescents tend to catch up with the new culture and learn the new language more rapidly than their parents, thus creating a potential conflict of values, particularly when parents cling to the old values. It is a period which requires the family, with the help of the therapist, to begin to examine roles and attitudes and initiate the complex process of changing some of its ways by throwing out some practices, retaining others, and acquiring new rules for the family members in order to adjust to the host country.

The *transgenerational period* is one in which there is a "clash between generations"; that is, whatever has been avoided in the first generation will appear in the second generation. An example, mentioned above, is when adolescents acquire new values and mores as a result of influences from school peers, television, and other formal and informal socialization processes.

There are neighborhoods that will mimic their country of origin by retaining many of their attributes such as language, newspapers, religion, food stores, herbal stores, and so forth. Chinatowns throughout the United States are a good example. These ethnic enclaves (Harlem, Spanish Harlem,

---

Hispanic/Latino Cultural Concepts

Agringado   an individual who after some time in the United States has been Americanized.

Ataque (de Nervios)   a hysterical reaction as a result of stressful events (i.e., death of a close relative, separation or divorce, witnesses to an accident). Symptoms include general sense of being out of control, attacks of crying, hyperventilation, sudden bursts of violence or verbal aggression, fainting, trembling. Amnesia may occur after the event. After the attack, the individual returns to his usual level of functioning. It is similar to panic attacks, except for the absence of acute fear or apprehension (American Psychiatric Association, 1994).

Barrio   a town or neighborhood

Bilis and cholera   also referred to as muina. The primary feature of this syndrome is strongly experienced anger or rage. Symptoms can include acute nervous tension, headache, trembling, screaming, stomach disturbances, and in some severe cases, loss of consciousness. Chronic fatigue may result from an acute episode.

Botanics   stores which sell herbs, statues of saints, books, and other products necessary for folk religious practices.

Compadrazgo   part of the extended family system. It may include a compadre (godfather) and/or a comadre (godmother). It sets up a relationship between the padrinos (godparents) and their godchildren, and another relationship with the parents. The responsibilities of the godparents are to be available as coparental figures and to provide support to the godchildren in case of the death of a parent.

Curanderismo   a folk healing system of beliefs practiced in Central and South America, the Caribbean, and the southwestern United States. It is based on the practice of healing with indigenous plants and herbs in the form of curative potions and the laying on of hands.

Espiritismo (Spiritism or spiritualism)   an indigenous healing practice among Puerto Ricans, Dominicans, and other Hispanic cultural groups. It is a folk system for the explanation and treatment of physical intrapsychic and interpersonal difficulties based on a belief of the existence of an "invisible world" of disembodied spirits that interact and communicate with living, incarnated ones (mediums or Espiritista) (Garrison, 1977; Harwood, 1977). It is based on the writings of Allan Kardec (1951), who taught that people must do their best to perfect their spirits by developing their facultades (mental faculties) so that their spirits can lead them through life's trials (pruebas) or difficulties. The level of spiritual development attained is based on how they deal with the trials in their life (Canino & Canino, 1993).

Hijos de crianza   nonblood-related children who have been raised by a family as their own. It is usually an informal (nonlegal) arrangement whereby children are adopted either by an extended-family relative or a significant other. It can be a temporary or permanent agreement.

Irijua   a child's disorder prevalent in Peru. Symptoms appear after the birth of a sibling or after weaning. It is characterized by sadness, melancholy, irritability, hypersensitivity, anorexia, loss of weight, and tearfulness (Canino & Spurlock, 1994).

Machismo   means manliness and virility. Within Hispanic cultures it means that the man is responsible for the welfare and honor of his family. It is usually associated with sexual prowess with women, and expressed in romanticism and a jealous guarding of the wife or fiancee, as well as in premarital and extramarital relationships (Fitzpatrick, 1976). The concept is inaugurated at an early age, where set rules are identified for boys and girls. Boys are discouraged from playing with girls and encouraged to engage in more aggressive and manly activities (Badillo-Ghali, 1982).

Mal de ojo (the evil eye)   common in Mediterranean cultures and other parts of the world. Symptoms include agitated sleep, crying without apparent cause, diarrhea, vomiting, and fever in a child or an infant. Children are particularly vulnerable.

Mal de pelea   similar to **amok.**

Mal puesto   a folk illness in which a hex has been placed on an individual by another (friend or lover) with the help of a witch.

Marianismo   the counterpart of **machismo.** It is based on the concepts of the Virgin Mother within the Catholic religion. Women are expected to suffer in silence with regard to their husband's double standard, and to be self-sacrificing in favor of their children and husbands. They are expected to remain virgins until their marriage, which is the responsibility of the father and brother. They are expected to be good homemakers, and overseers of the health care of their family (Ramos-McKay et al., 1988).

Nervios   general states of vulnerability as a result of worries regarding stressful life events or life circumstances. Common symptoms include headaches, irritability, sleep disturbance, tingling sensations, easy tearfulness, dizziness.

Personalismo   a cultural concept which emphasizes the personal quality of an interaction in which an individual maintains a relationship with another particular individual instead of an institution. This concept has significant consequences in the therapeutic relationship, particularly if the clinician leaves the agency. The new clinician should be introduced before the final session.

Respeto   literally means respect, common among many Hispanic ethnic groups, as well as many other ethnic groups. It is the appropriate behavior given or expected to oneself or one's family because of age, sex, social, or economic status. It dictates the appropriate behavior given to figures of authority, older people, parents, relatives, husband, and others (Ramos-McKay et al., 1988).

Santeria is both an alternative religion and a folk-healing system. It is a religious cult practiced by Hispanics in general and Cubans in particular. Essentially, it is a syncreation of various African (Yoruba), European, American Indian, and other folk religions and healing practices. It blends African religion with Christianity. Negro slaves in Cuba and in the United States were prohibited from practicing their religion (including the use of African drums) so they masked their African deities by projecting their characteristics into facsimiles of the Roman Catholic saints, a practice which is still continued today. It involves witchcraft, magic, and ritualistic use of herbs in order to affect the influence of spirits in helping the individual with their request. In formal Santeria rituals the sacrificial offering of birds and animals may be required. Priests in this religion are known as Santeros for males or Santeras for females (Martinez & Wetli, 1982).

Susto a folk illness of "fright" or "soul loss," common among Hispanic cultural groups, particularly Mexicans. Characterized by various symptoms of anxiety, appetite disturbance, sleep problems, and depression; thought to be caused by loss of the soul following the fright experience (Gaw, 1993). Somatic symptoms may include muscle aches and pains, headache, stomachache, and diarrhea. Can be cured by ritual healing by calling the soul back to the body and cleansing the person's bodily and spiritual balance (American Psychiatric Association, 1994). Susto is also referred to as espanto, pasmo, tripa ida, perdida de alma, or chibih. It may appear days to years after the initial fright.

Ventosas (Cupping) see **Hua-Guan** in Asian Concepts.

Asian Cultural Concepts

Amok (running amok) originally reported from Malaysia. It is a dissociative episode in which people are at first in a period of brooding, followed by an outburst of violent impulses or homicidal behavior directed at people and objects. This state is precipitated by a perceived slight or insult and is more common among males. It is also found with similar characteristics in Laos, Philippines.

Bah tschi a Thai word for "easy startle" syndrome. It is an episode of dissociative, mimetic behavior in which the person is highly suggestible. Similar to **Latah** (Simons & Hughes, 1993).

Bangungut   a Philippine term. It is a nightmare death syndrome in which the person develops nightmares after a heavy meal and during the dream panics and tries to awaken. Failure to awaken may result in death (Gaw, 1993).

Ch'i   a Chinese medical term. It is believed to be an all pervasive force that permeates the universe and the human body, which are regulated by Yin-Yang and the five evolutive phases (Gaw, 1993). Essentially, the body has different conduits or meridians that allow for the flow of Ch'i. Impediments in this flow of Ch'i result in illness which can be treated by acupuncture, massage, or other traditional Chinese method, such as herbs. The impediments are detected by listening to the pulse (from the right and left wrist) of the individual to determine the strength of the main forces in the body: Jing which resides in the kidneys, Qi which originates in the lungs, and Shen which is contained in the liver (Shen, 1990).

Dhat   a folk illness in India referring to severe anxiety and hypochondriacal concerns associated with the discharge of semen, discoloration of urine (whitish), and feelings of weakness and exhaustion.

Flushing response   among Asians, a response to alcohol consumption which includes facial flushing, dyspnea, tachycardia, nasal congestion, and subjective discomfort (Yamamoto, 1982).

Gua-sha (coining)   a Chinese medical practice, common among southeast Asian refugees, also known as Cao Cio (Buchwald et al., 1992). A coin is dipped in oil and scraped along the chest and back. Then it is scraped along the four limbs, the arms and legs bent as they are scraped. If the skin turns purplish, it shows that the body has been affected by the elements. The excess weather (cold, dampness, heat) is forced out through the pores (Shen, 1990).

Hua-guan   practiced by Chinese and southeast Asians. It is an ancient Chinese treatment in which a flame is burned inside a glass jar or cup for a moment, creating a partial vacuum. Before the air escapes, the cup is rapidly placed down on a specific part of the body. The flesh is pulled up a bit into the cup (producing a slight puff). A number of cups are used in one treatment session, are left in place about twenty minutes, and are then removed. It is used when the individual is exposed to cold weather, or in certain cases of muscular pains from other causes (Shen, 1990).

Hwa-byung   a Korean culture-bound syndrome also known as "anger syndrome," characterized by the suppression of anger. Some of the symptoms include insomnia, fatigue, panic, anorexia, palpitations, indigestion, generalized aches and pain, and heavy feelings in the chest or abdomen.

Koro   reported in south and east Asia, occasionally in the Western Hemisphere. It is a fear or intense anxiety that the penis in males and the vulva or nipples in females will recede into the body and may cause death (Heyman & Fahy, 1992; Yap, 1965).

Latah   a Malaysian term. It is a hypersensitivity to sudden fright. The term denotes hypersensitivity and hypersusceptibility to a startle reaction. It has been found in many parts of the world, such as Mali-Mali and Silok in the Philippines (American Psychiatric Association, 1994).

Morita therapy   a Japanese therapy for the treatment of *shinkeishitsu* neurosis. Based in Zen Buddhism, it is aimed at freeing the patient from excessive self-preoccupation and intellectualization.

Moxibustion   based on the therapeutic value of heat, in contrast to acupuncture, which is a cold treatment. It is performed by heating pulverized wormwood (or eucalyptus oil, or incense) and applying it directly to the skin over specific meridians. It is helpful for women during the labor and delivery periods (Buchwald et al., 1992; Reinhart & Rhus, 1984).

SUNDS   Sudden Unexplained Nocturnal Death Syndrome, reported among young, male Southeast Asian refugees. Evidence suggests that individuals with SUNDS experience "night terrors" (not to be confused with nightmares) which occur immediately after falling asleep. It is also associated with stress and depression. Characterized by vocalization, agitated, sometimes violent movements, an inability to be roused, and severe discharge of the autonomic nervous system. In some cases the heart rate increases to 160–179 within 15–45 seconds of onset (Hardt, 1991).

P'a-leng   a Mandarin Chinese term. It means "morbid fear of the cold." Symptoms include loss of vitality and a strong desire to wear excessive clothing (Simons & Hughes, 1993).

Shen-K'uei   a Chinese folk illness, similar to **Dhat.** Excessive semen loss is feared because of fear of losing one's vital essence; fear of death is also present.

Shin-byung   a Korean folk illness characterized initially by anxiety accompanied by somatic complaints of weakness, dizziness, fear, anorexia, insomnia, and gastrointestinal problems. It is accompanied by dissociation and belief of possession by ancestral spirits (American Psychiatric Association, 1994).

Taijin kyofusho   a unique Japanese folk illness, also known as *Anthropophobia*. An intense fear that an individual's body or body parts embarrass or are offensive to other people in appearance, odor, facial expression, or movements. Resembles a social phobia in DSM-IV, (American Psychiatric Association, 1994).

Wind illness   translation for **P'a-leng,** fear of the cold.

Yin-Yang   a Chinese medical term for theory of balanced energy. A metaphysical concept of bipolarity that is simultaneously both opposite and complimentary (Gaw, 1993). There are five yin viscera and five yang organs, each responsible for a bodily function, and each associated to an external part of the body physiology. Yin is the female principle and makes up the negative, passive, weak, destructive power resulting in darkness, cold, and emptiness. Yang, the male principle composes the positive, active, strong, constructive energy or power resulting in warmth and light (Spector, 1991).

North American Cultural Concepts

Bulimia   prevalent in industrialized nations. A serious eating disorder chiefly of females that is characterized by compulsive overeating usually followed by self-induced vomiting or laxative or diuretic abuse. In the United States this disorder occurs primarily among whites, but it has been reported among other ethnic groups as well.

Falling out   in southeastern United States, between American and Caribbean blacks, and other ethnic groups, a sudden collapse or seizure or losing consciousness preceded by feelings of dizziness as a response to some type of traumatic event. The eyes are usually open but people cannot see and are powerless to move. Among Bahamians, who seem to have the highest incidence, it is known as "indisposition" (Simons & Hughes, 1993).

Ghost sickness   well known among the Navajo Indians. A disorder caused by belief that witches and evil supernatural forces have overwhelmed an individual (Simons & Hughes, 1993).

Pibloktoq   among native people of the Arctic, also known as **amok**

among Asians and **frenzy** witchcraft among the Navajo. Characterized by sudden onset of high level of activity, a trancelike state, potentially dangerous behavior in the form of running or fleeing, followed by exhaustion, sleep, and amnesia.

Sweat lodge among Native Americans it is a ceremony usually held in a tepee with steam provided by pouring water over very hot rocks. It is used for spiritual cleansing, or healing.

Wacinko a distinctive syndrome among Oglala Sioux Indians. It includes symptoms of anger, withdrawal, mutism, and immobility, and may lead to suicide in some cases. Usually as a response to disappointment and interpersonal problems.

Windigo observed among the Ojibwa Indians of southern Canada. This syndrome is characterized by melancholia and a delusion of the transformation of the victim into a monster who eats human flesh (Canino & Spurlock, 1994).

Other Cultural Concepts

Boufee delirante observed in West Africa and Haiti. It is characterized by a sudden outburst of agitated and aggressive behavior, marked confusion, and psychomotor excitement. Sometimes accompanied by visual and auditory hallucinations or paranoid ideation.

Brain fag term used in West Africa to a refer to university or high school student's response to the challenges of schooling. Symptoms include difficulties in concentrating, remembering, and thinking. Students report their brains are "fatigued." Somatic symptoms may include pressure, tightness around neck and head, pain, or blurring of vision. Brain tiredness or fatigue, found in many cultures, as a result of too much thinking can resemble anxiety, depressive, and somatoform disorders (American Psychiatric Association, 1994).

Zar in North Africa and Middle East. A dissociative episode in which a person feels possessed by spirits. A person may resort to shouting, laughing, hitting the head against the wall, singing, crying, or withdrawal, and may refuse to perform daily tasks. The person may develop a long-term relation with the possessing spirit, which is not considered pathological locally (American Psychiatric Association, 1994).

and Little Italy in New York City, for example) seem to buffer the cross-cultural exposure and essentially slow down the adaptive transformation phase. This conflict between the generations is also present within the Anglo- and African-American communities in the United States. In summary, the clinician needs to determine the acculturation level as well as the migration history of the client.

Lee (1990) provides another framework which identifies the migration history, determines the person's background, including their baseline functioning level, and describes the patient's life experiences in their native country prior to the migration. Among the major areas addressed in this outline are:

1. *Premigration history*: country of origin, socioeconomic status, family support, political issues, war

2. *Experience of migration*: migrant or refugee? Why did they leave? Who was left behind?

3. *Degree of loss*: family members, properties or business losses, cultural milieus

4. *Trauma experiences*: physical or psychological (depression). Are there any signs of post traumatic stress disorder?

5. *Work and financial history*: occupation or line of work

6. *Support systems*: family, community, and religious social supports

7. *Medical history*: practices and beliefs (coining, moxibustion, herbal treatments, acupuncture, etc.). What somatic complaint does a client report?

8. *Family's concept of illness*: What does the family think the problem is? What do family members do to get help? Can they help with identifying the cause and treatment?

9. *Level of acculturation*: first or second generation, bicultural, traditional, marginal, or assimilated

10. *Impact on development*: How have patients and their children adjusted in terms of developmental stages?

Additionally, the clinician needs to know the English language proficiency level of the client, and whether the client feels comfortable in expressing him- or herself in English or in his or her native language (*see* language assessment and mental status examination, below).

Somatization

Somatization is an idiom of distress in which emotional disorders are expressed by the presentation of physical symptoms. There are several reasons why somatic complaints are presented in such a manner. Among them is that seeking help for mental health problems is taboo in many cultural groups, but it is socially acceptable to present physical problems. Somatic complaints are common among Hispanics, Asians, and people from Islamic cultures. In these cultural groups, mental health problems are stigmatized, not talked about, and conceptualized as somatic (Lu et al., 1995). Often a patient will be reluctant to give personal information to a clinician, particularly one from a different cultural group or from the dominant host country. Asian cultures have traditionally encouraged coping strategies such as not thinking too much about gloomy problems and becoming involved in activities, rather than talk therapy (Huang, 1991). Family elders will often persuade an individual to be more family oriented, less absorbed, and not to think about personal problems (Uba, 1994). This attitude is based on Buddhism, which stresses that one should accept and endure one's problems, and that suffering is a normal part of life for everyone (Nguyen, 1982).

With the influx of migrant individuals and families from many parts of the world into the United States, it has become important for the clinician to become familiar with culture-bound syndromes as well as other cultural concepts that will help them in the assessment and treatment plan development for culturally diverse patients. "Culture-bound syndromes" are "recurrent patterns of culturally shaped aberrant behavior that are indigenously considered pathological, but that have no place in official diagnostic taxonomies" (Simons & Hughes, 1993). They incorporate local symptom constellations which are important to identify, because the patient's conceptualization of the illness and treatment operates within his cultural belief system (Lu et al., 1995).

Some of the culture-bound syndromes and cultural concepts that a mental health provider or clinician should be aware of are explained in the following section of selected cultural concepts. Clinicians are advised that not all people are the same, and that while particular culture-bound syndromes are normal, others go beyond normality (Mezzich et al., 1996). The authors provide these lists to give the reader information about cultural concepts and syndromes which could be used within the context of the biopsychosocial assessment of patients who have come for mental health services.

Religion and Spirituality

It is unquestionable that religion plays a major role in the mental health status of individuals from diverse cultural groups. One can see from the previous section on cultural concepts that many of the folk illnesses are spirit related and may possibly require folk treatment. In addition, many people from cultural ethnic groups often turn to their particular religion for social and religious support.

Based on religious beliefs and on herbal knowledge, folk medicine has been practiced throughout time and has taken root in most cultural groups. In the United States these practices were transplanted over time by each of the cultural groups that migrated here. When Puerto Ricans migrated to the United States in the late 1940s, they brought with them a number of cultural characteristics and traits. Besides the Spanish language, they brought their newspapers and their "bodegas" (Spanish grocery stores), as well as their religion (Catholicism, Protestantism, Pentecostalism), including "Espiritism" (Spiritism). They brought their herbal folk medicine practices as well as the "botanicas" (herbal stores), where a variety of prescriptions were and are still filled. Prescriptions are usually made by an "Espiritista," who prepares the prescriptions for potions of all sorts. Individuals usually turn to help from the "Espiritista" when they have problems, particularly during periods of crisis when explanations for and causes of misfortune are sought. In essence,

> The *espiritistas* believe in visible and invisible worlds populated by spirits, some of which are presently incarnated and some of which are not. Disincarnated spirits communicate with incarnated spirits through mediums or people who have "developed their spiritual faculties," or they may directly intervene for good or ill in the lives of the incarnated. Each spirit is "subject to the law of progress, or the law of spiritual evolution." According to Kardec's *Book of the Mediums,* there are three levels and ten grades of spiritual development through which all spirits must pass and on all of which both incarnated and disincarnated spirits are to be found. (Garrison, 1972)

Each incarnated spirit has special relationships with certain disincarnated spirits: each has a

> guardian angel (angel guardian) and one or more spirit guides (guias), collectively known as spirit protectors (protectores). These spirit protectors help the individual master the *causas* or "misguided spirits"

which might otherwise afflict him, and if he develops his spiritual
faculties (facultades) so that he can communicate directly with them,
they help him to help others who have not developed their spiritual
faculties. (Garrison, 1972)

Once the nature of the cause of the problem(s) (a particular spirit or
spirits) is identified, much of the anxiety surrounding the illness is allevi-
ated and the individual can face the outcome calmly (Delgado, 1977). In
addition to potions that the medium or "Espiritista" can prescribe, the
medium may also need to make referrals to a physician for more complex
physical problems that are beyond the scope of the medium. Mediums
have also worked closely with other mental health professionals in col-
laborative efforts for the good of the client; for instance, when the client is
not in compliance with medication prescribed by a physician (MERTI,
1995).

Dr. Pedro Ruiz for many years has advocated close cooperation between mental health practitioners and folk healers. As director of Lincoln
Hospital Community Mental Health Center, he was able to successfully
initiate and implement a close working relationship with his staff psychiatrists and clinicians and the "Espiritistas" in the South Bronx, New
York (Ruiz & Langrod, 1976).

Among Asian Americans, the celestial world is believed to be populated by departed ancestors, gods, ghosts, demons, criminal spirits, and
deified heroes of the Chinese history. Among the Chinese peasantry a variety of folk therapies, known as popular medicine, have developed which
are deeply rooted in folk traditions traceable to ancient Taoist, Buddhist,
and Confucian teachings (Gaw, 1993). One of the principal folk leaders is
the shaman, or wu. He is called upon to intercede on behalf of a person
sick with either physical or mental problems since many times physical
problems are correlated with or caused by mental problems. Very briefly,
in this belief,

the human body is thought to be infused with both *Shen* and *Kuei* at
birth. At death, *Shen* returns to the *Yang* of heaven and *Kuei* to the *Yin*
of the earth. *Kuei* can become a free-floating spirit called *Hseigh-chi.*
The presence of human transgressions such as family strife, failure to
render filial obligations, interpersonal quarreling, and social immo-
rality is thought to create a human anomaly that can invite the inva-
sion of *Hseigh-chi* into the human body and inflict illness. When
Hseigh-chi invades the body, a person is considered possessed. (Gaw,
1993)

The treatments are performed by the shaman, who acts as a medium to conduct a curing ritual which can include exorcisms, healing, and ceremonies to call back lost souls. The shaman attempts to diagnose by deterring the *Kuei* in the family. Once the offending spirit is identified, the healer intercedes on the patient's behalf by appealing to the offending spirits to drive out *Kuei* from the distressed individual.

In examining traditional Indian life, one has to understand and view Indians in a broad context and recognize that they are a diverse group of people referred to as tribes, each possessing a distinct tribal culture. According to their preserved oral histories American Indians believe they are indigenous to this continent, and the accounts of their beginnings as a people are contained in their sacred creation stories and ceremonies, which vary from tribe to tribe. Generally, American Indian creation accounts can be grouped into four broad categories: (1) Earth, (2) emergence, (3) sky fall, and (4) other.

In the earth-diver category, an animal of one kind or another brings up some mud from the bottom of the ocean from which the all-powerful Creator makes this earth and all life, which he orders in perfect harmony. The creation accounts of the Arapaho, Blackfeet, and Cheyenne fall into this particular category. Other tribes like the Navajo, Pueblo, and Kiowa narrate their emergence to earth from successive worlds below, which embodies a spiritual as well as a historical journey. The Senecas of the Iroquois Confederation, among others, believe that a beautiful spirit woman fell from the sky, and to keep her from drowning in the turbulent seas, the Great Spirit, with the assistance of the water people, made the earth upon which she and her children were to live (Mann, 1995).

To the American Indian and Alaska native the concept of origin is very important. Origin not only provides the ingredients of definition, but also structures the reality for the individual from which the world view will evolve. The presence of the reservation within these conceptual frameworks is significant, because reservations are homelands for the people. Reservation residents are able to interact, observe, and honor various aspects of their environments on a daily basis, and are reminded of the sacredness of the life they share with others. The interaction of their kin and relatives reinforces the individual's sense of relatedness and interdependency. The reservation homeland shapes the person's demeanor and style (Blanchard, 1995).

> . . . the homeland as a place where one gets one's bearings; where one
> takes in a part of the world, keeps another part at a distance and learns

how to use one's given attributes with some sense of achievement and satisfaction. The homeland as a "security blanket," as a source of nourishment, as a place that gives sanction to some of one's urges and strivings—while enabling one to discard others as foreign, as belonging to one "them" or another. The homeland also boosts one's forceful side, one's urge to forge ahead, make a mark upon the world. (Coles, 1986)

Some Indian and Native people identify their place of origin in the same place where they presently live, which is characteristic of tribes who have lived on their land for a very long time. Additionally, places of extreme importance and significance within the reservation boundaries have a vital role in the final decision to settle in a particular place. These places are among the many shrines that have been recognized over time. These shrines are regularly maintained by individuals designated with responsibility for them. They are a part of the ceremonial or religious life of members of the community. The shrines are a living connection between the individual and the earth from which one is created (Blanchard, 1995).

The creation accounts of some tribes are preserved in story form and in the ceremonial life of the people. For instance, the creation of the Cheyenne world is conserved in story form as part of their sacred traditions, and is also preserved in their two major ceremonies.

These accounts serve as the source from which all life flows, and lays out the American Indian world view and the Indians' interdependent relationships with their environment. The creation experience provides the people with the sustainment and structure for their religious beliefs and practices, as well as for the formation of moral guideposts from which questions of right and wrong are addressed.

Evil and the concept of evil are very important in the interpretations of life's vicissitudes in the Indian and Native world, and are the basis for perceived causes and outcomes of mental or physical dysfunction. All peoples struggle with evil, and with the world crises that result in daily suffering that devastates the lives of multitudes of people. Ortiz (1972) explains, "It is not that the Pueblos have not accepted evil as part of the reality of life; it is just that they do not know how to handle it" (Blanchard, 1995).

There is acknowledgment that evil represents an extension of an idea and that everything has two faces. The soft, warm island breezes can turn swiftly to hurricanes that kill and destroy. Consequently, everything has the face of good and the face of potential evil and destructiveness. Ortiz (1972) states that among the Pueblos, who set careful limits to the boundaries of their world and order everything within it, "there is the clear notion of things inside and things outside" (Blanchard, 1995).

Every individual in the tribe is expected to live in respectful interdependence with the earth and the environment as a part of the great sacred circle of life; however, within the tribe there are unique individuals with special, sacred, and sometimes secret knowledge, who intervene when things are out of balance with an individual. They are known by different names, but generally they may be referred to as ceremonial or medicine people, or as keepers of sacred knowledge or sacred ways. These medicine people integrate the spiritual ways and tribal values into their respective ways of living. They are expected to be honorable people and to live impeccable lives, because otherwise they would contaminate the healing and sacred power entrusted to them (Mann, 1995).

Ceremonial medicine people live by a strict spiritual code, which governs their relationships with all people. The lives of spiritual medicine people are to be above reproach, because of the deep spiritual roots and demanding spiritual expectations and responsibilities placed upon them. In addition, they are community role models, since many tribes strive to maintain high standards of leadership and life.

Indians have always had expectations of maintaining a high quality of life characterized by wholeness, which guides them to become whole individuals in a physical, spiritual, intellectual, and emotional sense. When a person is ill, they treat all aspects of the individual. Native Americans believe in a holistic orientation toward life, and some tribes, including the Cheyenne, for instance, do not believe in amputation. When a person descends into a state of imbalance or ill health, Indian medicine people and ceremonies can restore the person to balance, wholeness, and good health, or beauty as the Navajos have conceptualized it. To the Navajos, walking in beauty implies balance, wholeness, harmony, and goodness. A code or way of life by which many Indians live is simply stated:

> Love and respect all people and all things.
> Speak your words and your heart in a good way.
> Be compassionate and understanding of all people.
> Overlook all wrongs and be a forgiving individual. (Mann, 1995)

This is a way that American Indians maintain their traditional life in a contemporary setting (Mann, 1995).

As you can see from the above review, there are a number of "spirit worlds" and much to learn about the beliefs and attitudes held by the many different patients and clients we see in institutional settings. The importance that is given to the "spirit world" by varying percentages of different cultural ethnic groups when they present physical or mental health problems is essential for the provider to understand in order to maintain the provider or doctor/patient relationship. Also remember that mental health problems are usually presented to the physician in the form of somatic (physical) problems, and that many ethnic cultural groups believe that mental and physical problems are caused by evil spirits and that the church, prayer, and spirituality have the power to treat their problems.

Assessment of Culturally Diverse Populations

Language and the Mental Status Examination

There is no doubt that language plays an important part in the assessment and treatment of mental health illness among multicultural patients. Consider if you will the same types of miscommunications illustrated in the medical delivery system (chapter 3), but now presented within a mental health clinic. Since talking therapy in and of itself implies speaking and communicating, errors in assessment can be committed with greater harm either by (1) misdiagnosis of conditions or causative reasons for the illness or problem, or (2) inappropriate medical treatment based on the misdiagnosis. During the mental status examination, errors can be based on ignorance of cultural values and norms and/or by language disparities either on the part of the therapist or social service practitioner, or more likely on the part of the limited-English-speaking client.

In 1980 Marcos and Alpert, in a study of bilingualism and therapy, reported that bilinguals were seen as more pathological when interviewed in English as compared to interviews in Spanish. It seems that when the limited-English-speaking clients are forced to speak in English, it creates much stress. Their answers tend to be shorter and there is a hesitancy to speak English (a sense of shame in not mastering the language after so many years in the United States). The Spanish-speaking group in the study, however, disclosed more information in their native Spanish. With the limited-English-speaking group, the therapist or examiner gets an impression that the patient does not want to cooperate, but in reality the problem is the patient's difficulty communicating across the language barrier. Additionally, the client may feel uncomfortable to begin with, not only with disclosing personal information to a therapist (a stranger, and part of the "establishment"), but also with being forced to speak in English. There is a negative transfer; clients may think, "Damn, I've got to speak to this guy in English."

The same may be said for African-American clients. African Americans who use Black English as the dominant language with peers and in community or home settings may also show hesitancy as they look for a phrase or sentence in standard American English when they feel it is appropriate in a given situation such as in a job interview or business meeting (Haskins and Butts, 1972; Paniagua, 1994). Many African Americans consider that they too are bilingual. Black families must therefore focus on the dual responsibility of helping their children handle the peer pressure if they don't speak Black English and to help them be able to function with the skills and abilities to succeed in the outside world (Hale-Benson, 1982). Hence, Black English may be spoken at home and standard English in the workplace.

In their review of the effects of bilingualism on the Mental Status Examination, Marcos and Alpert state that in terms of *motor behavior,* when bilinguals are interviewed in English, there is usually more hand movement, which correlates with the client thinking in Spanish and then translating into English. This should not be confused with anxiety, tension, or hyperactivity. Essentially, it is the client struggling with or going from one language to another (compensating).

Another component to be aware of in the context of the mental status examination is *speech.* Spanish dominants will tend to use Spanglish, a hybrid language which substitutes some Spanish words in English (language mixing). Consequently, the limited-English-speaking client has a lower speech rate and long silent pauses. The impression the examiner gets is that the client is anxious, that there is a use of unusual words (neologisms), or that the client is illogical or confused because of sentence incompleteness, stuttering, repetition, omission, incoherent sound, tongue slip, and "Ah" sounds (Marcos & Alpert, 1980).

Because of the bilingual patient's struggle with the English language, the clinician may mistakenly perceive an *attitude* of unwillingness to cooperate. The slower speech rate and silent pauses also affect the way the examiner assesses the emotions or mood of the client. His or her immediate impression of the client may be that of a flat affect, or that the client is not concerned. To the examiner the client appears more depressed or emotionally withdrawn. Once again, the answers are not spontaneous only because the client is trying to give correct responses.

In addition to the above examples of misdiagnosis that could be made during the mental status examination, the instrument itself has been under criticism for its potential bias when used with different ethnic and racial groups. Several authors have recently recommended caution and avoidance of the mental status examination with multi-cultural client groups (Hughes, 1993; Mueller et al., 1992).

The primary reason for their concern is that the examination is based on the assumption that a specific range of behaviors and cognitive processes are shared by all normal persons, regardless of cultural backgrounds (Westermeyer, 1993). Some of the components of the mental status examination that are under question and possibly contain threats to its validity are:

1. The serial 7s test, which asks the client to subtract seven from 100 and then to continue subtracting seven from the previous answer (Hughes, 1993; Smith, 1967).

2. Orientation. "What is the name of this month?" Limited-English-speaking clients could have problems with the answer.

3. Assessment of general knowledge. "How far is it from Los Angeles to New York?" Recent immigrants would have problems with conceptualizing where particular cities are located. Even Americans do poorly with geographic locations. "Can you name the capital of three countries in the Middle East or the difference between the American flag and the Malaysian flag?" (Paniagua, 1994).

Other Assessment Instruments

Many other instruments are also under criticism for their bias when used in the assessment of different ethnic and racial groups. For instance the Minnesota Multiphasic Personality Inventory (MMPI) contains several sources of bias. In comparing MMPI research studies of Anglo-Americans and other cultural groups, inappropriate statistics were used, and the studies also failed to adequately equate the groups on socioeconomic criteria or to define ethnicity (Greene, 1987).

Greene found that there were statistical errors in 85 percent of the cultural groups under comparative study and that ethnic group membership was omitted in 77 percent of the studies. Considering that the MMPI has the widest application of any test, with more than 150 translations and application in 50 countries (Butcher, 1985), many of the translations were not controlled for accuracy or linguistic equivalence (Williams, 1986). The items were often translated without revisions or validity checks of the translated version (Guthrie & Lonner, 1986). These literal translations, which included back-to-English translation and sufficient test-retest reliability examination, could not have equivalent meaning. As a result, study findings from cross-cultural comparative profiles are not feasible, thus yielding interpretations of profiles in the United States that are not useful in other Spanish-speaking countries, for example. Consequently, there is an inadequate research basis to justify using interpretations from existing tests in original or translated adaptations for the multi-cultural groups in this country (Dana, 1993). Dana states that this bias within personality theories emanates from prevailing explanations systems developed by males of European and American origins, which have been applied to all assessments in American society regardless of cultural identities.

On other test instruments, African Americans continue to be misdiagnosed as schizophrenic by use of the Schedule for Affective Disorders and Schizophrenia (SADS) and the Global Assessment Scale (GAS) (Pavkov et al., 1990). This has important consequences for an individual, since the evaluator's diagnosis impacts on the choice of either the criminal justice or the mental health intervention system (Lewis et al., 1980), not to mention the selected treatment modality, including a medication regime.

Misdiagnosis is nothing new in the assessment process for African Americans. More than a hundred years ago, Dr. Samuel Cartwright, the prominent antebellum southern medical doctor, discovered two (implausible) diseases among blacks: (a) Drapetomania, a disease causing black slaves to run away from their plantations, and (b) Dysaethesia Aethiopica, a disease causing black slaves to be wasteful and destroy everything they handle (Jones, 1992).

In a comparative study, Li-Repac (1980) instructed five Caucasians and five Chinese-American therapists to rate Chinese and Caucasian patients in videotaped interviews. The Caucasian therapists perceived the Chinese patients as anxious, awkward, confused, nervous, quiet, and reserved, while the Chinese therapists perceived the same patients as alert, dependable, friendly, and practical.

The Diagnostic and Statistical Manual

Another instrument which has been used routinely as a diagnostic tool, including identification of psychopathology for multicultural groups in the United States, is the Diagnostic and Statistical Manual (DSM-III R). Until the development and recent publication of the DSM IV, DSM-III R had a number of problems in using it with cultural groups (Loring & Powell, 1988). Lopez and Nunez (1987) reported that the only cultural reference in the DSM III is the recognition that certain religious and cultural beliefs may be difficult to recognize from schizophrenic delusions or hallucinations, and that the assessor should be careful not to use them as certainty or evidence of psychoses.

Consequently, multicultural groups are susceptible or vulnerable to misdiagnosis, such as having dependent or paranoid personality disorders. For example, dependent personality disorder, according to DSM, includes the criteria of granting others the choice of assuming responsibility for one's major life decisions and a denial of one's own needs in favor of those of other persons. But among Asian Americans, for example, others are expected to assume those responsibilities, not as a result of the individual's inability to function independently, but because the self-concept places certain responsibilities on designated family members, who believe the welfare of others to be synonymous with the best interest of the other family member or individual. These issues are further complicated when a son or daughter is in the process of assimilation into a bicultural or dominant society orientation within a traditional family context (Dana, 1993).

Similarly, many African Americans have been diagnosed as paranoid or schizophrenic, with a failure to diagnose depression. However, paranoia may not necessarily be pathological, and can perhaps be considered a healthy or commonsense state, since paranoid behavior may be justified as a common, reality-based byproduct of the African-American experience of prejudice, discrimination, and racism (Newhill, 1990). If considered in a healthy paranoid sense, such behavior represents a legitimate coping skill. Mirowsky (1985) explains cultural paranoia as mistrust which is an adaptive response found where opportunities and resources are scarce, including protection by societal institutions and where exploitation and victimization are common.

Fortunately, the fourth edition of the *Diagnostic and Statistical Manual of Mental Disorders* (DSM IV) (American Psychiatric Association, 1994) has integrated a new section entitled "Specific Culture, Age, and Gender Features" for each of the listed mental disorders, where applicable. The author (Dr. Quervalú) has provided a summary of culture features for selected DSM IV diagnoses (see Table 4.1) which lists these cultural "considerations." DSM IV describes this integrated section as providing "guidance for the clinician concerning variations in the presentation of the disorder that may be attributable to the individual's cultural setting, developmental stage . . . or gender." It states, referring to the above example for dependent personality disorder, for example:

> Dependent behavior should be considered characteristic of the disorder only when it is clearly in excess of the individual's cultural norms or reflects unrealistic concerns. An emphasis on passivity, politeness and differential treatment is characteristic of some societies and may be misinterpreted as traits of Dependent Personality Disorder.

Essentially, the posture one needs to take in the assessment, diagnosis, and provision of services takes into account the individual's cultural, religious, and social background and realizes that what is considered deviant in one culture may be more acceptable among members of another cultural group. Although many clinicians do not consider the DSM IV to be the definitive assessment instrument, it is a big improvement from previous DSMs.

Dana (1993) states that in order for assessment instruments to be applicable to clients of diverse cultural origins, modifications are required. He urges the use of moderator variables, which are defined as corrections for cultural differences which can be applied informally as part of an interview or more formally in a questionnaire. Dana states the moderator variables are not only helpful but may be necessary because the majority of assessments of culturally different persons in the United States emanate from the stance of an imposed ethic. He writes

> An imposed ethic is applied whenever assessment is accomplished by using instruments and techniques developed in the dominant society on the basis of the prevailing Eurocentric model of science. The use of an imposed ethic assumes that culturally different assessees are, in fact, not culturally different but have been willing to assimilate and have acquired a world view and value system similar to individuals in the dominant society. However, many culturally different persons opt for biculturality or retention of an original culture almost exclusively, and still others will have a marginality orientation.

Assessors need to be careful as to which assessment instruments they use, and must take into account the acculturation or assimilation phase of the particular individual, and the extent to which the original culture has been retained. Dana (1993) provides an excellent review of a number of assessment instruments which can be utilized with the four major multicultural government-protected populations in the United States: African Americans, Hispanic Americans, Asian Americans, and Native Americans. It is therefore up to the assessor to determine and explore prior to assessment, not only the group identity, but the acculturation level of the client, which can be any of the following (Dana, 1993):

1. Retention of the original or traditional culture,

2. Identification with the dominant Anglo-American culture,

3. Identification with both an original and adopted culture (biculturality),

4. Rejection of both original and Anglo-American identities (marginality), and for Native Americans,

5. A transitional orientation in which individuals are bilingual, but question traditional values and religion.

DSM IV has also provided the "Outline for Cultural Formulation" that supplements DSM IV's multiaxial diagnostic assessment and addresses the concerns presented above.

1. Cultural identity of the individual. Besides providing a summary of the individual's ethnic or cultural reference group this includes a description of the language abilities as well as language use and preference, including multilingualism.

2. Cultural explanations of the individual's illness. As with Kleinman's explanatory model of sickness, the clinician is asked to identify (a) the meaning and perceived severity of the individual's symptoms in relation to their cultural group's norm, (b) the predominant idioms of distress through which symptoms or the need for social support are expressed, such as "nerves," possessing spirits, somatic complaints, and so forth, (c) any culturally known illness expressed by the individual's family and community to identify the condition, and (d) current and past practices with professional or informal (alternative folk healers) sources of care.

3. Cultural factors related to psychological environment and levels of functioning. The clinician is asked to identify social stressors along with community and family supports such as religion.

Supports include the kinship family networks, as well as the informal supports (such as spiritualists, Hougan priests).

4. Cultural elements of the relationship between the individual and the clinician. The clinician is asked to note the cultural differences between the client and him or herself, as well as potential problems in diagnosis and treatment as a result of the differences. These may include language difficulties, as well as difficulty in understanding the cultural significance of symptom presentation, or determining whether a behavior is normative or pathological. [Depending on the cultural competency level of the clinician, this may or may not require additional input from a culturally competent or culturally knowledgeable staff member.]

5. Overall cultural assessment for diagnosis and care. A written discussion of how a cultural factor in the assessment specifically impacts on the comprehensive diagnosis and care of the individual.

Table 4.1 Summary of Culture Features for DSM IV Diagnoses in Infancy, Childhood or Adolescence

319 Mental Retardation, Severity Unspecified

1. Ensure that intellectual testing procedures reflect adequate attention to individual's ethnic and cultural background. 2. Accomplished by using tests in which individual's characteristics are represented in a standardization sample of a test or by utilizing an examiner familiar with the ethnic and cultural background of individual.

315.31 Expressive Language Disorder

1. Assessment should take into account individuals' cultural and language context, particularly individuals growing up in bilingual environment. 2. Standardized measures for language development and nonverbal intellectual capacity must be relevant for cultural and linguistic groups.

315.31 Mixed Receptive-Expressive Language Disorder

See Expressive Language Disorder

315.39 Phonological Disorder

See No. 1 in Expressive Language Disorder

312.8 Conduct Disorder

1. Can be misapplied to individuals in settings where patterns of undesirable behavior are sometimes viewed as protective (e.g., in threatening situations, impoverishment, high crime). 2. Applied only when behavior is symptomatic of an underlying dysfunction of individual and not a reaction to immediate social or economic context.

313.81 Oppositional Defiant Disorder

1. In certain cultures, eating dirt or other seemingly nonnutritive substance is believed to be of value.

307.23 Tourette's Disorder (Motor and Vocal Tics)

1. Widely reported in diverse racial and ethnic groups.

309.21 Separation Anxiety Disorder

1. There are cultural variations when considered desirable to tolerate separation. Important to differentiate this disorder from high values some cultures place on strong interdependence among family members.

313.23 Selective Mutism (formerly Elective Mutism)

1. Immigrant children unfamiliar with official language of host country may refuse to speak to strangers in their new environment and this refusal should not be considered selective mutism.

DELIRIUM, DEMENTIA, AND AMNESTIC AND OTHER COGNITIVE DISORDERS

Delirium

1. Care should be taken in evaluation of individuals' mental capacity as some individuals from different backgrounds may not be familiar with a) general knowledge test items such as names of presidents, geographical locations, etc., b) memory: where certain cultures do not celebrate birthdays, and c) orientation: sense of placement conceptualized differently in some cultures.

Dementia

Same as Delirium, No. 1. The prevalence of different causes of dementia (e.g., infections, seizure disorders, substance abuse) varies significantly across cultural groups.

Amnestic Disorders

1. Individuals from certain cultural backgrounds may not be familiar with some memory test items such as date of birth or celebration of birthdays.

SUBSTANCE-RELATED DISORDERS

Substance Abuse Disorders

1. Wide cultural variations in attitude. Some groups forbid alcohol while in other cultural groups the use of various substances for mood-altering effects is widely accepted. Care should be taken in evaluation of individuals' pattern of substance use as well as patterns of medication use and toxin exposure, which vary widely within and between countries.

Alcohol-Related Disorders

1. Cultural traditions surrounding use of alcohol in family and social activities during childhood can affect both alcohol use patterns and the likelihood those alcoholic problems will develop.
2. Marked differences across cultural groups. The overall prevalence of alcohol-related disorders in most Asian cultures may be relatively low. Among almost 50% of Japanese, Chinese and Korean individuals, the absence of the form of aldehyde dehydrogenase that eliminates low levels of the first breakdown product of alcohol produces "flushed face" and palpitations. Prevalence rates are similar between white and African Americans in the U.S., while Latino males have a somewhat higher rate and Latino females have lower rates than females from other ethnic groups.

Caffeine-Related Disorders

1. Varies widely across cultures. An average caffeine intake in most of the developing world is less than 50 mg/day compared to 400 mg/day in Sweden, the United Kingdom and other European nations.

Cannabis-Related Disorders

1. Most widely used illicit substance. Used as a remedy for wide range

of medical conditions. Among first drugs of experimentation for all cultural groups in the United States, particularly among teenagers.

Cocaine-Related Disorders

1. Cocaine use and its attendant disorders affect all ethnic groups in the United States.

Hallucinogen-Related Disorders

1. Hallucinogens may be used as part of established religious practices with regional differences in their use.

Inhalant-Related Disorders

1. There is a high incidence among young people living in economically depressed areas [high rate among Native American teenagers].

Nicotine-Related Disorders

1. The prevalence is decreasing in the United States while increasing among the developing nations. In countries outside the United States, smoking is more prevalent among males.

SCHIZOPHRENIA AND OTHER PSYCHOTIC DISORDERS

1. Cultural differences must be taken into account. Thoughts or ideas that may appear delusional to one cultural group (i.e., witchcraft) may be commonly held by another cultural group. Visual or auditory hallucinations with religious content may be a normal part of religious experiences in certain cultural groups. The assessment of affect requires awareness and sensitivity to differences in styles of emotional expression, eye contact and body language. Careful assessment should be given to linguistic differences between the evaluator and the individual as well as linguistic variations across different cultural groups. There is a tendency to over-diagnose Schizophrenia instead of Bipolar Disorder among ethnic groups [particularly African Americans]. Catatonic behavior has been reported as relatively uncommon among individuals with Schizophrenia in the U.S. but is more common in non-western countries. Individuals with Schizophrenia in the developing nations tend to have a more acute course and better outcome than those in industrialized nations.

295.40 Schizophreniform Disorder

See No. 1 in Schizophrenia and other Psychotic Disorders above. Recent information suggests that recovery from Psychotic Disorders may be more rapid in developing countries, which would result in higher rates of Schizophreniform Disorders than of Schizophrenia.

295.70 Schizoaffective Disorders

See No. 1 in Schizophrenia and Other Psychotic Disorders above.

297.1 Delusional Disorder

1. An individual's cultural and religious background must be taken into account. The content of delusion varies across different cultural groups. As stated in Schizophrenia No. 1, some sanctioned beliefs can be considered delusional in some cultural groups while held as common beliefs in other cultures.

298.1 Brief Psychotic Disorder

1. In certain religious activities, individuals may hear voices during the ceremony, but the voices will not persist after the activity and hearing them is not considered abnormal by most members of the individual's community.

MOOD DISORDERS

1. Depression may be presented in somatic terms, rather than sadness or guilt, in the form of "nerves" and headaches, in Latino and Mediterranean cultures. In Chinese and Asian cultures depression may be presented in terms of weakness, tiredness, or "imbalance" [of yin and yang or Qi]. Complaints can be presented as problems of the "heart" among Middle Eastern cultures or as "heartbroken" among the Hopi Indians. Cultural destructive experiences such as being "hexed" or feelings of a crawling sensation of worms or ants or of being visited by those who have died must be distinguished from actual hallucinations. The clinician or evaluator should not routinely dismiss a symptom because it is viewed as normal within that culture.

Manic Episode

See No. 1 in Mood Disorders

Mixed Episode

See No. 1 in Mood Disorders

Major Depressive Disorder

See No. 1 in Mood Disorders

Bipolar Disorder

1. No reports of differential incidences based on race or ethnicity. Some evidence that clinicians over-diagnose Schizophrenia rather than Bipolar Disorder in some ethnic groups and in younger individuals.

ANXIETY DISORDERS

Panic Disorder

1. In certain cultural groups, Panic Attack may involve fear of witchcraft (being hexed) or magic. Cultural Bound Syndromes may be related to Panic Disorder. 2. Some cultural groups restrict women's participation in public life and this should be discriminated from Agoraphobia.

300.22 Agoraphobia

See No. 2 in Panic Disorder

300.29 Specific Phobia (formerly Simple Phobia)

1. Fears of magic and spirits should be considered specific phobias if they are excessive within the context of a particular culture or ethnic group and cause significant impairment or distress. 2. Children do not usually recognize when fears are excessive. Their anxiety may be expressed by crying, tantrums, freezing, or clinging.

300.23 Social Phobia (Social Anxiety Disorder)

1. In certain cultures (i.e., Japan, Korea) individuals may develop persistent and excessive fears of offending others in social situations (instead of being embarrassed), which may become extreme anxiety that blushing, eye-to-eye contact or one's body odor will be offensive to others.

300.3 Obsessive-Compulsive Disorder

1. Culturally prescribed ritual behavior may not be considered Ob-

sessive-Compulsive Disorder unless it exceeds cultural norms, occurs at places and times deemed inappropriate by others of the same culture, and interferes with social role functioning. Clinicians may not be familiar with life transitions and mourning which may lead to an intensification of ritual behavior(s) that may appear to be an obsession. Repeated washing, checking and ordering rituals by adults or children are more likely to occur at home than in front of peers, teachers or strangers.

309.81 Posttraumatic Stress Disorder

1. Elevated rates of Posttraumatic Stress Disorder may occur among recently emigrated individuals from areas of significant social unrest and civil conflict. Because of their vulnerable political immigrant status such individuals may be reluctant to discuss their experiences of torture or trauma. [Children of migrant individuals with PTSD should be considered for assessment and possible diagnosis. PTSD may be high among U.S. youth exposed to violence regularly in low income/high crime areas.]

308.3 Acute Stress Disorder

1. Culturally prescribed coping behaviors are characteristics of particular cultures. Dissociative symptoms may be more common in cultures in which such behavior is appropriate. See Posttraumatic Stress Disorder, No.1.

300.02 Generalized Anxiety Disorder

1. In some cultures, anxiety is expressed principally through somatic symptoms while in others it is expressed through cognitive symptoms. 2. Cultural context should be considered in the evaluation process when worries about certain situations are excessive. 3. Among children focuses of anxiety may be regarding their performance in school or school activities. 4. Children who worry about catastrophic events [civil war] may be overly conforming, perfectionist or concerned with a less-than-perfect performance.

SOMATOFORM DISORDERS

1. Somatic symptoms differ across cultures. Certain pseudo-neurological symptoms are more common in Africa and South Asia (i.e., burning hands and feet or nondelusional sensation of worms in the head or ants crawling under the skin). Symptoms regard-

ing the male reproductive function may be more prevalent in cultures where there is widespread belief and concern about semen loss, such as "dhat" syndrome in India. Reports of higher frequency in Greek and Puerto Rican men suggest cultural factors that may influence the sex ratio (rarely in men in the United States).

300.81 Undifferentiated Somatoform Disorder

1. Medically unexplained symptoms and worry about physical illness may constitute culturally shaped "idioms of distress" that are employed to express concern about a range of social and personal problems without necessarily indicating psychopathology.

300.11 Conversion Disorder

1. More common in individuals of lower socioeconomic status, in rural populations and in individuals less knowledgeable about medical and psychological concepts. Higher rates of conversion are reported in developing countries with the incidence declining with increasing development. Falling down with loss or alteration of consciousness is a feature of a variety of culture-specific syndromes. Changes resembling conversion symptoms are common aspects of certain culturally sanctioned religious and folk healing rituals.

300.7 Hypochondriasis

1. The diagnosis of hypochondriasis should be made cautiously if the individual's ideas about disease have been reinforced by traditional healers who may disagree with the reassurances provided by medical evaluations.

300.7 Body Dysmorphic Disorder

1. Cultural concerns may influence or amplify preoccupation about an imagined physical deformity.

DISSOCIATIVE DISORDERS

300.13 Dissociative Fugue (formerly Psychogenic Fugue)

1. Individuals with variously defined "running syndromes" (e.g., Pibloktoq among native people of the Arctic, grisi sickness among the Miskito of Honduras and Nicaragua, the "frenzies" of witch-

craft among the Navajo and some forms of Amok in Western Pacific cultures) may have symptoms that meet diagnostic criteria. Dissociative Fugue is characterized by a sudden onset of a high level of activity, a trance-like state, potentially dangerous behavior in the form of running or fleeing, followed by exhaustion, sleep and amnesia.

300.14 Dissociative Identity Disorder

1. Recent relatively high rates reported in the United States might indicate it as a culturally specific syndrome.

300.6 Depersonalization Disorder

1. Voluntarily induced experiences of depersonalization form part of meditative and trance practices that are prevalent in many religions and cultural behaviors and should not be confused with Depersonalization Disorder.

SEXUAL AND GENDER IDENTITY DISORDERS

1. Clinical judgements should take the individual's cultural, ethnic, religious and social background into account. In some societies, sexual desires of the female are given less relevance (especially when fertility is the primary concern).

Paraphilias

1. Diagnosis varies across cultures or religions. What is considered deviant in one culture may be more acceptable in another cultural group.

EATING DISORDERS

307.1 Anorexia Nervosa

1. Appears prevalent in industrialized societies. Immigrants from other cultures who assimilate thin-body ideals may develop the disorder. In some cultures disturbed perception of the body may not be prevalent and expressed motivation for food restriction may have a different content, such as epigastric discomfort or distaste for food.

307.51 Bulimia Nervosa

1. Prevalent in industrialized countries. Few studies have examined prevalence rates in other cultures. In the United States this disor-

der occurs primarily among Whites but it has also been reported among other ethnic groups.

SLEEP DISORDERS

307.47 Nightmare Disorder

1. Varies across cultures. Some cultures associate it to spiritual or supernatural phenomena, while other cultures view nightmares as indicators of mental or physical disturbance.

307.46 Sleep Terror Disorder

1. No reports have provided clear evidence but it is likely that causes attributed to this disorder differ between cultures.

307.46 Sleepwalking Disorder

See Sleep Terror Disorder, No. 1.

307.42 Insomnia Related to Another Disorder

307.44 Hypersomnia Related to Another Disorder

1. Individuals from certain cultural backgrounds may be more likely to present complaints of insomnia (physical problems) rather than depression or anxiety (mental health problems) because of the stigma associated with mental problems.

IMPULSE-CONTROL DISORDERS NOT ELSEWHERE CLASSIFIED

312.34 Intermittent Explosive Disorder

1. Similar to Amok, except Amok occurs as a single episode rather than as a pattern of aggressive behavior. Often associated with prominent dissociative features.

312.31 Pathological Gambling

1. There are cultural variations in the prevalence and type of gambling activities (e.g., paigo, cockfights, horse racing, the stock market).

ADJUSTMENT DISORDERS

1. Individual's cultural background should be taken into account and whether behavior is maladaptive or is in excess of what would be expected within his or her culture.

Personality Disorders

1. Personality Disorders should not be confused with problems associated with acculturation or values expressed in individual's culture of origin. Clinicians should obtain additional information from informants familiar with the person's cultural background.

301.0 Paranoid Personality Disorder

1. Individuals from different cultural backgrounds may display guarded or defensive behaviors due to unfamiliarity (i.e., language barriers) or in response to the perceived neglect or indifference of the majority society. Some ethnic groups may display culturally related behaviors [due to racism and discrimination] that can be misinterpreted as paranoid.

301.20 Schizoid Personality Disorder

1. Some individuals who have moved from rural to metropolitan environments may exhibit "emotional freezing" that may last for months and may be manifested by solitary activities, constricted affect and other deficits in communication. Immigrants from other countries may be perceived as cold, hostile or indifferent.

301.22 Schizotypal Personality Disorder

1. Pervasive culturally determined characteristics, particularly those regarding religious beliefs and rituals, can appear to be schizotypal to the uninformed outsider (e.g., voodoo, speaking in tongues, evil eye, spiritism, and magical beliefs related to health and illness).

301.7 Antisocial Personality Disorder

1. Associated with low socioeconomic status and urban settings. Clinicians should consider the social and economic context in which behaviors occur in assessing antisocial traits so as to not misapply the diagnosis if behavior is part of survival strategy.

301.83 Borderline Personality Disorder

1. Identified in many settings around the world. May be misidentified in adolescents and young adults with identity disorders particularly if accompanied by substance abuse.

> **301.50 Histrionic Personality Disorder**
>
> 1. Norms for interpersonal behavior, personal appearance and emotional expressiveness vary widely across cultures.
>
> **301.82 Avoidant Personality Disorder**
>
> 1. There may be variation in the way different cultural and ethnic groups regard diffidence and avoidance as appropriate.
>
> **301.6 Dependent Personality Disorder**
>
> 1. Degree of dependence varies substantially across different age and sociocultural groups. Dependent behavior should be considered when it is clearly in excess of the individual's cultural norms or reflects unrealistic concerns. Some societies emphasize passivity, politeness and deferential treatment and may be misinterpreted as dependent personality disorder.
>
> **301.4 Obsessive-Compulsive Personality Disorder**
>
> 1. Certain cultural groups place emphasis on work and productivity. Clinicians need to consider habits, customs or interpersonal styles that are culturally sanctioned by the individual's reference group.

Racism and Mental Health

There is no doubt that racism is alive and well in the United States. The proliferation of white supremacist groups throughout the country has verified that. These groups have targeted many ethnic groups, including African Americans, Jews, Asian Americans, and people of color in general. The same principles may be present in the mental health arena. When a national educational group of minority professionals was asked to respond to its major areas of concern, the group reported that institutional racism was the most often cited factor that impinges on the mental health of minority youth (CASSP, 1986). The group stated that black and Hispanic children are often overenrolled in classes for the mentally retarded and the seriously emotionally disturbed, while underrepresented in programs for the gifted and talented.

As stated earlier, psychiatric misdiagnosis can occur primarily because of ignorance of cultural factors, but it can also occur as a direct consequence of institutional racism, overt or covert. Depression, for instance, has been reported more frequently in white clients than in African-American clients (Wilkinson & Spurlock, 1986). The basis for the underdiagnosis of depression lies in the foundation set by the literature, which indicates that depression is not as common among blacks as among the white population. Paniagua (1994) has pointed out that Griffith and Baker (1993) indicate that the reason for the underdiagnosis is based on the "myth that African Americans could not . . . become depressed." Consequently, race plays a big role, whether consciously or not, in determining that if the client is black then this, or if the client is white then that, which is a reflection of racial biases in the determination of diagnosis (Wilkinson & Spurlock, 1986). In conclusion, clinicians need to be aware of the potential effects of the racism, stereotypes, and personal biases they harbor as the result of many years' training within a society that is still struggling with this problem.

Psychopharmacology and Ethnicity

It should first be said that the field of biological and cultural psychiatry has been one of the last frontiers to be explored by social scientists, and until recently it remained virtually neglected. After more than a century, psychiatry came of age when its researchers put aside its limited focus on the omnipotent theorems which assume that people are universally the same in terms of the efficacy of medical treatment. It was assumed, for example, that protein and fat were metabolized the same way by all people, and that pharmacological agents had the same effects on everyone, no matter who the individual.

It was only during World War II that scientists began to realize that there are variations in the dosage and effectiveness of medications on people of different ethnicities. This occurred when the medical status of African-American soldiers treated with primaquine for malaria did not improve, but worsened into the condition of primaquine hemolysis and other serious side effects (Lin et al., 1993). During the 1950s observations of ethnic differences in side effects were identified in isoniazid, a medication for tuberculosis (Weber, 1987). Weber reported on the genetically controlled slow versus rapid acetylation phenotypes of isoniazid. Acetylation has since become an active area of research, since it can determine the metabolism of a number of pharmacoactive agents, but, more importantly, it is a significant risk factor for the development of a variety of malignant conditions (Weber, 1987).

Observations of "flushing response" were also reported in large cross-ethnic variations of populations in response to alcohol consumption (Singh et al., 1989). Flushing is a response to alcohol which can be accompanied by dyspnea, tachycardia, nasal congestion, and general discomfort (Yamamoto, 1982). It is found primarily among Asian people.

One of the better known factors associated with ethnic racial difference in relation to metabolic variation is the inability to digest milk sugar (lactose). Ethnic groups that lack the enzyme lactase, which is needed for milk sugar digestion, experience bloating, flatulence, cramps, and diarrhea after drinking milk. During the 1970s the percentage of lactose intolerance was reported in the following groups (Chien, 1993):

Ethnic Group	Percentage
Asians	94%
African blacks	90%
American Indians	90%
Mexican Americans	50%
White Americans	15%

Asian herbal treatments and diets also influence the metabolism of some psychotropic medicines. Foods that include soy, fish, and fermented and pickled foods interact with monoamine oxidase inhibitors, which are used to treat depression, PTSD, and panic disorder, causing serious side effects, such as hypertension (Lin & Shen, 1991). Herbal drugs are also likely to cause or intensify side effects if they contain an atropinelike substance known to produce anticholinergic reactions (Chien, 1993).

Upon further study of chemical agents and their metabolic variations among cross-cultural groups, it was found that there are some people who are poor metabolizers and others who are extensive metabolizers of particular chemical agents. The metabolism of most psychotropic drugs is known to be dependent on a group of liver isoenzymes called cytochrome (P450). Of these groups of enzymes, debrisoquine hydroxylase (CYP2D6) and nephenytoin hydroxylase (CYP2C19) are generally found to be genetically controlled (Cholerton et al., 1992; Kalow, 1993).

The implications of these findings are significant in terms of dosages needed for particular ethnic groups. As an example, Table 4.2 (Lin & Poland, 1995) presents the ethnic variations and percentages of poor metabolizers for CYP2D6 and CYP2C19.

Since CYP2D6 is also involved in the metabolism of diazepam (Valium), a significant number of African Americans require a higher dose of diazepam as compared to Caucasians (Hassibi, 1995). Conversely, Caucasians may require higher dosages of these antidepressants and neuroleptics, since CYP2D6 is involved in the metabolism of SSRIs, and higher percentages of the Caucasians are poor metabolizers (3 percent to 9.2 percent).

TABLE 4.2

Ethnicity and Percentage of Poor Metabolizers

Percentages of Poor Metabolizers

Race	CYP2D6	CYP2C19
Caucasians	3 – 9.2	2.5 – 6.7
African Americans	1.9	18.9
East Asians	0 – 2.4	17.4 – 22
Amerindians	0 – 5.2	0
Hispanics	4.5	4.8

CYP2D6 is also involved in the metabolism of a number of major classes of psychotropic medications. Studies have shown that about 30 percent of those of Asian-American and African-American background are poor metabolizers of these drugs because they oxidate the enzyme debrisoquine more slowly. Some studies have shown that about 3 percent of Caucasians and about 20 percent of Asian and African Americans lack the enzyme CYP2C19, which is involved in the metabolism of benzodiazepines and the majority of antidepressants.

It is only within the past fifteen years that the pharmaceutical companies have begun using different populations for their clinical trials of effectiveness, dosage levels, and side effects. Previously their population for standardizing medications was basically white, male college students. Women, ethnic groups, and different subpopulations were not considered until recently, as a result of community advocacy and pressure and, most importantly, independent research studies by ethnically concerned, culturally competent scientists.

Hassibi (1995) has presented a chart of some recent findings comparing psychotropic medication levels most commonly used by patients in three ethnic groups with levels used by Caucasians. Table 4.3 shows

TABLE 4.3

Response to Medications in Three Groups in Comparison with Caucasians

Medication	African Americans	Asian Americans	Hispanic/Latino Americans
Tricyclics[1]			
Time to response	More rapid response	Not consistent	
Amount of dose to response	Lower dose		Lower dose
Reactions	Delirium at high dose		More side effects (complaints)
Haldol[2]			
Amount of dose to response	No difference	Lower dose	No difference
Lithium[3]			
Amount of dose	Lower dose	Lower dose	No difference
Benzodiazepines[4]			
Amount of dose	Higher dose	Lower dose	Not studied

[1]Ziegler & Biggs, 1977; Livingston et al., 1983; Marcos & Camcro, 1982
[2]Jana et al., 1992
[3]Lin et al., 1990; Ostrew et al., 1986
[4]Fleishaker & Phillips, 1989; Zhang et al., 1990

that in African Americans the response to tricyclics occurs earlier in the course of treatment, with about one third to one half of the dosage necessary for Caucasians. With African Americans on high dosages of tricyclics, delirium is a side effect. Another drug, lithium bicarbonate, used for mania and occasionally for intermittent explosive impulse disorder and aggressive behavior, can cause drug toxicity if used over a prolonged period of time, as the result of the drug accumulating in the body. The table also shows that higher dosages of benzodiazepines may be required for African Americans, because they metabolize it much faster than Caucasians. In comparison, Asians usually require small dosages, because a large number of Asians are slow metabolizers of neuroleptics and benzodiazepines.

However, Chien's (1993) review of the literature reports that there are inconsistent and conflicting reports in dosage surveys and pharmacokinetics studies of neuroleptics used to treat Asians and white patients; specifically there are conflicting results in the studies of tricyclic antidepressants. Chien goes on to say that "the notion that Asians require a lower dosage of psychotropic drugs than Whites cannot at this point be supported unequivocally for all four major categories of psychotropic drugs except benzodiazepines which still need more confirming clinical studies." In conclusion, he states that ethnopsychopharmacology is still in its pioneer phase, and that future studies should have larger samples of subjects, "preferably from patient populations," and adequate representation of subjects who are slow, intermediate, and fast excreters.

Comorbidity

Comorbidity is another area which needs attention, in addition to herbal interaction with medicines and metabolic rates of clients. Comorbidity is the combination of a pair of disorders, such as a physical illness and depression. Another example is the consumption or intake of a drug substance or alcohol in addition to a medical or mental health problem. It is obvious that the prevalence of substance abuse among the medically or the mentally ill hinders their recovery process and may affect the assessment as well as complicate their diagnosis. Cohen et al. (1991) administered a one-day survey to assess the prevalence of substance abuse in Adult General Care at Metropolitan Hospital Center in East Harlem, where residents are primarily Hispanic and African American. The results revealed that 51 percent of the Adult General Care patients had either reported using substances or incurred injury indirectly from substance abuse (e.g., acting as a drug courier and failing to return adequate money from a drug sale). Furthermore, 12 percent of the newborns in Metropolitan Hospital had traces of cocaine in their urine.

Another study in Harlem Hospital (Curtis et al., 1986), where community residents are primarily African American, found that the overall prevalence rate of patients with alcoholism in the Medicine Service sample was 30.2 percent, with men being three times more likely than women to be alcoholics. In the surgery department, the overall prevalence rate of alcoholism among patients was 43.8 percent, with men equally as likely to be alcoholics as women. Severely alcoholic patients were more likely to be severely depressed than mildly alcoholic patients, suggesting that progressively severe alcoholism is associated with progressively severe depression. Physical illness coupled with alcoholism and depression (triple morbidity) appears to slow patient recovery.

In a national sample, the National Comorbidity Survey reported that blacks and Hispanics were more likely than other groups to experience comorbid depression (Blazer et al., 1994). In a city-wide survey of the fourteen psychiatry departments' Consultation and Liaison Services (which provide a link between medical and psychiatric services) within New York City's Health and Hospitals Corporation, where the client's population is more than 80 percent from minority groups, findings showed that dual and triple diagnoses comprised 35 percent of the total consultations (54,392) seen during 1991–1992 (MERTI, 1993).

In a study of HIV/AIDS patients, Snyder et al. (1992) revealed that mental illness was prevalent in 61.9 percent of inpatients with AIDS. Although depression accounted for only 10 percent of the inpatients, increased severity of illness was associated with a higher prevalence of mental disorders. In addition, trends suggest a correlation between physical disability due to the onset of AIDS and anxiety and cognitive impairment. Bearing in mind the number of studies that correlate mental illness significantly with physical illness (Badger et al., 1992; Coyne et al., 1992; Goldstein & Niaura, 1992; Spitzer et al., 1992), improved provider understanding of these factors will likely assist in improved accuracy in the detection of mental illness in this population.

Among the HIV/AIDS population, several studies have reported that the prevalence of substance abuse in patients with HIV/AIDS ranges from 7 to 20 percent (Atkinson et al., 1988; Baer, 1989). Other studies have found that substance abuse suppresses the immune system, promoting the onset of AIDS in HIV-positive subjects. For example, Friedman et al. (1988) revealed that tetrahydrocannabinol (THC), a component of marijuana, suppresses the immune response system. Furthermore, Donahoe and Falek (1988) found that alcohol, cocaine, and opiates depress T-cell functioning. However, in some circumstances, morphine can actually enhance T-cell functioning. Donahoe and Falek caution that substance abuse, in general, can have a dichotomous effect on the immune system. Although substance abuse changes the strength of the immune system, various drugs have differing impacts on the direction of change. Contrary to Donahoe and Falek, Klein et al. (1988) suggest that cocaine has no toxic impact on lymphocytes. However, the authors state that their findings are preliminary and further studies are required.

In summary, clinicians, physicians, and social service providers should be aware not only of indigenous practices, but also of other ethnic and cultural variables such as metabolic rates for certain groups of people, the interactive effects of herbal treatments with conventional medicines (Crone & Wise, in press), and the comorbidity prevalence of mental illness in health services, including alcoholism and substance abuse among their populations.

References

Abad, V., Ramos, J., & Boyce, E. (1974). A model for delivery of mental health service to Spanish-speaking minorities. *American Journal of Orthopsychiatry, 44*, 584–95.

American Psychiatric Association (1994). *Diagnostic and statistical manual of mental disorders.* (4th ed.). Washington, DC: Author.

Antonovsky, A. (1974). Conceptual and methodological problems in the study of resistance resources and stressful life events. In Dohrenwend and Dohrenwend (Eds.), *Stressful life events: Their nature and effects* (pp. 245–258). New York: Wiley.

Atkinson, J., Grant, I., & Kennedy, C. (1988). Prevalence of psychiatric disorders among men infected with human immunodeficiency virus. *Archives of General Psychiatry, 45*, 859–864.

Attneave, C. (1982). American Indians and Alaska Native families: Emigrants in their own homeland. In M. McGoldrick, J.K. Pearce, & J. Giordano (Eds.), *Ethnicity and family therapy.* New York: Guilford.

Badger, L., Plant, M., deGruy, F., Anderson, R., Ficken, R., Gaskins, S., Hartman, J., Leeper, J., Maxwell, A., Rand, E., & Tietze, P. (1992). Predictors of psychiatric under diagnosis. In J. Gonzales (Chief), *Primary care mental health research: Concepts, methods, and obstacles.* Symposium conducted at the meeting of the National Institutes of Mental Health, Tysons Corner, Virginia.

Badillo-Ghali, S. (1982, January). Understanding Puerto Rican traditions. *Social Work,* 98–102.

Baer, J. (1989). Study of 60 patients with AIDS or AIDS-related complex requiring psychiatric hospitalization. *American Journal of Psychiatry, 146*, 1285–1288.

Billingsley, A. (1968). *Black families in white America.* Englewood Cliffs: Prentice-Hall.

Blanchard, E. (1995). Mental health services and reservation Indians - The concept of origin (Part three). In K. R. Argrette & J. Suarez (Eds.), *An introduction to Indian life: A Native American curriculum.* New York: Multicultural Education, Research and Training Institute, Department of Psychiatry, Metropolitan Hospital Center.

Blazer, D.G., Kessler, R.C., McGonagie, K.A., & Swartz, M.S. (1994). The prevalence and distribution of major depression in a national community sample: The National Comorbidity Survey. *American Journal of Psychiatry, 151*(7), 979–986.

Boyd-Franklin, N. (1989). *Black families in therapy—A multisystems approach.* New York: Guilford.

Brown, G.W., Bhrolchain, M.N., & Harris, T. (1975). Social class and psychiatric disturbance among women in an urban population. *Sociology, 9*, 225–254.

Buchwald, D., Panwala, S., & Hooton, T.M. (1992). Use of traditional health practices by Southeast Asian refugees in a primary care clinic. *Western Journal of Medicine, 156*(5), 507–511.

Butcher, J.N. (1985). Current developments in MMPI use: An international perspective. In J.N. Butcher & C.D. Spielberger (Eds.), *Advances in personality assessments.* Hillsdale, NJ: Erlbaum.

Canino, I.A., & Canino, G.J. (1993). Psychiatric care of Puerto Ricans. In A. Gaw (Ed.), *Culture, ethnicity and mental illness.* Washington, DC: American Psychiatric Association.

Canino, I.A., & Spurlock, J. (1994). *Culturally diverse children and adolescents: Assessment diagnosis and treatment.* New York: Guilford.

CASSP. (1986). *Developing mental health programs for minority youth and their families: Summary of conference proceedings.* Washington, DC: Child and Adolescent Service System Program, Technical Assistance Center, Georgetown University Child Development Center.

Chien, C.P. (1993). Ethnopsychopharmacology. In A.C. Gaw (Ed.), *Culture, ethnicity and mental illness.* Washington, DC: American Psychiatric Association.

Cholerton, S., Daly, A.K., & Idle, J.R. (1992). *Trends Pharmacol Sci, 13*(12), 434–439.

Cobb, S. (1976). Social support as a moderator of life stress. *Psychosomatic Medicine, 38,* 300–314.

Cohen, M., Aladjem, A., Horton, A., Lima, J., Palacios, A., Hernandez, I., Lefer, J., & Mehta, P. (1991). How can we combat excess mortality in Harlem: A one day survey of substance abuse in adult general care. *International Journal of Psychiatry in Medicine, 21*(4), 369–378.

Coles, R. (1986). *The political life of children.* Atlantic Monthly Press.

Coyne, J., Schwenk, T., & Fechner-Bates, S. (1992). Nondetection of depression by family physicians reconsidered: The Michigan Depression Project. In J. Gonzales (Chief), *Primary care mental health research: Concepts, methods, and obstacles.* Symposium conducted at the meeting of the National Institutes of Mental Health, Tysons Corner, Virginia.

Crone, C.C., & Wise, T. (Eds.) (in press). Use of herbal medicine among C-L populations: A review of current information regarding risks, interactions, and efficacy. *Psychosomatics.* Washington, DC: American Psychiatric Press, Inc.

Curtis, J., Millman, E., Joseph, M., Charles, J., & Bajwa, W. (1986). Prevalence rates for alcoholism, associated depression and dementia on the Harlem Hospital Medicine and Surgery Services. *Advances in Alcohol & Substance Abuse, 6*(1), 45–64.

Dana, R.H. (1993). *Multicultural assessment perspectives for professional psychology.* Needham, MA: Allyn and Bacon.

Delgado, M. (1977, October). Puerto Rican spiritualism and the social work professions. *Social Casework, 451–458.*

Dohrenwend, B.P. (1966). Social status and psychological disorder: An issue of substance and an issue of method. *American Sociological Review, 31,* 14–34.

Donahoe, R., & Falek, A. (1988). Neuroimmunomodulation by opiates and other drugs of abuse: Relationship to HIV infection and AIDS. In T. Bridge, A. Mirsky, & F. Goodwin. (Eds.), *Psychological, neuropsychiatric, and substance abuse aspects of AIDS,* (pp. 145–158). New York: Raven Press.

Fitzpatrick, J.P. (1976). The Puerto Rican family. In R.W. Habenstein & C.H. Mindel (Eds.), *Ethnic families in America: Patterns and variations.* New York: Elsevier.

Fleishaker, J.C., & Phillips, J.P. (1989). Adinazolam pharmacokinetics and behavioral effects following administration of 20–60 mg. oral doses of its mesylate salt in healthy volunteers. *Psychopharmacology, 99,* 34–39.

Friedman, H., Klein, T., Specter, S., Pross, S., Newton, C., Blanchard, D.K., & Widen, R. (1988). Drugs of abuse and virus susceptibility. *Advances in Biochemical Psychopharmacology, 44,* 125–137.

Garrison, V. (1972, February 24–26). Espiritismo: Implications for provision of mental health services to Puerto Rican populations. Paper read at eighth annual meeting of the Southern Anthropological Society, Columbia, MO.

Garrison, V. (1977). The Puerto Rican syndrome. In V. Crapanzano & V. Garrison (Eds.), *Psychiatry and spiritism: Case studies in spirit possession.* New York: Wiley.

Gaw, A.C. (1993). *Culture, ethnicity and mental illness.* Washington, DC: American Psychiatric Association.

Goldstein, M., & Niaura, R. (1992). Psychological factors affecting physical conditions: Cardiovascular disease literature review. *Psychosomatics 33*(2), 134–154.

Gorbea, C. (1975). The institute's program for new arrivals. In D.J. Curren et al. (Eds.), *Proceedings of Puerto Rican conference on human services.* Washington, DC: COSSMHO.

Greene, R.L. (1987). Ethnicity and MMPI performance: A review. *Journal of Consulting and Clinical Psychology, 55,* 497–512.

Griffith, E.H., & Baker, F. (1993). Psychiatric care of African Americans. In A.C. Gaw (Ed.), *Culture, ethnicity and mental illness.* Washington, DC: American Psychiatric Press.

Gurin, G., Veroff, J., & Feld, S. (1960). *Americans view their mental health.* New York: Basic Books.

Guthrie, G.M., & Lonner, W.J. (1986). Assessment of personality and psychopathology. In W.J. Lonner and J.W. Berry (Eds.), *Field methods in cross-cultural research.* Cross-Cultural Research and Methodology Series. Beverly Hills, CA: Sage.

Hale-Benson, J.E. (1982). *Black children: Their roots, culture, and learning styles.* (rev. ed.). Baltimore: Johns Hopkins University Press.

Hardt, E.J. (1991). *Discussion leader's guide for the bilingual medical interview I and the bilingual medical interview II: The geriatric interview.* B. Harrington, L.A. McElaney, M. Nash, & S. Simon (Eds.). Boston: Boston Department of Health and Hospitals.

Harwood, A. (1977). *Rx: Spiritist as needed.* New York: Wiley.

Haskins, J., & Butts, H.F. (1972). *The psychology of black language.* New York: Hippocrene Books.

Hassibi, M. (1995). Cultural diversity and psychopharmacology. In *Psychotherapeutic Drug Manual.* New York: Multicultural Education, Research and Training Institute, Metropolitan Hospital Department of Psychiatry.

Heyman, I., & Fahy, T.A. (1992). Koro-like symptoms in a man infected with the human immunodeficiency virus. *British Journal of Psychiatry, 160,* 119–121.

Hill, R. (1972). *The strengths of black families.* New York: Emerson-Hall.

Ho, M.K. (1992). *Minority children and adolescents in therapy.* Newbury, CA: Sage.

Hollingshead, A.B., & Redlich, F.C. (1958). *Social class mental illness.* New York: Wiley.

Huang, K. (1991). Chinese Americans. In N. Mokuau (Ed.), *Handbook of social services for Asian and Pacific Islanders.* New York: Greenwood Press.

Hughes, C.C. (1993). Culture in clinical psychiatry. In A.C. Gaw (Ed.), *Culture, ethnicity and mental illness.* Washington, DC: American Psychiatric Association.

Inclan, J. (1990). Understanding Hispanic families: A curriculum outline. *Journal of Strategic and Systemic Therapies 9*(3), 64–82.

Isaacs, M.R., & Benjamin, M.P. (1991). *Towards a culturally competent system of care* (Vol. 2). Washington, DC: CASSP Technical Assistance Center, Center for Child Health and Mental Health Policy, Georgetown University Child Development Center.

Jaco, E.G. (1959). Mental health of the Spanish-American in Texas. In M.K. Opler (Ed.), *Culture and mental health: Cross-cultural studies.* New York: Macmillan.

Jann, M.W., Chang, W.H., Lam, Y.W.F., et al. (1992). Comparison of haloperidol and reduced haloperidol plasma level in four different ethnic populations. *Prog Neuropsychopharmacol Biol Psychiatry, 16,* 193–202.

Jones, B. (1992). The administrative perspective: Minority mental health needs and priorities. In J. Suarez (Ed.), *Keynote addresses: The mental health forum to explore the role of cultural competency in the delivery of mental health services to ethnic/racial groups.* New York: Multicultural Education, Research and Training Institute, Department of Psychiatry, Metropolitan Hospital Center.

Kalow, W. (1993). Pharmacogenetics: Its biological roots and medical challenge. *Clinical Pharmacology and Therapeutics, 54,* 235–241.

Kardec, A. (1951). *El libro de los espiritus* [The book of the spirits] (1869). Mexico City: Orion.

Klein, T., Newton, C., & Friedman, H. (1988) Suppression of human and mouse lymphocyte proliferation by cocaine. In T. Bridge, A. Mirsky, & F. Goodwin (Eds.), *Psychological, neuropsychiatric, and substance abuse aspects of AIDS.* New York: Raven Press.

Kleinman, A., Eisenberg, L., & Good, B. (1978). Culture, illness and care: Clinical lessons from anthropologic and cross-cultural research. *Annals of Internal Medicine, 88,* 251–258.

Langner, T.S. (1962). A twenty-two-item screening score for psychiatric symptoms indicating impairment. *Journal of Health and Human Behavior, 3,* 269–276.

Lee, E. (1990). Assessment and treatment of Chinese-American immigrant families. In G.W. Saba, B.M. Karrer, & K.V. Hardy (Eds.), *Minorities and family therapy.* New York: Hayworth.

Lewis, D.O., Shanok, S.S., Cohen, R.J., Kligfeld, M., & Frisone, M. (1980). Race bias in the diagnosis and disposition of violent adolescents. *Psychiatry, 137*(10), 1211–1216.

Liem, R., & Liem, J. (1978). Social class and mental illness reconsidered: The role of economic stress and social support. *Journal of Health and Social Behavior, 19,* 139–156.

Li-Repac, D. (1980). Cultural influences on perception: A comparison between Caucasian and Chinese-American therapists. *Journal of Cross-Cultural Psychology, 11,* 327–342.

Lin, N., & Ensel, W.M. (1984). Depression mobility and its social etiology: The role of life events and social support. *Journal of Health and Social Behavior, 25,* 176–188.

Lin, N., Dean, A., & Ensel, W. (1986). *Social support, life events and depression.* Orlando, FL: Academic.

Lin, K.M., & Poland, R.E. (1995). Ethnicity, culture and psychopharmacology. *Psychiatric Times, XII*(3), 20–24.

Lin, K.M., Poland, R.E., & Silver, B. (1993). Overview: The interface between psychobiology and ethnicity. In K.M. Lin, R.E. Poland, & G. Nkasaki (Eds.), *Psychopharmacology and psychobiology of ethnicity.* Washington, DC: American Psychiatric Association.

Lin, K.M., Poland, R.E., & Chien, C.P. (1990). Ethnicity and psychopharmacology: Recent findings and future research directions. In E. Soral (Ed.), *Family, Culture and Psychobiology.* New York: Legas.

Lin, K.H., & Shen, W. (1991). Pharmacotherapy for Southeast Asian psychiatric patients. *Journal for Nervous and Mental Disease, 179,* 346–350.

Lin, N., Simeone, R., Ensel, W.M., & Kuo, W. (1979). Social support, stressful life events and illness: A model and an empirical test. *Journal of Health and Social Behavior, 20*(1), 108–119.

Livingston, R.L., Zucker, D.K., Isenberg, K., et al. (1983). Tricyclic antidepressants and delirium. *Journal of Clinical Psychiatry, 44,* 173–176.

Loo, C. (1982) Chinatown's wellness: An enclave of problems. *Journal of the Asian American Psychological Association, 7*(1), 13–18.

Lopez, S., & Nunez, J.A. (1987). Cultural factors considered in selected diagnostic criteria and interview schedules. *Journal of Abnormal Psychology, 96,* 270–272.

Loring, M., & Powell, B. (1988). Gender, race and DSM-III: A study of the objectivity of psychiatric diagnostic behavior. *Journal of Health and Social Behavior, 29,* 1–22.

Lu, F.G., Lim, R.F., & Mezzich, J.E. (1995). Issues in the assessment and diagnosis of culturally diverse individuals. In J.M. Oldham and M.B. Riba (Eds.), *Review of Psychiatry* (Vol. 14).Washington, DC: American Psychiatric Association.

Malzberg, B. (1956). Mental illness among the Puerto Ricans in New York City, 1949–51. *Journal of Nervous and Mental Disease, 123,* 262–269.

Mann, H. (1995). Part 1: An introduction to Indian life. In K. R. Argrette & J. Suarez (Eds.), *An introduction to Indian life: A Native American curriculum.* New York: Multicultural Education, Research and Training Institute, Department of Psychiatry, Metropolitan Hospital Center.

Marcos, L.R., & Alpert, M. (1980). Bilingualism: Implications for the evaluation of psychopathology. In R. W. Rieber (Ed.), *Applied psycholinguistic and mental health.* New York: Plenum.

Marcos, L.R., & Cancro, R. (1982). Pharmacotherapy of Hispanic depressed patients: Clinical observations. *American Journal of Psychotherapy, 36,* 505–512.

Martinez, R., & Wetli, C.V. (1982). Santeria: A magico-religious system of Afro-Cuban origin. *The American Journal of Social Psychiatry, 11*(3), 32–38.

McKinlay, J.B. (1973). Social networks, lay consultation and help-seeking behavior. *Social Forces, 51,* 275–292.

MERTI (1995). Seminar presentation by Dr. D. Korin-In I. Quervalú (Ed.), *Culture in Medicine* (September, 1994). New York: Multicultural Education, Research and Training Institute, Department of Psychiatry, Metropolitan Hospital Center.

MERTI (1993, May 6). *Teach out '93, a televised round table conference: The delivery of mental health services within the general health care sector.* New York: Multicultural Education, Research and Training Institute, Department of Psychiatry, Metropolitan Hospital Center.

Mezzich, J.E., Kleinman, A., Farbrega, H., & Parron, D.L. (Eds.). (1996). *Culture and psychiatric diagnosis: A DSM IV perspective.* Washington, DC: American Psychiatric Press.

Mirowsky, J. (1985). Disorder and its context: Paranoid beliefs as thematic elements of thought problems, hallucinations, and delusions under threatening social conditions. *Research in Community and Mental Health, 5,* 185–204.

Mitchell, R.E., & Moos, R.E. (1984). Deficiencies in social support among depressed patients: Antecedents or consequences of stress? *Journal of Health and Social Behavior, 25,* 438–452.

Moriwaki, S.Y. (1973). Self-disclosure, significant others and psychological well-being in old age. *Journal of Health and Social Behavior, 14*(3), 226–232.

Mueller, J.J., Kiernan, R.J., & Langston, J.W. (1992). The mental status examination. In H.H. Goldman (Ed.), *Review of general psychiatry.* San Mateo, CA: Appleton and Lange.

Newhill, C.E. (1990). The role of culture in the development of paranoid symptomatology. *American Orthopsychiatric Association, 176*–185.

Nguyen, S.D. (1982). Psychiatric and psychosomatic problems among South East Asian refugees. *The Psychiatric Journal of the University of Ottawa, 7,* 163–172.

Ortiz, A. (Ed.). (1972). *New perspectives on the Pueblos.* Albuquerque: University of New Mexico Press.

Ortiz, C.G., & Vazques-Nuttral, E. (1987). Adolescent pregnancy: Effects of family support, education and religion in the decision to carry or terminate among Puerto Rican teenagers. *Adolescence, 22*(8), 897–917.

Ostrow, D.G., Dorus, W., Okonek, A., et al. (1986). The effect of alcoholism on membrane lithium transport. *Journal of Clinical Psychiatry, 47,* 350–353.

Padilla, A., & Ruiz, R. (1973). *Latino mental health: A review of the literature.* Washington, DC: U.S. Government Printing.

Paniagua, F.A. (1994). *Assessing and treating culturally diverse clients: A practical guide.* Thousand Oaks, CA: Sage.

Pavkov, T.W., Lewis, D.A., & Lyons, J.S. (1990). Psychiatric diagnosis and racial bias: An empirical investigation. *Professional Psychology: Research and Practice, 20,* 364–368.

Quervalú, I. (1990). Stressful life events, symptomatology, and social support resources among the Puerto Rican family system in a low socioeconomic community. (Doctoral dissertation. University of Michigan.) (University Microfilms) No. ADG 90-34946.9101.

Ramos-Mckay, J.M., Comas-Diaz, L. & Rivera, L.A. (1988). Puerto Ricans. In L. Comas-Diaz & E.E.H. Griffith (Eds.), *Clinical guidelines in cross-cultural mental health.* New York: Wiley.

Reinhart, M.A., & Rhus, H. (1984). Moxibustion: Another traumatic folk remedy. *Clinical Pediatrics, 24*(1), 58–59.

Rodriguez, O. (1987). *Hispanics and human services: Help-seeking in the inner city.* New York: Hispanic Research Center, Fordham University.

Rogler, L. (1978). Help patterns, the family and mental health: Puerto Ricans in the United States. *International Migration Review, 12,* 248–58.

Rogler, L., & Hollingshead, A. (1965). *Trapped: Families and schizophrenia.* New York: Wiley.

Rogler, L., & Santana-Cooney, R. (1985). *The Puerto Rican families in New York City.* Maplewood, NJ: Waterfront Press.

Ruiz, P., & Langrod, J. (1976). The role of folk healers in community mental health. *Community Mental Health Journal, 17*(4), 392–398.

Shen, J.F. (1990). *Chinese Medicine.* (2nd ed.). Shanghai, China: Chinese Medicine Research Foundation of Dr. John Shen, 381 Fifth Avenue, New York, NY.

Simons, R.C., & Hughes, C.C. (1993). Culture bound syndromes. In A.C. Gaw (Ed.), *Culture, ethnicity and mental illness.* Washington, DC: American Psychiatric Association.

Singh, S., Fritz, G., Farg, B., et al. (1989). Inheritance of unitochondrial aldehyde dehydrogenase: Genotyping in Chinese, Japanese and South Korean families reveal dominance of the mutant allele. *Human Genetics, 83,* 119–121.

Sluzki, C.E. (1979). Migration and family conflict. *Family Process, 18*(4), 379–387.

Smith, A. (1967). The serial sevens subtraction test. *Archives of Neurology, 17,* 78–80.

Snyder, S., Reyner, A., Schmeidler, J., Bogursky, E., Gomez, H., & Strain, J. (1992). Prevalence of mental disorders in newly admitted medical inpatients with AIDS. *Psychosomatics, 33*(2), 166–170.

Spector, R. (1991). *Cultural diversity in health and illness.* (3rd ed.). Norwalk, CT: Appleton and Lange.

Spitzer, R., Williams, J., Kroenke, K., Linzer, M., deGruy, F., Brody, D., Matthews, D., Kathol, R., & Mahon, C. (1992). Prime-MD: Initial results. In J. Gonzales (Chief), *Primary care mental health research: Concepts, methods and obstacles.* Symposium conducted at the meeting of the National Institutes of Mental Health, Tysons Corner, Virginia.

Srole, L., Langner, T., Michael, S., Opler, M., & Rennie, T. (1962). *Mental health in the metropolis: The midtown Manhattan study* (Vol. 1). New York: McGraw-Hill.

Sue, S., Allen, D., & Conaway, L. (1975). The responsiveness and equality of mental health care to Chicanos and Native Americans. *American Journal of Community Psychology, 45,* 111–118.

Sue, S., McKinney, H., Allen, D., & Hall, J. (1974). Delivery of community health services to black and white clients. *Journal of Consulting and Clinical Psychology, 42,* 794–801.

Sue, S., & McKinney, H. (1975). Asian Americans in the community mental health care system. *American Journal of Orthopsychiatry, 45,* 111–118.

Sue, S., & Sue, D. (1990). *Counseling the culturally different: Theory and practice.* (2nd ed.). New York: Wiley.

Sussman, M.B., & Burchinal, L. (1962). Kin family network: Unheralded structure in current conceptualizations of family functioning. *Marriage and Family Living, 24*(3), 231–240.

Taeuber, K.E., & Taeuber, A.F. (1976). The black population in the United States. In M.M. Smythe (Ed.), *The Black American reference book.* Engelwood Cliffs, NJ: Prentice Hall.

Torrey, E. (1969). The case for the indigenous therapist. *Archives of General Psychiatry, 20*(3), 365–373.

Torrey, E. (1973). The irrelevancy of traditional mental health services for urban Mexican-Americans. Paper presented at the meetings of the American Orthopsychiatry Association, 1970. In Padilla and Ruiz (Eds.), *Latino mental health: A review of literature.*

Uba, L. (1994). *Asian Americans: Personality patterns, identity and mental health.* New York: Guilford.

Veroff, J., Kulka, R., & Donovan, E. (1981) *Mental health in American patterns of help-seeking from 1957 to 1976.* New York: Basic Books.

Warheit, G.J. (1979). Life events, coping, stress and depressive symptomatology. *American Journal of Psychiatry, 136*(4b), 502–507.

Weber, W. (1987). *The acetylator genes and drug responses.* New York: Oxford University Press.

Westermeyer, J.J. (1993). Cross-cultural psychiatric assessment. In A.C. Gaw (Ed.), *Culture, ethnicity and mental illness.* Washington, DC: American Psychiatric Association.

Wilkinson, C.B., & Spurlock, J. (1986). The mental health of Black Americans: Psychiatric diagnosis and treatment. In C.B. Wilkinson (Ed.), *Ethnic psychiatry.* New York: Plenum.

Williams, A.W., Ware, J.E., & Donald, C.A. (1981). A model of mental health, life events and social support applicable to general populations. *Journal of Health and Social Behavior, 22,* 324–336.

Williams, C.L. (1986) Mental health assessment of refugees. In C.L. Williams & J. Westermeyer (Eds.), *Refugee mental health in resettlement countries.* New York: Hemisphere.

Yamamoto, J. (1982). *Japanese Americans, in cross-cultural psychiatry.* A.C. Gaw, Ed. Littleton, MA: John Wright-PSG Company.

Yap, P.M. (1965). Koro—a culture bound depersonalization syndrome. *British Journal of Psychiatry, 111,* 43–50.

Zhang, Y., Reviriego, J., Lou, Y., et al. (1990). Diazepam metabolism in native Chinese poor and extensive hydroxylators of S-mephenytoin: Interethnic difference in comparison with white subjects. *Clinical Pharmacology and Therapeutics, 48,* 496–502.

Ziegler, V.E., & Biggs, J.T. (1977). Tricyclic plasma levels: Effect of age, race, sex and smoking. *Journal of the American Medical Association, 238,* 2167–2169.

CHAPTER 5

Cultural Competency and Child and Family Services

Culture is the learned, repetitive, characteristic way of behaving, feeling, thinking, and being of a societal group. It is transmitted from one generation to another through language, role-modeling, child enculturation, and other means. Behaviors like dietary preferences; religious practices; establishment of hierarchies; and values, mores, and beliefs are all culturally transmitted. Culture gives meaning to individuals of a social group (Brown & Ballard, 1990). Humans are ethnocentric. They experience the world through their primary culture, which has been adaptive in the history of society. Culture is humanity's most powerful nonbiological mechanism of adaptation and is what has made our species so dominant. Conversely, ethnocentricity, with its emphasis on relatively subtle differences—as opposed to overwhelming similarities—among human beings, has become the fulcrum of discord, tension, and even culturally motivated war, like the wars in Bosnia and Rwanda. This is worrisome, especially for a pluralistic society like ours, with its immense ethnic diversity.

Multicultural tolerance and sensitivity, more recent attitudes, are essential if humans are to maintain world cooperation and peace or to provide, at the local level, professional services for those who need them.

This chapter explores children and family services from a cultural relevance viewpoint. This necessitates a brief incursion into families' and

Joao V. Nunes, acknowledges the collaboration of Amy Winnick, MSW, Director of the Foster/Kinship Care Program of Boys Harbor, Inc., New York, in the authorship of this chapter.

children's lives in America today. A cultural emphasis is supported by the systems theory–based biopsychosocial model (Engel, 1977). This model abandons reductionistic notions and embraces all-encompassing ones which are truer to human beings' life complexities. Human life exists in the space where biological, psychological, and social factors interact. Simultaneously, each factor influences and is influenced by the other two. Social experience, for example, modifies biological functioning and vice-versa. In this context, the family can be seen as the unit of biopsychosocial consolidation.

Family in America

Life is lived in groups. The primary unit of group living is the family. The role of the family and of its members is extremely sensitive to cultural variations, which is very apparent in the subcultures of our society. One cannot help but notice regional and ethnic differences in societal expectations of families and family members. These differences have become more pronounced with the changing role of women (and of men), the increasing prevalence of two-career couples, and of divorce (Dulcan, 1994). Families, in this post-modern era, have several faces. They may be headed by a single parent or by two same-sex parental figures; they may have a father who works outside of the home while the mother is the homemaker and main caregiver or vice-versa. Families may have none, few, or many children; they may be headed by a woman who receives public assistance; they may be well-to-do, the children being entrusted to nannies. There are many other possible variations, as the cultural norms for family life are changing in America. Pertinent statistics corroborate this.

The United States Bureau of the Census (1986) reported that the "traditional" family—bread-winning father; homemaking, child-rearing mother; and children—accounts for around 8 percent of American families; most families are now run by two-income or single parents, are step-families, or are childless couples. Twenty-seven percent of all families with children are headed by a single parent, a woman 90 percent of the time. Sixty percent of black children and 15 percent of white children are born to unwed women, 22 percent of all births.

But, despite their diverse outward appearances, families share specific functions. They are expected to form and sustain: (1) a marital coalition that meets adults' emotional and other needs; and (2) a parental coalition to benefit the children. Families are also expected to: nurture the children; maintain relatively flexible boundaries among family members within and between generations; enculturate offspring, perpetuating and interpreting familial and cultural values to children; promote emancipation of the young; and be capable of crisis-resolution (Fleck, 1966).

Child Abuse: An Example of Family Failure

When the family fails in its functions, its cohesiveness and homeostasis suffer and its viability as a system is compromised. Although all family members suffer, children are especially affected, a vulnerability inherent in the formative years.

Consider child abuse as an example of family failure. In the United States, an estimated 1 million to 4 million cases occur each year. (The wide range is due to most cases going unreported.) Child abuse is responsible for 10 percent of the injuries in children less than five years old who are brought to an emergency room. It also accounts for around 2,000 deaths per year (Foye & Sulkes, 1990). Many abused children are

1. Under the age of five years
2. Male
3. Disabled
4. Foster children; or have:
5. Difficult temperament or
6. Unsettling behavior, like hyperactivity

Although abuse also happens in middle- and upper-class families, poverty is a strong contributing factor. Unemployment, social isolation, geographic mobility, poor housing, parental discord, parentified children (those who take on family responsibilities traditionally assigned to parents), and unwanted child status also contribute to the high prevalence of child abuse (Foye & Sulkes, 1990).

Child-abusing adults frequently show low self-esteem, signs of depression, substance-related and personality disorders, and poor child-rearing techniques. They have unrealistic expectations of children, and are often survivors of abuse themselves. This last point suggests that a self-perpetuating *child-abusing culture* exists.

Family and Children Services

Children and families are inextricably connected. The younger the child, the less likely he or she is to seek help outside of the family, when troubled. Older family members also first rely on the family, when troubled. If the family proves ineffective, the person in need of help will seek it elsewhere, moving from source to source in a culturally acceptable order. Only after this natural chain is exhausted do families or individuals seek professional help. It is plain that this process is much less individually driven where children are concerned. Families overtly seek help for members identified as troubled, rather than for systemic failures.

Professional services for children and families are sought primarily through referral by community leaders and concerned professionals, and only secondarily through self-referral. Most lay people think of the need for such services only when families are no longer able to function as expected, as evidenced by domestic violence, substance abuse, child abuse and neglect, mental illness, joblessness, and so on. The professional community, politicians, and others, it seems, think the same way: How else could we explain the relative paucity of educational and preventive services compared to treatment services?

Services provided to children and families vary with the difficulties that motivate referral. Educational, psychiatric, and social support services are among them, each branching out into further categories. Children and families come to professionals, not as blank slates but steeped thoroughly in their culture. They come with specific ideas of the nature of what afflicts them and of what is likely to help, which professionals must take into account to avoid treatment failures. A good understanding of culture, then, is essential for a good therapeutic outcome.

Historical Overview of Foster Care Placement

This section offers a brief history of the foster care movement, demonstrating the interdependence of family and children's services. Since the inception of foster care in the mid-1800s, the cultural characteristics of its recipients have been an afterthought.

The creation of the first foster boarding agency—the New York Children's Aid Society in 1853—was based on the philosophy, perpetuated by Charles Loring Brace, that children need to be *rescued* from their parents in "evil" urban environments (CWLA, 1993; Kadushin & Martin,

1988; Wiltse, 1985). Children were easily transferred to families of strangers: There was an "increased physical movement from one locality to another, thus decreasing the frequency and intimacy of contact among members of a kin network" (Goode, 1968).

> Children were placed in state supervised foster boarding homes which flourished from 1890 to 1980 (Bell & Vogel, 1968; Gordon, 1983; Sussman, 1965). Supporters promised that placement would produce sociable, independent, productive, and reliable citizens (Kadushin, 1988; Tiffin, 1982; Trattnor, 1989) to meet the industrial revolution's new demand for able factory workers. The practice was aided by social science theories on the decline of the extended family. An ancillary theory of the increased role of the mother in the family was concomitantly being voiced (Scott & Wishy, 1982). By the 1850s, "a social and cultural transformation as great as any in American history had changed the mother into the moral and spiritual guardian of the American Republic" (Scott & Wishy, 1982). In agrarian societies men and women worked together in the fields. In industrial society the mother stayed home to tend to the family's needs while the father was in the labor force. Mothers' role in child rearing increased further as extended kin networks gave way to isolated nuclear families. (Gibson, 1972)

Talcot Parsons in the 1930s and 40s theorized that small nuclear families were more easily transferable from one work place to another, a necessity in a rapidly growing industrial society. Parsons had observed less mutual aid and functional support within extended kin networks in urban centers (Gibson, 1972). Family needs were being met in the new social structures of industrialization. For example, instead of turning to kin for loans, isolated nuclear families had to use the new banking system (Gibson, 1972; Kadushin & Martin, 1988; Sussman, M., 1965).

Goode (1968) outlined pressures industrialization exerted on traditional extended-kinship networks, which propelled the predominance of the nuclear family. Only the nuclear family, it was concluded, was compatible with industrialized society (Bell & Vogel, 1968). Shanas & Sussman (1991) summarized the theory: "the large-size family, multigenerational and with bilateral kin or extended kin groups as units of being and analysis, was relegated to the museum of ancient history."

In the beginning of the foster boarding home movement, most institutionalized children were white. Black children were in separate institutions or in informal foster care (Hogan & Siu, 1988; Stehno, 1982). Three factors accounted for the marked increase in the number of black children in the child welfare system by the 1940s (Hogan and Siu, 1988):

1. Increased northward migration of black families,
2. Replacement in the public system of poor white children, whose numbers dwindled, with poor black children, whose numbers soared, and
3. The effects of a new national focus on racial integration.

Theories then prevailing about black families formed the basis for the placement of black children in foster boarding homes (Dodson, 1981; Hogan & Siu, 1988). E. Franklin Frazier saw black families at the mercy of a larger urbanized society's forces, which prevented the development of stable family relationships (Allen, 1978; Gutman, 1983). He assumed that to survive, black families needed to function like white families. This comparative approach led to viewing black families as culturally deficient (Allen, 1978; Billingsley, 1968; Gutman, 1983; Platt & Chandler, 1988). "Frazier, in 1939, concluded that matriarchal orientations, marital instability and sexual permissiveness were prevalent in black family life and represented the results of an evolutionary process which dissolved the cultural bases for kinship and family relations among blacks. . . . At the center of the deterioration of the fabric of Negro society is the deterioration of the Negro family . . . female-dominated—thus dysfunctional— households lay at the center of widespread family disorganization and pathology in lower income black communities" (Allen, 1968).

Extended-family networks were seen as not suited for the industrialized way of life. They were remnants of an agricultural past. Black extended-family networks, economic assets of the agricultural era, became too static for the industrialized north and were forced to adapt through forming more compatible nuclear families (Martin & Martin, 1978).

It followed that children were put in foster homes to be "rescued" from the perceived deleterious effects of urbanization (Kadushin & Martin, 1988). The practice grew, but failed to achieve its prescribed goals: Children began paying a psychological toll. Christopher Lasch, looking at family development in the early twentieth century, saw the family as an institution fighting against the threatening forces of an anonymous and sometimes ruthless society "filled with new guardians who have become specialists" in fulfilling responsibilities previously discharged by extended kin networks (Gordon, 1983).

Criticism of the foster boarding home movement peaked with the publication "Children in Need of Parents" (Maas & Engler, 1959). The authors' surveys of children in foster homes around the country concluded that the system failed children by denying them a feeling of permanency. Children were being raised "in limbo," often carrying for very long periods the stigmatizing label "foster children."

Afrocentrism

Reacting to the view of Negro society as culturally deficient, Africentrist sociologists suggested that earlier models of family life considered all peoples and cultures to operate in the same mode as did white culture, failing to see the distinct qualities of nonwhite families (Wilson, 1991). Africentrist sociologists put forth a model of African-American family which allowed for significant relationships to kinship networks. Derived from literature in the 1960s and 70s on black family and community life, this model provided a view of black families that took into account their strengths (Billingsley, 1968; English, 1974; Williams & Stockton, 1973). These theories were put forth while the African-American population in foster care grew, as did the negative effects of placement.

Billingsley (1968) found that whereas white Americans view family as composed of immediate members, African Americans include nuclear, consanguineous, affinal, and fictive relations. Billingsley refuted Parsons's earlier theory of nuclear families by demonstrating how traditional family functions were still being carried out in nuclear, extended, or augmented black families. Hays and Mindel (1973) concurred, explaining that, "minority status tends to strengthen kin ties in Black families because of a need for mutual aid and survival in a hostile environment." These ideas support viewing black families as culturally competent, a view supported by research.

Ethnographic studies have shown how kin serve as resources for poor blacks in the struggle against poverty and high rates of male unemployment, and, especially, in efforts to achieve upward mobility. Stack's (1974) study of urban life in Chicago recorded the vital role extended family relationships play in maintaining sound black communities in the face of severe economic deprivation. She reported women raising sisters', nieces', or cousins' children and regarding them as the same as their legitimate grandchildren. "Fosterage" was the term used to describe these relationships (Burton & Anderson, 1991). Instead of formal, legal adoptions as in "mainstream" America, many black families adopt informally, maintaining children's connections to parents (Peters, 1981; Stack, 1974).

> The extended family is a more salient institution among blacks than among whites. African Americans tend to help their kin in every respect, especially with child care and financially. This is consistent across economic lines. (Hays & Mindel, 1973)

Billingsley (1968) and Staples (1971) turned to history to show the strengths of black families. During slavery, they reported, elderly relatives—major sources of cohesiveness and fortitude—often reared children. Thousands grew up this way (Burton & Anderson, 1991). Many black grandparents have continued to serve as surrogate parents to their grandchildren since then, providing temporary or permanent homes in response to family needs (Burton & Anderson, 1991). During the great north and westward migration of young adult blacks, grandparents kept their children, returning them when parental finances permitted (Burton & Anderson, 1991; Wilson, 1991).

In a study of black grandparents more than sixty years old, 47 percent reported having raised children other than their own; the same percentage reported having raised fictive grandchildren. Compare this figure to 8 percent of older Anglos who reported having raised children other than their own (Bengston & Robertson, 1985).

The history of foster care shows that its philosophies, theories, treatments, laws, labels, and names have been changing; not so much its methods or results (Pelton, 1989). Yet kinship care is the new optimistic alternative in child welfare. But is it really the answer?

Government failed to continue funding institutions that kinship care replaced. Since 1980, "return to the family" has meant reduced federal spending and increased roles of family members and kin networks. This trend, however, fails to address minority families' limitations (Boyd-Franklin, 1989).

Our experience in a mental health program for foster and kinship care children shows that the latter demonstrate emotional strengths not found in the former. As advocates anticipated, we have seen that separation issues are less prevalent and less severe in kinship care. Kinship children feel better off than foster care children. Nevertheless, kinship children, especially the younger ones, are still pained by separation from biological parents. Although these children may see their parents more often, visits can be confusing, as parents promise to take them home, beg for money for drugs, or show up obviously intoxicated. Kinship adolescents struggle with grandparents "from the old school," who attempt the difficult task of limit-setting. Intergenerational conflicts result in adolescents experiencing divided loyalties between parents and grandparents.

Existence of urban extended kinship networks and history of informal adoptions give credence to kinship care as a sound, culturally sensitive supplement to traditional foster care. But, given its problems, we cannot say it is *the* answer, but only one aspect of the wide range of services that ought to be available to children in need.

Latinos and Others

Latinos comprise the segment of American population originating in Latin America. Latinos speak two major languages, Portuguese and Spanish, and several dialects or native languages. Although Portuguese-speaking Latinos can generally understand Spanish, the reverse is not true. Spanish varies in pronunciation, inflection, meaning, usage of words, and even in rate and success of incorporation of native words in regular parlance, according to the country and region speakers come from. Latinos come in all shades of skin color and cultural hues. Yet there is more that unites than separates them culturally.

Although they also vary in socioeconomic status, Latinos are among underrepresented minorities, participating in the benefits afforded by the American dream in a much lower proportion than their numbers in American society. Conversely, they are overrepresented in all indices of poverty and social deprivation. This, coupled with their having a higher birth rate, being substantially younger than the Anglo population, and being primarily urban dwellers, supports their high rate of foster care utilization.

Latino immigration patterns peaked in the post–World War II years and has since gone through cycles of intensification and disintensification. The arrival of families that were struggling economically in the motherland made plain that there were prerequisites to admission to opportunity. A painful process of disillusioned adaptation ensued. This included less reliance on extended-kinship networks, with forced increased reliance on the nuclear family, a transition as difficult for

Latinos as it has been for African-Americans. It is useful to consider the African-American family experience as a model to guide understanding of the Latino family experience. The same could be said of more recent immigrants who in their motherland relied on extended kinship networks, but were forced to diminish or abolish that reliance by the realities of urban American life. Among these are Asian and Haitian refugees, who are now more represented than ever before in the foster care system.

Contemporary Foster Care

A large number of children in foster care face overwhelming deterrents to becoming responsible, mature adults capable of good parenting (Maluccio, 1991). These children are being enculturated to perpetuate dysfunctional families, parental care-deprived children, and therefore, the foster-care culture.

Fein (1991), Kadushin and Martin (1988), and Pine (1986) quote studies documenting long-term emotional consequences of being in foster boarding homes. Identity disorders, adjustment problems, and loyalty conflicts are among them. Children in foster boarding homes feel abandoned and angry at themselves and at their biological parents. They feel ambivalence and guilt about attaching to unrelated foster parents (Fein, 1991).

Several evaluations of the foster boarding home system identified major shortcomings: inadequate monitoring of foster parents and children; and failure to provide physical, mental health, and educational services (Dubowitz et al., 1993). Removal and separation of children from their families, communities, and values are often as harmful as the abuse or neglect from which the children are being "rescued" (Child Welfare League of America, 1991; Dubowitz, 1993; Fein, 1991). In short, children are not being rescued; rather, they are being damaged further (Kadushin & Martin, 1988).

Legislative Action

To address these findings, the Adoption Assistance and Child Welfare Reform Act of 1980—PL-272, was federally approved (Chipungre, 1991; Takas, 1993). PL-272 was designed to (1) support with more money and services the "front end" of delivery, and to prevent family breakup; and (2) insure implementation of a "permanency plan" for every child (Everett,

1991; Maluccio & Sinanoglu, 1992; Task Force on Permanency Planning, 1990). PL-272's guiding principle is that a sense of permanency, of belonging, can be created through sound child welfare practice (Fein, 1991; Kadushin & Martin, 1988; Maluccio & Sinanoglu, 1991). If a child's own biological family is unable to provide a proper home, then a new family, unrelated by blood, can be permanently assigned. PL-272 requires that placements be in the least restrictive and most family-like setting possible, opening the door for relatives as guardians (Child Welfare League of America, 1994; Task Force on Permanency Planning, 1990). In June of 1987, a policy statement by the Federal Administration for Children, Youth and Families was issued to include the homes of relatives as legitimate foster placements (Child Welfare League of America, 1994).

In the early days of foster care, it was difficult for reformers to convince state and federal governments to provide financial assistance for strangers to care for abused and neglected children. Recently, procuring reimbursement for relatives has been fought against in the courts even harder (Iglehart, 1994; Mayor Dinkins' Task Force, 1993).

Kinship care policy is based on administrative law (Gleeson & Craig, 1994). The precedent for the most recent court decisions is in Title IV of the Social Security Act of 1962. It authorized grandparents, siblings, stepsiblings, aunts, and uncles to receive AFDC grants to care for dependent children (Child Welfare League of America, 1991; Gleeson & Craig, 1994; Task Force on Permanency Planning, 1993). Requirement of parity was brought before the Supreme Court by Miller V. Youakim in 1979 (Child Welfare League of America, 1994; Takas, 1993; Task Force on Permanency Planning, 1993). In Illinois, a couple caring for the wife's younger siblings contested the state's practice of paying them AFDC rates while non-kin received higher foster boarding rates (Task Force on Permanency Planning, 1993). The ruling states, ". . . for any children entering the child welfare system due to findings of neglect or abuse by the birth parents, it was contrary to the intent of Congress to exclude relatives who care for children of their kin from eligibility for federal foster care benefits if the case meets standards that aligned the case with those of the foster care" (Task Force for Permanency Planning, 1993). In states like New York and Maryland, courts have been accepting of kinship care, awarding payment for the same types of services to kin as to strangers.

New York State has one of the most clearly defined policies on kinship care (Gleeson & Craig, 1994). Following a 1989 federal audit, the legislature passed a law strengthening the focus on placement with relatives. The law delineates process and criteria for approving relatives as foster parents and licensing their homes. In fact, New York City began licensing kinship homes in 1987 (Task Force on Permanency Planning, 1993).

Wulczyn and George (1992) postulate that the increase of kinship foster homes, especially in New York City, is due solely to the social need to make up for a decline in traditional foster homes. Although it was not its explicit intent from the start, kinship care is a culturally sensitive alternative to traditional foster care.

Demographics

Child welfare systems in the United States fund 442,000 children in foster and kinship care. That number grew from 243,000 in 1982 and was projected to reach 500,000 or more by 1995 (Child Welfare League of America, 1994, p. 15; Wulczyn & George, 1992). The Child Welfare League of America (1994) reported that during the 1980s the number of available foster homes declined by 27 percent while the number of children needing placement rose by 47 percent.

Meanwhile, three states—New York, Illinois, and California—have seen the greatest rise in kinship care placements (Takas, 1993; Wulczyn & George, 1992). In New York City the number of such placements increased from just 45 in 1986, to 24,000 in 1990 (Takas, 1993). This growth owes more to a shortage in traditional foster homes than to a societal commitment to the importance of relatives in the lives of abused and neglected dependent children (Gleeson & Craig, 1994). With the dramatic rise in the ranks of children coming into foster care in the late 1980s due to the crack-cocaine epidemic, major urban areas had to turn to relatives as guardians (Child Welfare League of America, 1994; Wulczyn & George, 1992).

Children entering foster care are no longer just "dependents." They are increasingly "infants and young children with medical complications and physical and mental limitations" (Child Welfare League of America, 1991). Foster care roles have changed from finding homes for homeless dependent children to developing social service agencies which oversee 442,000 children with severe emotional, behavioral, and psychological problems (Child Welfare League of America, 1994). Most of these children now come from families where the parents are substance abusers, may have AIDS or be homeless, or are incarcerated. Many of the children have suffered physical or sexual abuse (Child Welfare League of America, 1991).

Out of a sample of 11,648 children in kinship foster care in New York City in 1991, 70 percent were African American, and 25 percent Latino. Most foster kinship parents in New York City are older than fifty-one and, most likely, African-American grandmothers (Mayor Dinkins' Task Force, 1993). This corresponds to a national demographic trend.

New Social Science Theory

Social science theorizing has come full circle. In 1965, Sussman reported that an extended, albeit modified, kinship network has always existed in modern urban societies (Gibson, 1972). The complexity of—and transition to—life in urban America, they claimed, had previously made it difficult to detect existing kinship structures and roles (Shanas & Streib, 1965). Nonetheless, these kin networks were important in both the provision of material and nonmaterial aid and as a locus of social activity (Shanas & Streib, 1965).

Clavan (1978), too, claimed that the kinship structure had always existed for particular groups of urban families, especially in the African-American culture and that of other minorities.

Cultural Strategies for Intervention

To propose strategies for intervention is a difficult business, regardless of the angle of approach. Each individual and situation are unique, defying one-size-fits-all solutions. Yet it is important to offer some generalities that could guide professional interventions as appropriate. As different helping professions emphasize characteristically different aspects of the help continuum, we assume that each one will use cultural knowledge, skills, attitudes, and values in ways that fit their emphasis. This, too, compels us to focus on generalities. Besides, although we consider diverse cultures subcultures of American pluralistic society, here, too, like in their place of origin, they reflect traditional mechanisms for dealing with all aspects of the human condition. These must be paid attention to if professional work is to be effective.

Professionals must know well the cultural background of those they works with. An illustrative case, published in the *Annals of Behavioral Science and Medical Education* (Nunes, 1994), follows.

Robin, a fifteen-year-old girl recently arrived from Jamaica, was brought by her mother to the Pediatric Emergency Room with suicidal ideation and intent. She had not slept the previous two nights since receiving news that an "old lady" had died in her hometown. Robin was very apprehensive and clung to her mother.

Her history revealed no psychosis, gross organicity, major mood disorder, alcohol or drug use; she used no prescribed or over-the-counter medication. Toxicology screening was negative. Her physical health was good. She reportedly did well in school and enjoyed a fulfilling social life.

Six months before, Robin had come to live permanently in New York with her mother and stepfather. Although still adapting to her new life, she got along with them. Her father, with whom she had a warm relationship, and maternal grandmother, who raised her, remained in Jamaica. She came to New York to further her education. No strain in the family was reported. Robin remained an only child. There was no history of psychiatric disorders in the family.

Robin was cooperative, alert, fully oriented, and had intact memory. No thinking disorders were found. Clinically, her intellectual functioning was above average. She was not particularly impulsive. Her affect was intense. Although visibly frightened, she could converse calmly, but quickly panicked, with attendant physiologic signs, if staff asked if she could go back home or if her mother so much as moved away from her. Hospitalization in the Pediatric Adolescent Unit was necessary. She agreed, eventually feeling confident enough to allow her mother to leave. As she appeared so much improved the next day, staff suggested her possible discharge. She panicked. Staff suspected child abuse, which turned out to be unfounded.

The deceased, Robin said, had "put a curse" on her five years before when Robin had naughtily "disrespected" her. The woman, Robin recalled, promised to get revenge even if in spirit, after death. Robin's mother, upon hearing the tale, suggested independently that her daughter was being persecuted by an evil spirit.

Robin woke up three times that night, screaming, saying she saw the "old lady" hovering outside the hospital window, threatening to come in. The third time, the psychiatrist on call ordered a minor tranquilizer and waited with her until she fell asleep.

After examining her midmorning, the treatment team concluded that her visions were indistinguishable from dream imagery. Yet she was still convinced that "the deceased" was ever closer to getting her soul. The team decided to add culturally syntonic approaches to therapy. A psychologist familiar with such approaches suggested that patient and family needed a concrete symbol of the healing process. His prescription: (a) mother was to give Robin a "protection"—a garlic clove in a small cloth bag purchased in a Botanica, capable of keeping evil spirits at bay—to be worn on a necklace; (b) the family was to buy a specified cologne to be sprinkled around the house, in the corners, around doors and windows; (c) the family was to maintain a Bible open to a specific passage; (d) mother was to bring fresh flowers into the house every Friday and throw them away every Monday; (e) prescriptions were to be carried out for one month. These instructions were to be given to the family behind closed doors.

Prescriptions emphasized making the home safe for Robin's return and the treatment team's acceptance of the family's culture and beliefs. Instructions were carried out and Robin slept well. She requested to be discharged the following day, serene, confident, and thankful. After one month, the family stopped following the prescription. Robin continued in brief psychotherapy for six additional months, demonstrating she had integrated the experience appropriately into her life.

Comments

Although not a fostered care case, Robin's suggests cultural interventions which are readily applicable in diverse situations. Effective treatment requires cultural sensitivity. The treatment team did not quickly understand the need for culturally specific interventions. In retrospect, several clues existed: Robin's recent arrival from Jamaica; her history and clinical presentation; precipitating events; absence of psychosis; unresponsiveness to conventional interventions; her belief—shared by family—that she was being chased by a spirit. Eventually, specific therapeutic steps were designed to address several points: (1) Robin needed a concrete, symbolic protection against what she experienced as vivid, "concrete," and extremely frightening reality; (2) her house must be made safe for her return; (3) the whole family needed a *ritual* to reaffirm members' common cultural ground; (4) powerful symbols—the Bible, ritual cleansing—lent credibility and force to the entire process; (5) a major goal of the treatment was to reestablish the family as a unit.

These techniques are useful in foster care situations, where focus on culture and families is imperative. It is also necessary to include child welfare agencies responsible for placement of the children in question. Welfare agency case workers and supervisors should be helped to understand the family and culture such children come from in order for them to intervene constructively and work synergistically with outside professionals in behalf of the children. While belonging to families and subcultures that can be classified, each child and context is unique. Therefore, professionals should understand the generalities about children and their environments, while getting the all-important specific nuances from children and families directly. Preconceived ideas are of limited value here.

Whenever possible children are to be matched with foster parents of the same cultural subset. If this is impossible, foster parents should always be—or be helped to become—culturally sensitive and knowledgeable, which will enhance the lives of all involved.

References

Allen, W. (1978). The search for applicable theories of black family life. *Journal of Marriage and Family, 40,* 117–129.

Barranti, C. (1985). The grandparent/grandchild relationship: Family resource in an era of voluntary bonds. *Family Relations, 34,* 343–351.

Bengston, V., & Robertson, J. (Eds.). (1985). *Grand parenthood.* Beverly Hills, CA: Sage.

Berrick, M.J., Barth, R., & Needell, B. (1994). A comparison of kinship foster homes and foster family homes: Implications of kinship care as family preservation. *Children and Youth Services Review, 16*(1/2), 33–63.

Billingsley, A. (1968). *Black families in white America.* Englewood Cliffs, NJ: Prentice Hall.

Black Task Force on Child Abuse and Neglect. (1992). Position paper on kinship foster care. Brooklyn, NY.

Boyd-Franklin, N. (1989). *Black families in therapy* (pp. 42–64). New York: Guilford Press

Brown J.P., & Ballard, B. (1990). Culture, ethnicity, and behavior and the practice of medicine. In A. Stoudemire (Ed.), *Human behavior. An introduction for medical students.* Philadelphia: Lippincott.

Burton, L. (1992). Black grandparents rearing children of drug addicted parents: Stressors, outcome, and social service needs. *Gerontologist, 32,* 744–751.

Burton, L., & Anderson, P. (1991). The intergenerational family roles of aged black Americans. *Marriage and Family Review,* 311–329.

Child Welfare League of America. (1991). *Blueprint for fostering infants, children, and youths in the 1990s.* Washington, DC: Child Welfare League of America.

Child Welfare League of America. (1994). *Kinship care, a natural bridge.* Washington, DC: Child Welfare League of America.

Chipungre, S.S. (1991). A value-based policy framework. In J.E. Everett, S.S. Chipungre, & B.R. Leashore (Eds.), *Child welfare: An Afrocentric perspective* (pp. 290–305). New Brunswick, NJ: Rutgers University Press.

Clark, M.M. (1983). Cross-cultural medicine. *West J Med. 139.*

Clavan, S. (1978). The impact of social class and social trends on the role of grand-parent. *Family Coordinator, 27,* 351–357.

Dodson, J. (1981). Conceptualizations of black families. In McAdoo (Ed.), *Black families* (pp. 23–25). Beverly Hills, CA: Sage.

Dubowitz, H., Feigelman, S., & Zuravin, S. (1993). A profile of kinship care. *Child Welfare, 72*(2), 153–169.

Dulcan, M. (1994). Psychiatric disorders of children and adolescents. In A. Stoudemire (Ed.), *Clinical psychiatry for medical students.* Philadelphia: Lippincott.

Engel, G.L. (1977). The need for a new medical model: A challenge for biomedicine. *Science, 196,* 129–136.

English, R. (1974). Socialization and black family life. In L. Gary (Ed.), *Social research and the black community, selected issues and trends* (pp. 39–49). Washington, DC: Institute for Urban Affairs and Research.

Fein, E., Malliccio, A.N., & Kluyer, M.P. (1990). *An examination of long-term aftercare.* Washington, DC: Child Welfare League of America.

Fleck, S. (1966). An approach to family pathology. *Compr Psychiatry, 7,* 307–320.

Foye, H., & Sulkes, S. (1990). Developmental and behavioral pediatrics. In R.E. Bherman & R. Klugman (Eds.), *Nelson Essentials of Pediatrics.* Philadephia.

Gibson, G. (1972). Kin family network: Over heralded structure in past conceptualization of family functioning. *Journal of Marriage and Family, 42,* 13–22.

Gleeson, J., & Craig, L. (1994). Kinship care in child welfare: An analysis of states policies. *Children and Youth Services Review, 16*(1/2), 7–31.

Goode, W. (1968). Industrialization and family structure. In N. Bell & E. Vogel (Eds.), *A modern introduction to the family.* New York: Free Press.

Gordon, M. (Ed.). (1983). *The American family in social historical perspective* (pp. 1–21, 54–61, 459–482). New York: St. Martin's Press.

Gray, S. & Nybell, L. (1990). Issues in African American family preservation. *Child Welfare 69*(6), 513–523.

Gutman, H. (1983). Persistent myths about the African American family. In M. Gordon (Ed.), *The American family in social historical perspective* (pp. 459–482). New York: St. Martin's Press.

Hays, W., & Mindel, C. (1973). Extended kinship relations in black and white families. *Journal of Marriage and Family, 33,* 51–56.

Hogan, P., & Siu, S. (1988). Minority children and the child welfare system: A historical perspective. *Social Work, 33*(6), 439–498.

Iglehart, A. (1994). Kinship foster care: Placement, service, and outcome issues. *Children and Youth Services Review, 16*(1/2), 107–122.

Jendrek, M. (1994). Grandparents who parent their grandchildren, circumstances and decisions. *The Gerontologist, 34*(2), 206–216.

Kadushin, A., & Martin, J. (1988). *Child welfare services* (pp. 35–77, 344–434). New York: Macmillan.

Maas, H., & Engler, X. (1959). *Children in need of parents.* New York: Columbia University Press.

Maluccio, A. (1991). The optimism of policy choices in child welfare. *American Orthopsychiatric Association, 61*(4), 606–609.

Maluccio, A., & Sinanoglu, P. (1981). *The challenge of partnership: Working with parents of children in foster care* (pp. 3–22). New York: Child Welfare League of America.

Martin, E.P., & Martin, J.M. (1978). *The black extended family.* Chicago: University of Chicago Press.

Mayor Dinkins' Commission for the Foster Care of Children. (1993). Family assets: Kinship foster care in New York City. City of New York.

Parsons, T. (1968). The Stability of the American Family System. In N. Bell, & E. Vogel (Eds.), *A Modern Introduction to the Family* (pp. 97–102). New York: Free Press.

Nunes, J.V. (1994). Hovering menace. *Annals of Behavioral Science and Medical Education 1,* 49–51.

Pelton, L. (1989). *For reasons of poverty: A critical analysis of the public child welfare system in the U.S.* New York: Praeger.

Peters, M. (1981). Parenting in black families with young children, a historical perspective. H.P. McAdoo (Ed.), *Black families* (pp. 211–244). Beverly Hills, CA: Sage.

Pine, B. (1986). Child welfare reform and the political process. *Social Service Review,* 339–359.

Platt, T., & Chandler, S. (1988). Constant struggle: E. Franklin Frazier and black social work in the 1920s. *Social Work, 33,* 293–297.

Poe, L. (1992). *Black grandparents as parents.* Berkeley, CA: Library of Congress.

Shanas, E. (1980). Older people and their families: The new pioneers. *Journal of Marriage and the Family, 42,* 9–15.

Shanas, E., & Streib, G. (Eds.). (1965). *Social structure and the family generational relations* (pp. 2–10). Englewood Cliffs, NJ: Prentice Hall.

Shanas, E., & Sussman, M. (1991). Reflections on Intergenerational and Kin Connections. *Marriage and Family Review, 2,* 3–9.

Stack, C.B. (1974). *All our kin: Strategies for survival in a black community.* New York: Harper & Row.

Staples, R. (1971). Toward a sociology of the black family: A theoretical and methodological assessment. *Journal of Marriage and the Family 33,* 119–135.

Stehno, S. (1982). Differential treatment of minority children in service systems. *Social Work, 1,* 39–44.

Streib, G., & Beck, R. (1980). Older families: A decade review. *Journal of Marriage and the Family, 42,* 937–955.

Streib, G. (Ed.). (1995). *Social structure and the family generational relations* (pp. 62–93). Englewood Cliffs, NJ: Prentice Hall.

Sussman, M. (1965). Relationships of adult children with their parents in the United States. In E. Shanas & G. Streib (Eds.). *Social structure and the family generational relations* (pp. 62–93). Englewood Cliffs, NJ: Prentice Halls

Takas, M. (1993). *Kinship care and family preservation: A guide for states in legal and policy development.* Washington, DC: American Bar Association.

Task Force on Permanency Planning for Foster Children, Inc. (1990). *Kinship foster care: The double edged dilemma.* New York: Author.

Taylor, R., Chatters, L., & Tucker, M. (1990). Developments in research on black families: A decade review. *Journal of Marriage and the Family, 52,* 993–1013.

Tiffin, S. (1982). *In whose best interest? Child, in welfare reform in the progressive era* (pp. 88–107). Westport, CT: Greenwood Press.

Timberlake, E., & Chipungu, S. (1992). Grand motherhood: Contemporary meaning among African American middle class grandmothers. *Social Work, 37*(3), 216–221.

Thorton, J. (1991). Permanency planning for children in kinship foster homes. *Child Welfare, 70,* 593–601.

Trattnor, W. (1989). *From poor law to welfare state* (pp. 103–129). New York: Free Press.

William, R., & Stockton, R. (1973). Black family structures and functions: An empirical examination of some suggestions made by Billingsley. *Journal of Marriage and Family,* 39–47.

Wilson, M. (1991). The context of the African American family. In E. Everett, S. Chipungu, & B. Leashore (Eds.). *Child welfare: An Afrocentric perspective* (pp. 85–119). Rutgers, NJ: Rutgers University Press.

Wiltse, K. (1985). Foster care, An overview. In J. Laird & A. Hartmann (Eds.). *A handbook of child welfare* (pp. 565–585). New York: Free Press.

Wulczyn, F., & George, R. (1992). Foster care in New York and Illinois: The challenge of rapid change. *Social Service Review,* 278–294.

PART II
Organizational Issues

CHAPTER 6

Cultural Competency and Services to the Minority Aged and Frail

Nesecitas creer en Dios y portate bien. Si haces lo que te digo, todo saldra bien. Ahora ten esto para los ninos y vamos para que te ayuden. [You need to believe in God and behave. If you do what I tell you then every-thing will turn out well. Take this for the children and let's go get you help.]— The late Delfina Pedroza

La Senora Pedroza was an eighty-two-year-old Mexican-American woman who raised nine sons and daughters, buried three husbands, a sister and a brother, and two sons. More importantly, she helped raise, counsel, and nurture more than thirty grandchildren and at least twelve great-grandchildren. She also provided her family with wisdom, love, and support every day of her life. The quotation above reflects the traditional elderly Latino form of advice, "consejos"—counseling and advice—that could have been given to any of her children or grandchildren when in need of guidance and assistance. It is our elderly minorities, especially Latinos and females, who continue to serve as the pillars of support and wisdom for many of today's minority families. The advice given was to believe in God, be good, accept her help, and then to go with her to find assistance. She probably gave the family member some financial support as well. It is common, especially among Mexican Americans, to have elderly Latinos take charge of family decision making. This is not an infrequent scenario, especially with the ever increasing number of households that are headed by single females, who often have the help of an elderly relative. And yet, as the minority elderly grows older, who will take care of them and how will this be done?

Today, the need to take care of the elderly and provide appropriate health care services is a challenge facing both practitioners and our communities. In large part, the stress and concerns are based on the premise that the values in the current health care delivery system do not reflect the real needs of the minority elderly. Today's mainstream health care delivery system does not provide for our minority elderly in an appropriate, culturally competent fashion. This is evident in the Latino community, for example, where the extended family plays an important role in the care of elderly Latinos, a fact which in many cases is still not accepted by today's practitioners. This situation could be caused by the simple fact that practitioners simply don't know about the cultural values and norms of minority elderly. For example, it is common for Latino elderly to be cared for at home and not in long-term care facilities or nursing homes. As an important cultural sign of respect, elderly Latinos are taken care of by a family member, thus assuring that no harm comes to them. Even if minorities wanted to put their elderly family members in nursing homes, the financial constraints of poverty prohibit this. Latino elderly as well as other minority elderly continue to live in severe poverty, which directly and indirectly affects their health and well-being.

Demographers state that by the year 2010 the face of America will be completely different. In fact, Dr. David Hayes Bautista of the University of California at Los Angeles (UCLA) School of Medicine, Center for the Studies of Latino Health, states that many of our traditional and larger inner cities will have a majority population consisting of Latinos, African Americans, Asians, or a combination of these groups. Although this is already true in states such as Arizona, Colorado, New Mexico, Southern California, and South Texas, it is also happening in certain city sectors in other states; Illinois, Florida, and New York primarily, but also Connecticut, Maryland, New Jersey, Pennsylvania, Wisconsin, Minnesota, Washington, and Oregon. Furthermore, the impact of this growth has many long-lasting ramifications on health and human services programs.

Another important thing about so-called elderly growth is the "graying of America." It is estimated that by the year 2030 there will be 70 million elderly; of these, 25 percent will be elderly minority. However, the number of elderly, and especially minority elderly, will continue to grow at a fast rate. This is especially true of the Latino population, which in general is very young, with a median age of twenty-six. However, the Latino elderly, Mexican American in particular, are the fastest-growing groups of all elderly. What this means to current social services programs, housing, labor, and the health care delivery system is very important. The current system of human and social services will have to adapt and change with the graying of America. That graying will be dominated by Asian, African American, and Latino elderly. This has major implications for the way the current health and human services delivery system provides care to minority elderly.

Latino "ancianos" (elderly), for example, represent a large and diverse ethnic group that comprises 4.9 percent of the total Latino population (more than 1 million, according to the 1990 Census Bureau). This group consists primarily of 60 percent Mexican Americans, 13 percent Cuban Americans, 9 percent mainland Puerto Ricans, 6.5 percent other Central and South Americans, and 11.5 percent other Hispanics. Among Latino elderly, the median age is 60–64; the ratio of men to women is about 85 to 100, decreasing to about 60 to 100 after age 85. Many Latino elderly come from a rural/agrarian background (which also has health care implications); however, the number of minority elderly that actually live in rural America is less than the number of Anglo elderly. The majority of Latino elderly live in five southwestern states, which have large concentrations of Mexican Americans. This is an important factor, because the overwhelming majority of the Mexican American elderly were born in the United States and are life-long residents.

This is not the case for Cuban Americans, many of whom are immigrants. Among all the Latino elderly subgroups, the Cuban Americans have the most elderly. The Puerto Rican population is generally very young and is concentrated in the eastern states, but Puerto Ricans maintain a vital relationship with Island Puerto Ricans. Asian Americans, Central Americans, and African Americans also have a population of recent immigrants that needs special culturally based health care services.

Although the Latino elderly growth rate is approximately 26 percent, the fastest-growing subgroup of all elderly, Latino elderly continue to be largely ignored, as do other minority elderly. In part, this is due to the American cultural value system which adores and glorifies the young and ignores the elderly population. Since a majority of minority elderly continue to live in poverty, are less educated, are more likely to live with another family member, and are underinsured or have no insurance, they also suffer disproportionate disabilities, illness, poverty, and discrimination (Espino, 1989; Sotomayor, 1993). The health care service paradigm currently in place does not appropriately treat and reach minority elderly. Practitioners will have to consider a paradigm shift from their current way of providing health care services to a more appropriate culturally based model that accepts the client's customs, culture, language, and identity. If this is not done, then 25 percent of our elderly population will continue to be disenfranchised. However, we should not make the mistake of thinking that minority elderly are just sitting around doing nothing. On the contrary, they have recognized that they are a strong buying power, voting block, and lobbying group, and as a consequence, we will begin to see more and more activism on the part of minority elderly in the future.

Minority elderly today are a vibrant part of society and need to be included in the decision-making process on issues that affect them. While at a recent National Latino Conference on Aging held in Denver, Colorado, March 7–9, 1996, many Latino elderly voiced a concern that they are usually ignored by health care practitioners. While the minority elderly expect extended family members to care for them, they also expect to be treated with respect and not be ignored. If the needs of the minority elderly are to be confronted, then the issues of minority health at the national policy level must be changed to address the elderly's needs. The following areas pose some very serious questions on the future of elderly minority health care services that we must all begin to ponder.

1. Do we include cultural diversity in all aspects of health and human services?

2. Do we address health and economics together, because the current policy on aging doesn't include these two very important aspects?

3. Do we include models of bicultural/bilingual culturally competent health care and human service delivery systems, including an appropriate education and information system so that the elderly understand their health care? Are they consulted in this process?

4. What is the national aging policy and does it include elderly in the decision-making process?

5. Do health care and human service issues include concerns about nutrition, chronic diseases, advanced directives, mental health, abuse and trauma, quality of care, transportation, and housing?

6. Are health care and social services affordable, accessible, assessable, available, and acceptable?

7. Does a policy statement exist that addresses the financing of primary and urgent care services? Is it clearly defined, and easily understood by minority elderly? (This must also address the issue

of uninsured patients, Medicare, Medicaid, and managed care services.)

8. Are the current recruitment, retention, and training programs of minority health care practitioners adequate and producing enough practitioners?

All of these issues present a challenging effort for everyone who delivers services to the elderly, everyone who develops health care policies for the elderly, and for everyone who cares for and lives with the elderly. Within the context of minority services we must also include other factors that play an important role in the lives of minority elderly, such as acculturation, education, language, and immigration. We must understand what these factors mean to our elderly minorities, especially Latinos, and how they affect access to health care delivery. For example, some research supports the concept that acculturation could adversely affect health. Some studies and research conducted by Latinos such as Drs. David Hayes Bautista, Marta Sotomayor, David Espino, and others, suggest that the more assimilated the younger generations, the more prone minority elderly are to smoking, infectious diseases, certain chronic diseases (such as diabetes), substance abuse, and mental health problems.

Two major events have recently occurred that tried to focus and address the health and human service concerns of minorities: the National White House Conference on Aging (NWHCoA) and its subsequent regional meetings, and the National Latino Conference on Aging held in Denver, Colorado, sponsored by the Mexican American State Legislators Institute, Inc. (MASLPI). Both of these events tried to address the concern about services to the elderly and fragile. Although NWHCoA had very good intentions for the national aging agenda, it did not provide a forum for minority health care issues. It did, however, play an important role in the discussion about creating a national policy statement for elderly; it recommended that the Older Americans' Act (OAA) be reauthorized; it called for strengthening the elderly's independence; it promoted personal security; it encouraged empowerment of the elderly; and it recognized the elderly as a resource. Drs. David Espino and Marta Sotomayor, who have done extensive research on the Latino elderly and have provided both social and primary care services for primarily Latino elderly, have stated that services need to be more comprehensive and culturally appropriate if we are to promote well-being and prevention as an integral part of the health care delivery system for

Latino elderly; if we do not, we will have additional health care problems with our elderly in the future.

The second event, the National Latino Conference on Aging, tried to address the need for culturally appropriate health care services for Latino "ancianos" (elderly). It brought together Latino experts on aging and researchers, such as Drs. Marta Sotomayor, Manuel Miranda, and Steve Applewhite Lozano; federal officials and policy makers, such as Drs. Fernando Torres Gil, Assistant Secretary on Aging, and Ciro Sumaya, Director of the Health Resources and Services Administration (HRSA); and other important health care advocates and practitioners, such as Drs. David Hayes Bautista, Elisa Facio, Melissa Talamantes, Ben Obregon, and Rita Barreras. What was more important is that the conference included both elderly and community members in the same conference as panelists, speakers, moderators, and "consejeros" (counselors and trainers). Some of these panelists were Juanita Morales Putnam, Mary Moreno, and Mario Obledo. The conference discussed major health care concerns for Latino "ancianos," developed a plan of action, and made specific policy recommendations for health care delivery, cultural competency, and financing of health care for preventive primary, urgent, and long-term care. It was an event that merits credit for bringing together community, elderly, and experts to work side by side. A short summary in the last section of this chapter will convey the recommendations for solutions and future actions.

Currently, the leading causes of death for elderly minorities are heart disease, lung cancer, diabetes, stroke, chronic obstructive pulmonary disease, colorectal cancer, and osteoporosis. Among Latinos, especially Mexican Americans, diabetes is an important morbidity concern. Among Asians it is osteoporosis, and among African Americans, lung cancer. There is some research that suggests, however, that certain diseases such as hypertension have a lower incidence among Latinos (especially Mexican Americans) (David Hayes Baustista, AARP).

To provide adequate and appropriate health care services to minority elderly, providers must reevaluate the current services paradigm. They must also ensure that the new forms of health care delivery, such as managed care, incorporate comprehensive health care services that include prevention and health education, mental health, substance abuse, and other counseling and educational services, as well as long-term care, and that these be provided in a culturally appropriate manner. Providers are also encouraged to seek and study current comprehensive models that may already exist and have already incorporated these components. Perhaps these can be replicated.

Direct Care

Practitioners and providers will have to understand that their patients will not only get older, but will belong to a minority majority. This is important to note, because the way health care delivery is designed and provided will need to change. For example, providers who want to assure compliance must realize that when treating the Latino elderly, they must be ready to consult with the oldest family member, usually a daughter, if not with the entire family (David Espino, Marta Sotomayor, Center for Health Policy Development). While this may not be true for all minority groups, it does illustrate the point that health care delivery as we know it now will have to change. Too many times practitioners fail to realize that understanding the elderly minority's values and customs can assist in the provision of health care and facilitates the patient's compliance.

Many also need to realize that geriatrics is a fairly new field of focus; the majority of our efforts has been in providing services at the other end of the spectrum, the young and the unborn. Medical schools and other health professional programs often do not include extensive training in geriatrics, much less in Latino aging issues. Practitioners must know the community where they practice or provide services and should also incorporate community resources that could be available to them. At the Denver Latino Anciano Conference, for example, many Latino elderly expressed concern that practitioners did not really understand them; language was only part of the reason for the problem. Elderly cited the concern that the delivery system was too complicated, bureaucratic, and confusing. In addition, they felt that many practitioners were patronizing and spoke through them and not to them, which was infuriating and frustrating. Also mentioned at the conference (and elsewhere) was that Latino and other minority elderly prefer being treated by someone of their own ethnic group. With the change to managed care and Medicaid services, minority elderly patients could lose their minority provider, possibly resulting in a disruption of health care services.

We need to question what type of practitioner the health care system is creating for the minority elderly. If it is true that the minority commonly takes care of its own, then we may be creating two systems of care: one for minorities by minorities, and the other for Anglo elderly. In any event, although elderly minorities prefer their own minority health care practitioners, the reality is that there are not enough minority or minority-trained practitioners to treat them. Thus, in addition to having minority practitioners, we must ensure that postgraduate programs and

residencies include cultural competency training. Furthermore, partnerships should be formed with existing community-based resources, programs, and practitioners that can serve as models of service. Through
these partnerships, community-oriented staff could also serve as mentors
and faculty to new and upcoming practitioners. Let me cite as an example
an elderly "anciana" who is monolingual and receives medication for her
thyroid problem, but leaves the clinic thinking that she is all right and
only has a throat problem. She may not understand that she needs additional testing and follow-up. It is not until she returns to her "barrio,"
when she asks another family member and/or a neighbor to explain what
she has, does she begin to realize her problem and that she needs to return to the clinic. This may have been avoided through better communication: if a family member who was bilingual went with her, or if there
was bilingual medical staff (not a janitor or secretary who many times are
asked to step into the office to interpret). Practitioners often not only do
not know how to communicate to elderly minority, but also fail to realize
the special circumstances of these persons. Sensitivity, cultural competency, ethics, and language should be considered as part of the health care
delivery paradigm by practitioners, if they are to treat elderly minority.
Practitioners should recognize, for example, that advance directives is another very serious and new concept to minority elderly. Among minorities, advanced directives may not be accepted as a normal and routine aspect of their health care. Furthermore, some cultures (including Latino
"ancianos") may not accept predetermining the right to life and death,
yet the health care delivery system must address these concerns with minorities. Latinos, for example, are fatalistic and will resort to the statement that the time of death is destined; they will find it difficult to decide.
Family members will also have trouble with this issue, a situation that
could be addressed with an outreach and education program for minority elderly and their families.

There are other cultural customs that affect health care delivery and
need special attention from the practitioner. Among Mexican Americans,
for example, the elderly may be more inclined to accept therapies and
treatments if home remedies, folk medicines, natural teas, and herbs are
combined with current treatment regimens. Practitioners may find this
hard to accept, but if we know that the folk remedy is harmless (and in
some instances it may truly help), and our goal is to provide care, then
why not accept the regimen and convince the minority elderly that the
therapy, medication, and treatment can be used in combination with
their own remedy.

Among other factors influencing the health of minority elderly is when an elderly person takes care of another, older elderly person. This is becoming a more common and frequent happening among minority elderly. This is an important factor for practitioners to understand, because when explaining therapies, treatments, medications, and general care (especially among Latinos), they may find a 60–65-year-old taking care of a 75–80-year-old. This has implications for both the patient and the caregiver. If one gets ill, the other may subsequently become ill also, and if there is no one to care for both of them, there now is a dilemma. It is also interesting to note that factors such as transportation, language, sensitivity, office hours, location of the clinic or office, the promotion and understanding of the health care system, as well as minority staff, could affect the number of clinic visits and the compliance of minority elderly patients. Many elderly in large inner city neighborhoods, for example, will not leave their homes after sunset, making it difficult to keep appointments later in the day.

Other minority elderly direct-care issues that the practitioner must recognize are common community-based cultural health conditions. These, if not understood, could create a barrier between the patient and the provider. For example, within the Latino community there are many complaints of illness and syndromes unfamiliar to the nonminority practitioner, which in many instances are as real as any other symptoms. Latino elderly may, for example, complain of being ill from "susto" (being scared), from "un ataque" (fainting), "fatiga" (shortness of breath), "mal de ojo" (evil eye), or "dolor de rinones" (back pain). These descriptions are somewhat vague, but real for Latinos, and they usually have some biological foundation that requires a careful and sensitive evaluation. Some nonminority practitioners might dismiss these symptoms as superstition or nonsense and hence, miss a very important diagnosis. Therefore, considerations of the chief complaints must include an understanding of the patient's cultural symptoms and concerns. A "fatiga," for example, may just be tiredness, but, it may also be the patient's own explanation of an underlying neurological or nutritional problem. He or she has probably disregarded the "fatiga" for quite some time, but is finally coming to the practitioner because it has continued, is prolonged, and is now a matter of concern.

Language also plays an important factor in health care delivery, especially for minorities that are monolingual and/or more proficient and more comfortable in their native tongue. Unless there is a bilingual person on staff, the elderly minority patients may never divulge their true complaints.

It is up to the practitioner to probe until the elderly person feels comfortable and discloses the pertinent signs and symptoms. Although this factor in many instances is dealt with in bilingual materials, the information often is translated into a language form or dialect that is also foreign to the patient. During the acculturation process, many minorities have adopted a different version of the mother tongue, and like many other immigrants, in many instances the elderly have adopted a modified language that is a combination of both English and Spanish (Tex-Mex, as it is called in many South Texas Mexican-American communities). In addition, even if they have retained their native tongue, many are illiterate and cannot read or write. There is a case that Dr. Juan Chavira, a medical anthropologist and judge, frequently uses when he makes presentations on cultural competency in the health care field. He cites the case of an elderly Mexican-American couple who bring their daughter to the doctor because she has a severe stomachache, has been vomiting, and has diarrhea. A very capable Latino practitioner examines her and provides a diagnosis and treatment. The practitioner tells the elderly couple that their daughter has "gastroenteritis." The woman seems relieved, but doesn't understand and again asks the practitioner what her daughter has. He again calms her fears, tells her the daughter will be fine, and provides a prescription. When the husband asks the wife what the daughter has, she replies that the doctor told her the daughter ate "un gato enterito" (ate a whole cat). This is an example of when it is not enough to speak to minority elderly bilingually or even, as in this case, in Spanish. What the practitioner needs to know is that elderly minority need to be spoken to directly, sensitively, and simply. In the southwestern United States, where there are a majority of Latinos, this is certainly a challenge for eastern-trained practitioners who come to train and practice with Latinos.

Past health and medical conditions need to be explored carefully, because many Latino elderly still travel and receive care in their homeland. This is especially true of Mexican Americans who live on the United States–Mexico Border, and may also be of concern with Puerto Ricans, Dominicans, or Caribbeans from the islands. Elderly minorities many times receive medication and other therapies from nontraditional and traditional practitioners, both in the United States and abroad. Practitioners need to realize that for many poor elderly, there is no other choice. It is important for Latino elderly, for example, to be able to receive health care treatment on both sides of the United States–Mexico border. However, there are differences in prescribed medication regimens, dosages, and, at times, formulas. Many pharmaceutical companies in Latin

America and the United States have different formulas for the same medication; for example, a medication for hypertension may have the same name on both sides of the border, but in Mexico it may contain an added diuretic. In addition (although fortunately less and less common) there are folk remedies and treatments, as well as some food products, that are either made or stored in lead-tainted pottery, or are processed with some quantities of metals such as mercury. Both the Mexican and United States public health officials, as well as the Food and Drug Administration, provide a strong, vigilant deterrent and inspection system; however, there are continuous leaks in the system, which sometimes places elderly Latinos at risk. Some researchers have also expressed concern about hormone therapies given to elderly African-American women. They suggest that the dosage could cause serious ill-health effects, in part because the dosage is calculated for young white males that may cause a different response. Since we really don't have extensive data on minority drug therapy reactions and their physiological and pharmacological health effects, practitioners should keep this in mind, especially when medicating elderly minorities. Specific drug therapies and treatments may not produce the side effects expected with other elderly.

As previously mentioned, extended families are an important cultural ritual and support system, especially for Latino elderly. Not giving extended-family members active participation in the health care delivery of minority elderly can make the difference between success and compliance and failure and noncompliance, even death. This is illustrated in the case of sixty-seven-year-old diabetic who knew of his diabetes only by accident when his daughter took him for an exam. Although his physician knew of his condition, he could never get him into the office for checkups and follow-up visits. The communication and dialogue were totally conducted through the daughter. When he worsened and needed hospitalization, it was the daughter and wife who finally convinced him to see the doctor. When the time came for him to leave this world, it was only the family, especially the daughter, who could reason with him. If the practitioners and medical support team had not included the family members, this person would not have lived as long as he did.

The participation of extended family members can also cause problems. Many practitioners will use as a translator a younger family member who is too young to understand the health condition and may not relay the message correctly. For example, an elderly monolingual Mexican-American woman was found to have breast cancer, and the only one available to translate was her eleven-year-old granddaughter. The information was totally miscommunicated and misunderstood, because the granddaughter didn't understand the terminology and was embarrassed to discuss breast cancer with her grandmother. In addition, the granddaughter did not want to show disrespect to her elder, because some matters (like sex) are simply not discussed with an elder. Other language barriers may exist that impede extended-family members from interpreting and translating for the elderly minority. For the most part, when dealing with the elderly, this may not pose a serious problem. It is usually the oldest daughter that intervenes in the communication, therapy, and treatment of the elderly family member.

When it comes to institutional care for example, it is very important to have the support of the extended family, because, as stated in the example given earlier, it is the family members who on many occasions intervene and convince the elderly patient to accept hospitalization, or other institutionalization. The decision to institutionalize could be one of the most difficult decisions a minority family member makes regarding elderly family members. Many times a minority elderly remains the patriarch of the family, and may not wish to pursue a certain therapy or treatment which requires hospitalization. Here again, extended-family members play important roles in serving as mediators and liaisons between the health care system and the ill elderly person.

As an adjunct to health care services for elderly minorities, there is a severe need to recruit and retain ethnic and minority practitioners at all levels of the career spectrum: physicians, nurses, health staff technicians, laboratory staff, research staff, dentists, pharmacists, social workers, dietitians, and so forth. Over the last twenty years, the federal government has implemented different strategies that promote increasing the pool of minority providers, and yet areas like the southwest United States, South Texas, and other rural areas continue to have severe provider shortages, adding to the problem of underrepresentation in the already medically underserved areas. We are encouraged with the new support that calls for the establishment of several demonstration projects that will test and pilot comprehensive models which will try to increase the pool of minority disadvantaged students in the health professions. What is even more important is that these programs will include community-based agencies and programs. The models should also promote the development of partnerships, coalitions, and associations with other academic, private, educational, and community-based agencies and programs that have traditionally served minority populations. Many of these same services are also provided by traditional, community-based practitioners, and by other minority elderly service delivery programs. Some of these programs and providers have not only provided services for many years, but have also been providing quality health care services. These programs, and other programs of "motherland" origins that seem to work, must be evaluated and studied in terms of different models of health care. If these models are successful, we should try to replicate and adjust them for our needs, communities, and programs.

Prevention and Health Education

It is astonishing that even though the United States is the most advanced nation technologically and medically, prevention is still not part of routine health care delivery. In the United States, we stress "illness care" and not wellness. When we look at health care for elderly minority, prevention is an important concept to include. Although Latinos traditionally have considered health to be the well-being of the soul, mind, and body, modern medicine today has assimilated and to an extent destroyed this philosophy. The practitioner should recognize that to provide good comprehensive health care to the elderly, prevention and health education need to be coupled intimately with primary and urgent care, as well as long-term care services.

As stated in earlier chapters, cultural competency is extremely important in the delivery of health care services to minority elderly. This is even more important when we consider prevention, wellness, and health education. Those who provide community-based health care service know that education, wellness, and prevention are the keys to good health. However, many policy makers, health care administrators, and public officials unfortunately have not recognized this importance. They fail to realize that paying now (even if it costs more in the short term) will save lives later and is less costly in the long run. Some policy makers feel that providing health care to minority elderly is very costly because they are sicker and their health status is lower than that of white elderly in the United States; however, prevention will save dollars. A classic example is the recent Medicare inclusion of certain health care benefits such as cardiovascular and diabetes health education, nutritional counseling, colorectal exams, and influenza immunizations. As recently as two years ago some of these benefits were not covered by Medicare. In fact, many preventive measures and health educational services today are still not covered by either Medicaid or Medicare.

With the changes in health care and the advent of managed care, sweeping changes, especially in prevention and education, are taking place. Whenever these changes take place, the elderly are swept off their feet by the changes and the mandates they impose. Many of these prevention services have not been thoroughly evaluated and studied; the implementation processes in particular are usually not completely thought through. It is no wonder that elderly minorities don't understand the changes, much less follow them. The never-ending changes do keep our elderly very alert, anxious, and many times frustrated with what is supposed to be good for them. As a result of service delivery changes many elderly do not even try to seek services. Consequently, they fail to comply with their health care directives. Needless to say, this also causes extreme frustration and anguish for practitioners and other health care providers.

Imagine walking through a large medical center to a diabetes education and nutrition class to receive instructions on insulin administration, diet, and how to measure your glucose level. Next imagine that all of your instructions and directions were given to you in a foreign language and in a very formal manner. If the medical center environment didn't scare you, your education instructions will. This is how many minority elderly feel when they are first diagnosed with a condition and are then told they must go to an educational prevention program (a service that is totally fragmented). Again, the elderly minority must adjust and become familiar with another aspect of health care among total strangers who are expounding even stranger words. This is not a fictitious scenario; I have seen many minority elderly people totally lost in the halls of giant medical centers and not understanding what is being told to them in their health education class. This is, again, why minority elderly, especially monolingual Latinos, rely on extended family members. Family members can accompany them to their health appointments; they can explain and teach them what they didn't understand. They are probably the main reason for the minority elderly's compliance and adherence to health care directives.

There are many other examples of how language, staff, and the physical environment play an important role in the treatment for the elderly. For example, until recently, directions, instructions, and health education materials for services such as nutritional counseling, exercise, chronic diseases, and other wellness programs, were all written in English, targeting mainstream Anglo elderly. Furthermore, any audiovisuals, pictures, and other promotional efforts only portrayed Anglo elderly Americans, and were not produced in a culturally appropriate fashion to which minority elderly could relate. Today, traditional print and media systems continue to be used, even though for years marketing experts have advised that minorities need to be reached in a compatible fashion. Certainly, the tobacco, alcohol, and pharmaceutical industries have learned this and use a culturally sensitive model approach in order to reach the consumer power of the minority community, especially the minority elderly. It is the United States health care industry that has not performed well in providing health education and prevention services to our elderly.

The concepts of adapting to the needs of the target population, however, are there, and the health care industry needs to learn to use them. First, practitioners need to learn that the elderly minorities are very diverse, even among same ethnic groups. Each group is different, and each has special health care needs. This is one of the reasons that health education and prevention services have not made significant inroads with minority elderly. The minority elderly, in fact, have not participated in traditional health care prevention services or taken advantage of them, either because they didn't understand them, or because they were not accessible. By inaccessible we mean that they were either too costly or never part of the practitioner's comprehensive approach to therapy and treatment.

Today, prevention and health education services have become more readily available and accessible, yet they remain out of reach for many minority elderly. We know that minority elderly have higher rates of lung and colorectal cancer and diabetes. Education and prevention services continue to be provided in an inappropriate fashion that is not culturally competent, and thus continues to distance minority elderly. This is because practitioners and programs do not consider language, customs, diets, and cultural differences of the minority elderly. For example, when a diabetic diet is presented to a Mexican American elderly person, he or she is given a basic diet with the appropriate calories for a person of his or her age and stage of diabetes. This diet may consist of wheat bread, yogurt, salad with no oil, boiled white rice, mashed potatoes, and a portioned amount of meat. In many cases among Latino elderly this diet is totally foreign. A normal diet for minority elderly may be totally different from the one presented above, and thus the prescribed diet will not be followed. It is not uncommon that the minority patient may be consuming the wrong diet, but honestly feels in compliance, because he or she is not eating his or her usual diet. In the patient's mind he or she is following directions, and either eating what he or she thinks should be eaten or strictly following directions and not eating certain foods he or she thinks shouldn't be eaten. Among the Latino elderly, especially Mexican Americans, the recommended diet mentioned above might be misunderstood because these are not the standard foods for them. A normal diet for Mexican-American elderly people might be flour tortillas, pinto beans cooked in animal lard, sauteed rice in tomato sauce, fried pieces of meat, and a soda. A culturally appropriate alternative for a Mexican-American elderly person could be presented in the following manner: corn tortillas, pinto beans cooked in vegetable oil, boiled rice with tomato sauce, sauteed meat, tea, water, or a diet drink. This culturally appropriate diet would be more appropriate and relevant to a diabetic Latino elderly person and thus conducive to compliance. Such an example can be altered to suit any minority elderly. However, if the practitioner and the rest of the team of nurses, dietitians, social workers, and health education staff insist on the routine and normal health education and prevention norms and materials that are inappropriate to the cultural customs of the minority elderly, health care delivery could continue to be inadequate. There is a saying in Spanish, "Hablando se entiende la gente y siesde cara a cara es mejor" [Speaking to one another promotes understanding and when done face to face, it's even better]. The minority elderly need to be reached through their own environment, in their churches, and through their elderly programs. This approach would be more personable, contrary to those relationships and services presented through seminars or in large auditoriums. In addition, if the environment is not comparable to the elderly's known and familiar one, try to recreate that environment and make the elderly feel at home.

Other means of reaching out to the elderly community are being explored. Some of these include health screening services provided in schools, hospitals, and health fairs. Services that have been provided are mammograms, blood pressure taking, and glucose and vision screening. Some efforts have been made to include these in elderly service programs by piggy-backing them to meals-on-wheels programs, and through health information bulletins sent by Medicare or other service providers. Although the intent was good, the means was not appropriate. Minority elderly should be provided with health education and prevention services through nontraditional methodologies that are culturally appropriate and community-based. These should also be presented in a bilingual/bicultural fashion by minority staff. In addition, dedicated follow-up services should be provided to assure a continuum of care. As stated earlier, for some minorities extended families need to be part of the equation and should be incorporated into every action that affects the elderly's health. If culturally appropriate family-oriented services for minority elderly are not provided and they continue to receive fragmented services, they will feel isolated, and consequently become even more disenfranchised. A good way to provide health education to minority elderly is by carefully choosing and identifying other minority elderly to deliver the prevention message. This could be done by using religious and civic leaders who are known by the elderly. Another very important minority elderly motivator is to have elderly community leaders, known and accepted locally by the elderly, serve as mentors in their own neighborhoods. For Latino elderly, especially Mexican Americans, an accepted community-based leader who speaks about health issues is a good source of prevention and education.

For example, one could have local minority leaders take an influenza vaccination campaign on television or radio and discuss the vaccine process in Spanish, which would be understood by the elderly minority community. This was done by the San Antonio Metropolitan Health District in Texas, and the results were astonishing. The flu vaccine program was offered to elderly programs that incorporated other services for the elderly and was presented by elderly minority volunteers. Immunization services were also introduced to long-term care facilities and institutions. This required the added responsibility of training staff and providers, even for those who had traditionally cared for minority elderly. When service providers seek accepted minority norms of living and incorporate them into their goals and objectives, then services are more readily accepted, and stronger inroads in prevention and wellness can be made for the minority elderly. In summary, prevention and educational services are a required part of wellness that practitioners should include in their everyday practice with minority elderly. This outreach, however, needs to be provided in a culturally competent manner that incorporates the distinct customs of the elderly.

Long-Term Care

Besides culturally appropriate and family oriented programs, long-term care planning should also include issues of financial resources. As mentioned earlier, minority elderly in large part live in extreme poverty. Without appropriate resources, many minority elderly patients and their practitioners are having to face an additional problem added to the already very difficult decision of long-term care, home health care, nursing homes, and rehabilitation services. This is another health care issue that our current delivery system paradigm does not take into account and needs to include in the equation for health care services. Tertiary care for many minority elderly is an especially difficult and sensitive decision, one that may require a special support system within health care delivery. Imagine being a productive, contributing person, and then one day you are told that you must go to an institution for the rest of your life. There are different factors in this decision-making process that affect both the elderly person and the family: (1) guilt in sending away the elderly loved one, (2) consequences of the disease that affects the elderly person, (3) the care facility itself. For many Latino families this is a decision that is dreaded, but one which is being confronted on an increasingly frequent basis. It is traditional that the youngest daughter care for the elderly parents, especially the mother, until her death. Sending an elderly Latino person away is considered a sin.

Consider, for example, a case involving a Mexican-American family with nine grown children, all with families of their own. The eighty-nine-year-old matriarch, who was still active and living alone, became very ill with diabetes, emphysema, hypertension, and arthritis. All of a sudden the family was confronted with the fact that their mother could not care for herself. Although still very coherent, agile, and independent, she had three cerebral vascular accidents/strokes that left her with more and more sequelae each time. The family decided that she would move in with one of the daughters, disregarding any thought of additional personal or financial responsibilities. There all of her needs were cared for. All of the other daughters and sons came to see her as frequently as they could. Her other children, and her grandchildren as well, took turns taking her to the doctor and assisting with her everyday chores. Even though she lived with the daughter, she still maintained her home and cared for her animals, which included two dogs, a parrot, two chickens, and fish. Even when she worsened, discussion of a long-term care facility never arose. Although the individual conditions may differ, this scenario typifies the Latino (minority) experience in which the elderly are cherished and taken care of by family members.

In many cases, being taken care of by one's own family contributes to the well-being and health of the elderly person. Practitioners and other health care providers may disagree with this approach, but the custom still exists. While this has proved to be a sensitive topic, when a decision on treatment and therapy is needed that may require long-term care, most minority elderly will comply. It does, however, pose very important concerns to the families that the medical community and practitioners should recognize. Home health care, hospice, intermediate and assisted care, as well as other chronic health care services, need to be evaluated as they relate to minority elderly.

Although some minority groups may not look favorably at long-term facilities as a health care alternative, more and more elderly are faced with this decision. Practitioners, minority elderly, and their families must deal with this situation together. By ensuring that these facilities provide an environment that is acceptable, assessable, and culturally compatible the facilities might prove beneficial and more relevant to minority elderly and their families. For example, community minority groups and families may better support long-term care facilities and nursing homes that provide services that are more family and community oriented, that are culturally appropriate, and where the minority elderly are not excluded from society. There are a number of community groups and programs that already provide culturally based, relevant services for the elderly. It behooves new programs to go into partnership with them, since these are already accepted by the community and minority elderly. When the elderly see people they already know in these institutions, adjustment becomes a little easier, and life is happier. To access these facilities and services, minority elderly and their families must understand them. Owners, administrators, and health care providers need to understand that cultural competency education and training should be provided for staff. If these services are provided early enough, the elderly might access them before they become rehabilitative services.

By combining community services, family, and other prevention programs, rehabilitative needs may not be needed, or at least deferred. After all, do we not wish to make living conditions better for all of us? Other alternative services, such as home health care and assistance living, need to be presented to minority families of the elderly as a support system that will help during those times that require health care outside of hospital setting. It is these institutions and programs that need to establish a dialogue between community-based programs and families to assure that elderly minorities are cared for in a culturally competent fashion. By doing this, the elderly and their families may better accept these types of services. There are a few nursing and home health care programs that understand minorities, are able to provide services in a culturally appropriate manner, and incorporate the family members who assist with the care. Examples of some of these programs are "Casa Central" in Chicago and the "El Paso Elderly Services" in El Paso, Texas. Other models and programs that incorporate different services for the elderly including health, home health care, nutrition, and prevention services, as well as other social support services, need to be studied for their success and/or failures, and should be replicated in other parts of the country.

Death, dying, and anguish also play an important role for the elderly and their families. Although there are frequent discussions on advanced directives for everyone, the challenge for minority elderly is a special approach. When we discuss advanced directives with minority elderly, we need to ensure that they understand what is being asked of them and that they recognize what their responsibility is in this process. This is difficult for Latino elderly because of both religious and cultural beliefs; they feel that it is the will of God (or destiny) that determines such matters, and we do not have the right to intervene. Thus, family and elderly minorities may not readily accept advance directives as do other elderly. Dr. David Espino suggests that these ethical decisions need to be discussed not only by the practitioner and the patient, but with all members of the family, as well as community support groups. As we grow older, these other challenges pose very important questions as to how we manage health care services for the elderly.

As we move into other forms of health care delivery systems, such as managed care, the above mentioned concerns must be taken into account. Although for some, managed care has not been an appropriate means of health care delivery, it is an option that is here to stay. Therefore, when the issue of health care for the elderly is discussed, assurances need to be made that managed care provides comprehensive, culturally based services that also incorporate community-based prevention and education programs targeting the specific needs of minority elderly. Managed care must also ensure that the quality of care is maintained when we address health care issues of the elderly. Lastly, elderly minority need to be included in all the decision-making boards, advisory groups, and review panels within the managed care system. Dr. Marta Sotomayor urges us to take our time evaluating managed care and how it addresses the health care delivery issues for minority elderly. Becoming involved in the system is part of the answer.

Other Health Care Concerns

There are a number of other health care issues that also affect minority elderly in a special way. Some of these health concerns are nutrition, substance abuse, elderly abuse and neglect, injury and trauma, homelessness, rural health, and mental health. As stated previously, poverty among minority elderly is prominent, and certainly contributes to additional adverse health conditions. When we speak of elderly abuse, minorities tend not to be as abusive as other persons, especially as it relates to Latino elderly women. Rather, they are more caring and supportive. There may be concern about self-deterioration and self-abuse because minority elderly also have a lot of pride and tend to care for themselves. This sometimes leads to neglect because elderly who live by themselves don't reach out for help, and elderly minorities tend to live in less than adequate housing, which can lead to adverse health conditions. Homelessness also contributes to this problem, causing a number of health conditions to worsen, such as diabetes, cardiovascular disease problems, and mental illness.

Trauma and injury are another concern. However, there has been insufficient research and documentation to correlate any special health conditions of the minority elderly of which practitioners should be made aware. Injuries from past or present occupational hazards need to be considered, for example, among people who have spent years as farmworkers/migrants. Interested researchers may wonder if there is any correlation between that occupation and hand and other musculoskeletal conditions that frequently cause trauma and injury in Latino elderly. Another occupation-related hazard is past exposure to chemicals and pesticides which affect the nervous system and cause chronic allergies and poor respiratory conditions.

Mental health, already briefly mentioned, remains a special challenge for practitioners. Because many minority elderly people are simply considered "senile," or "just getting old," by their family members, certain conditions may not be uncovered until an advanced stage of illness. Family members may continuously dismiss these conditions and may at times prolong the clinical diagnosis of a mental/psychiatric condition that could deteriorate and cause additional problems. Practitioners should be aware of this, especially when treating Latinos. This awareness may help in prevention and outreach programs that target mental health services for minority elderly. As with other health care concerns, mental health practitioners must also incorporate cultural customs and language issues. In addition, the physical conditions of the individual and his or her cultural beliefs need to be understood. Elderly minorities are much more likely to believe that the body, soul, and mind are totally connected, so that if one's mental health is sound, then his or her physical self is also well.

Among minority elderly, there is also more tolerance of mental health conditions. It is very common, for example, to say that he is "el loco de la familia" (he is the crazy one of the family). Most of the time these persons are not ostracized, but on the contrary, are treated as an integral part of the family. Other physical conditions and disabilities are also treated with more tolerance as well. Minority practicing psychiatrists and mental health practitioners, who have provided extensive clinical therapy and mental health counseling, frequently express their concerns about the mental health of the minority elderly. There are mental health conditions that may affect minority elderly in a different fashion than that manifested by other groups. For example, the clinical manifestations, causes, and therapy of dementia and Alzheimer's disease as it relates to Latino elderly could be different; there are simply not enough research, data, and studies on minority elderly. Other practitioners have also expressed their concerns about "social mental health" problems that also contribute to the well-being and stability of the elderly. For example, the current mode of elderly people taking care of even older family members, and what that means to their mental and general health, is a concern still under observation and study. In mental health, as in Health Care Delivery, other models of care from the homelands of the minority elderly need to be evaluated for the kinds of services provided and the methods of implementation.

Recommendations for Today and Tomorrow

The health care concerns of the minority elderly need immediate attention. These can most readily be addressed by assisting the practitioner with the understanding that they need to provide comprehensive, culturally competent services. There are additional factors regarding minority elderly health care that need discussion. It was mentioned earlier that when introducing any health education and prevention program, elderly minority needs to be included, and that the positive aspect of aging also needs promotion, not just the negative health conditions. Although there is not enough minority-specific research on the health and medical conditions of the elderly, there are some limited studies which provide us with very interesting facts which show that at least some Mexican-American elderly have better health conditions than Anglo elderly. For example, in 1993 the following observations were reported by Dr. David Hays Bautista:

TABLE 6.1

1993 Morbidity and Life Expectancy for Latino Elderly in Comparison to Anglos ≥ 65 yrs of age per 100,000

	Anglos	Latinos
Heart disease	4,000	1,089
Life Expectancy (in LA County)	16.8 yrs	19.2 yrs

TABLE 6.2

Mortality Rates for Anglos in Comparison to Latino Elderly ≥ 65 yrs of age per 100,000

	Anglos	Latinos
Cancer	1100	631
Strokes	409	235

Similar lower rates were found for chronic obstructive pulmonary disease (COPD), pneumonia/influenza, and suicide. On the other hand, the Latino elderly had higher rates of diabetes and cirrhosis. Utilizing the Medicare and Medicaid billing process, the number of bed stays was tracked and reported to be less for Latino elderly than for Anglo elderly, by almost 50 percent. Whether this means that Latino elderly are less prone to severe disease and subsequent hospitalization, or that their state of poverty prohibits them from entering the hospital, is simply not known.

Recommendations for Interventions, Actions, and Solutions

In 1993, the surgeon general's report on Hispanic health conditions was written after numerous regional community-based meetings were held throughout the United States. Some very good information, recommendations, and actions were adopted, but have not yet been put into action. Part of the reason is the reversal of universal health care. Although elderly health care issues were not specifically addressed, many of the strategies discussed comprehensive health care services for all Latinos, which included services for the young, elderly, rural, and urban Latino populations. (For this discussion, comprehensive health care takes into account all of the support services, transportation, location, translation, and traditional and nontraditional providers at all levels, including mental health and adjunct social services.) Based on those strategies and recommendations, MASLPI decided to conduct a follow-up conference that would build on the report, focusing on Latino "ancianos." The conference was held in Denver, Colorado, March 7 to 9 1996. There were excellent input and dialogue that provided the following preliminary draft summary of twelve recommendations. MASLPI suggested that these recommendations be reviewed, evaluated, and analyzed for implementation and application consideration. The review process, however, should be conducted in combination with the elderly, academicians, clinicians, policy makers, researchers, and health care administrators. The overriding theme throughout the conference focused on the use of "respeto" (respect); the application of culturally appropriate services; communication and understanding; and the inclusion of the elderly. These are very basic, common, human dignity issues that would probably benefit society to include in everyday living. If we pay attention to these recommendations and goals, the end result could be good health care and "bienestar" (well-being) for the minority elderly.

1. Provide comprehensive health care services that are culturally based and family and community oriented and which also include the active participation of the elderly in the decision-making process of their health care delivery. (This was overwhelmingly expressed in all of the strategies.)

2. Include in services a review of current community-based services and programs that are presently providing good health care. These should be kept intact, and we should enhance them, and replicate them as well. If needed, we should also develop new models of health care services in primary care, urgent care, long-term care, health education, and prevention that are culturally appropriate for the minority elderly.

3. Enhance collaboration and build new partnerships with public and private entities, corporate and business partners, and most important, with historical (traditional and nontraditional) and community-based providers.

4. Consider as partners in providing health care services to the minority elderly resources such as community health care centers,

migrant health care centers, alternative health care programs, and other community-based organizations and programs, as well as social and human service programs.

5. Conduct massive and comprehensive community-based health education, prevention, and promotion services, and ensure these are culturally competent, with appropriate educational instruction, with communication and language that is bilingual and bicultural, and that the materials used for education and training are visual, three-dimensional, and culturally appropriate for both patients and providers at all levels. Only in this fashion can we ensure that minority elderly and their families will understand, and thereby become medically compliant.

6. Ensure that all services and physical plants are accessible, available, and user friendly with good transportation, helpful personnel, a bright and cheerful atmosphere, special accommodations for the disabled, bilingual and bicultural staff and not just translators; that they are open when it is convenient for the elderly, and that they provide services in places where the elderly congregate (malls, shopping centers, churches, schools).

7. Enhance efforts to recruit, retain, and further train minority and nonminority health care providers in health care delivery methodologies with culturally based curricula and training that must be included as part of the instruction in medical (and other health professional) schools, including allied health programs.

8. Develop policies on health care delivery services with the ideas of "grassroots" participation that includes local, regional, state, and national participation.

9. Promote active participation in the electoral process among the elderly, including registering the elderly to vote at every opportunity.

10. Promote, support, and conduct applied research that is greatly needed to define the health care needs and problems of the minority elderly, as well as verify, correlate, and analyze current research to ensure that it is appropriate, competent, reflective, and relevant for minorities.

11. Actively review and participate in the decisions of alternative health care systems such as managed care, private insurance,

Medicare, and Medicaid, and ensure that they meet the needs of the minority elderly and provide quality care, through a system of checks and balances.

12. Promote positive health care data, such as low incidences of hypertension among Mexican Americans, as a healthy well-being effect that is prosperous and economically profitable. Provide and promote health education data that alert the minority elderly to relevant health care problems such as diabetes, heart disease, lung cancer, mental health, and long-term care.

Finally, the public needs to be reminded that until current U.S. attitudes on the elderly change, culturally appropriate health care services for the minority elderly, and for the elderly in general, will not be achieved. In the absence of change of attitude, health care for the minority elderly will continue to suffer.

References

American Association of Retired Persons (AARP). (1990). *Aging and old age in diverse populations.* Research papers presented at the Minority Affairs Initiative Empowerment Conference, San Antonio, TX.

American Association of Retired Persons (AARP). (1995, March). *Grandparents as caregivers: Options for improving access to federal public benefit programs.* Public Policy Institute, no. 9503.

American Association of Retired Persons (AARP). (1990). *Hispanic elders discuss health interests and needs.* A qualitative study conducted in New York City and Los Angeles, CA.

Closing the gap. (1996, June). *Health and older minorities.* Washington, DC: Office of Minority Health (OMH), Public Health Service (PHS), & U.S. Department of Health and Human Services (DHHS).

Espino, D.V. (1989). *Health policy and the elderly Hispanic.* San Antonio, TX.

Espino, D.V. (1995, May 17). Physician race and care of minority and medically indigent patients. *JAMA, 273*(19).

Espino, D.V. (1996, January 17). Personal interview. *UTHSC-SA.*

Gil, F.T. (1991). *Aging in Hispanic America.* Washington, DC: Office on Aging, National Council of La Raza (NCLR).

Gil, F.T. (1991). *Becoming involved in the aging network: A planning and resource guide for Hispanic community-based organizations.* Washington, DC: Policy Analysis Center and Office of Institutional Development, NCLR.

Hispanic-American elders. (1995, February). In *Clinics in Geriatrics Medicine, 11*(1). New Rochelle Hospital Medical Center, New Rochelle, NY; and New York Medical College, Valhalla, NY.

Sotomayor, M. (1988). *Hispanic elderly: A cultural signature.* Edinburg, TX: Pan American University Press.

Sotomayor, M., & Garcia, A. (1993). *Elderly Latinos: Issues and solutions for the 21st century.* Washington, DC: NHCoA.

Surgeon Generals' National Hispanic/Latino Health Initiative. (1993, June). *Recommendations to the Surgeon General to improve Hispanic/Latino health.* Washington, DC: Department of Health and Human Services.

Sotomayor, M. (1994). *In triple jeopardy—Aged, Hispanic, women: Insights and experiences.* Washington, DC: NHCoA.

United States Office on Aging. (1995). *White House conference on aging resolutions and recommendations.* Washington, DC: Author.

CHAPTER 7

Cultural Competency and Practitioner Issues

Rumblings about the kind of health care reform that will result in a full-fledged, efficient national health care system have existed for decades. The institution of Medicare and Medicaid in 1965 was one such attempt that did not completely suffice and whose cost now compounds the problem. However, the drive toward national health care still exists and has spawned new thinking and planning regarding just how American society will provide health care for its members (Becker, 1995).

Recently, the White House put forth a major effort toward the creation of a single-payer national health system which was rejected by Congress as politically unpalatable. Hindsight shows that the plan's approach was flawed, which considerably complicated matters.

The demise of President Clinton's health care plan produced momentum for the creation of at least fifty potentially different plans, as the states joined the fray. Hope exists that if one of these plans is greatly successful, it may be adopted nationwide. One thread runs through all state-sponsored plans (as with President Clinton's plan): to a higher or lesser degree they rely on *managed care* to control costs.

American health care is among the very best in the world. In the last few decades, however, its cost has been soaring out of control. The care citizens receive bears little relation to its cost, which has outpaced that of other goods and services. A two-tiered system came to exist that screens out those unable to pay. Although the United States spends more per capita on health care than any other industrialized nation, many millions of people do not have access to decent medical and dental care, primarily for lack of insurance. The cost of health care is too high, and access is denied to those—the poor, children, minorities, and even lower-middle-class people—who potentially need it most. Meanwhile, the economic principle of scarce resources, under which society operates, suggests that resources are finite. Since any type of expenditure contributes to the exhaustion of finite resources—in this case, money—once health care expenditures go up, there is less money left over for the purchase of other desirable goods and services. As health care costs ran out of control (the estimate is that by the year 2000 they will reach $1.6 trillion, or 16.6 percent of the Gross Domestic Product [Sonnenfeld, Waldo, Lemieux, & McKusick, 1991]), certain societal sectors started to react strongly to the limitations on the latitude and diversity of their expenditures imposed by the state of health care finances. Employers, responsible for paying for the health insurance of their employees, find the practice too costly, as it exceeds after-tax profits (Levit, Letsch, & Cowan, 1991), and they are seeking to limit growth of their insurance premiums and benefits cost (Bixler, Gartner, & Lindeman, 1994). Average Americans fear the bankrupting potential of the cost of catastrophic illness. Medicaid and Medicare are approaching insolvency. Of necessity, cost containment has been proposed and implemented. Nevertheless, before focusing attention on cost containment techniques and their consequences, we intend briefly to review, for the sake of providing background information, key aspects of the traditional American health care system.

Origins of Spiraling Health Care Costs

Traditionally understood economic factors are invoked as a partial explanation for the high cost of medical care. General inflation, introductions of new services and new technologies to keep up with the fast pace of advances in the medical field, increasing income levels, and demographic and social changes in the population, are some of them. There are, however, other, murkier, explanations (Lewis-Hall, Sierles, & Conway, 1993). For example,

1. It is often suggested that the health care market does not perform like other economic markets, but rather follows its own unique, idiosyncratic ways.

2. Health care workers are said to induce demand for the services they provide.

3. The increasingly malpractice-laden environment has had a serious inflationary effect on the cost of health care.

4. Complex administrative practices have driven up costs.

Whatever the explanation, the fact remains that the growth rate of health care expenditures in 1991 was four times that of the national economy (Letsch, 1993). Medicaid's $199 billion cost in 1992—double the figure for 1988—equalled Medicare cost (Holahan, Rowland, Feder, & Heslan, 1993).

Structure of the Health Care System in the United States

Five distinct but interdependent components comprise the structure of the health care system in the United States: resources, organization, management, financing, and provision of services. (In this discussion, we rely especially on the structure provided by Lewis-Hall, Sierles, & Conway, 1993.)

Labor, facilities, commodities, knowledge, and information are all aspects of health care resources. Labor produces and uses all features and functions of the health care system. More than 8 million people work within this system: 54 percent work in hospitals, 16 percent in nursing homes, 11 percent in physicians' offices, 6 percent in dentists' offices, 0.5 percent in chiropractors' offices, 12 percent in other sites (Jonas, 1990; U.S. Department of Labor, 1988). (All professions related to or concerned with the provision and delivery of health care at the biological, psychological, social, or biopsychosocial level, figure as resources.)

Organization is usually understood together with financing. Management and provision of services are also intertwined with the former two. In this section we will briefly explore all of them together. It is also important to note that the system's financing and organizational complexities preclude cohesive monolithic movement in any direction. This makes health care reform a very difficult proposition, so the tendency is for the status quo to be maintained. To that end, unwittingly though it may be—many interests, both private and governmental, influence health care decision making. Private professional associations and organizations and governmental concerns at the local, state, and federal levels all influence, administer, and/or finance services.

Within the federal scope is the Department of Health and Human Services whose division, the Health Care Financing Administration, runs Medicare and Medicaid. Medicare, the federal program enacted in 1965, supplies medical insurance for retired persons sixty-five or older, disabled persons who receive Social Security benefits, and persons of all ages with chronic renal disease who require dialysis. The program has two subdivisions. Part A covers hospital and long-term care, but not nursing home care. Part B covers physicians' services, certain medications, and equipment—for example, wheel chairs—purchases and rentals. Eligible persons do rely on this coverage for second opinions and some ambulance services.

Nearly 34 million persons were enrolled in Medicare in 1989. The Health Care Financing Administration estimates that by the year 2050, some 69 million people age sixty-five and older will be eligible for this form of medical insurance, as will 15 million people age eighty-five and older.

Medicaid is the other piece of federal health care legislation, passed in 1965. It is intended to finance health care for the poor. Poverty is defined according to a certain formula that takes into account family income and number of dependent children, low income single-parent households with dependent children, and low income aged and disabled. Both the federal and state governments finance Medicaid benefits, according to formulas that vary greatly. States differ in their eligibility criteria for recipients, which leaves many who cannot afford private insurance without coverage (Davis & Rowland, 1983).

Compounding the alphabet soup—made up of the initials of agencies—the Department of Health and Human Services administers the Public Health Service which, in turn, controls the Centers for Disease Control, the Food and Drug Administration, the National Institutes of Health, the Indian Health Services, and the Alcohol, Drug Abuse, and Mental Health Administration. Other cabinet-level offices are also involved in the business of health care delivery, providing mine workers with health benefits; farm workers with health care along with control of disease in their livestock; health care for active duty military personnel and their families; health care for disabled veterans; and health care in the prisons, to name several areas (Lewis-Hall, Sierles, & Conway, 1993).

State and local government also play a role through established public health programs. Four areas of endeavor result from the effort: personal health, environmental health, health resources, and laboratory services. State and local health care agencies also provide administration and services, the scope of which varies from state to state. As a fairly general trend, a separate agency controls state expenditures for mental health services. Mental health services are not adequately funded and provided at the community level. Therefore, the vast number of deinstitutionalized patients during the 1960s and thereafter do not receive appropriately comprehensive community mental health services. Many of them have joined the ranks of the homeless.

Most of the close to 3,000 local public health departments (Health Insurance Association of America, 1991; 1989 data), especially those in urban communities, are facing increasingly dire financial circumstances. Therefore, they find it increasingly harder to keep up with the ever greater and ever costlier health care demands of the urban poor.

In the private sector, a staggering number of professional associations and organizations influence the health care system through lobbying and other efforts. For example, the American Medical Association, in addition to lobbying for physicians, runs the Joint Commission on Accreditation of Health Care Organizations and oversees local medical societies.

The government, since 1979, has been funding close to two fifths of the national expenditures on health care through: Medicare and Medicaid; programs for veterans and the military and their families; programs for civilian federal employees; and programs for Native Americans. In 1989, the total cost of federally funded health care represented more than 42 percent of the total national expenditures for health care (Lazenby & Letsch, 1990). The government also functions as a third-party payer, reimbursing a portion of personal, out-of-pocket cost. The remainder is funded through private insurance, out-of-pocket expenses, and, to a much lesser degree, other varied sources, such as, for instance, contributions from philanthropic organizations. The overall health care expenditure in the United States in 1993 was more than 14 percent of the Gross Domestic Product, nearly one out of every seven dollars being spent on health care (Letsch, 1993).

Impact of Health Care Reform on Social and Human Services

Not only this worrisome economic picture, but public opinion and political concerns provide the impetus to overcome inertia. The United

States health care system is, therefore, rapidly changing. As it does, it departs somewhat from the general structure delineated above. This departure is partial and incremental, as a wholesale revamping of the system was rejected by politicians and, to a large extent, by the public. Although there is no single national health care program as such, there have been more focused initiatives, both at the federal and state levels. In all such efforts, managed care features prominently.

But what is managed care? It is a set of techniques with the purpose of insuring that consumers receive care that payers support. Additionally, effort is made so that excessive or unnecessary care is not delivered and if delivered, not reimbursed. Managed care was instituted as a means of controlling the tendency that the system of fee-for-service has of encouraging the delivery of more services and more expensive services. Techniques dedicated to such controls, like utilization review, have been used for over a decade. As a more recent phenomenon, certain organizational structures have formed to deliver treatment in a climate in which clinical management and financial incentives are put in place to encourage preventive care and control cost increases (Bixler, Gartner, & Lindeman, 1994). Given that these organizations contract with payers to deliver a certain volume of services, the payer may be a private corporation, an employer, or the government through Medicaid and Medicare. To the group of managed care organizations belong many Health Maintenance Organizations (HMOs), Preferred Provider Organizations (PPOs), and behavioral health managed care organizations (MCOs). In a 1994 survey, Oss showed that 45.9 percent of insured Americans, or 102 million people, were enrolled in some type of MCO (which provide both mental health and alcohol and substance related services).

Managed care has become a primary cost containment and organizational method in health care in America today. For example, since 1993 most Fortune 500 companies and over half of HMOs have been operating under managed care to purchase substance abuse treatment. Many states have "carve-out" (not under managed care; financing carved out from Medicaid pools) substance abuse and mental health services for Medicaid recipients (U.S. Department of Health and Human Services, 1994). Changes in the way services are provided, financed, and structured, as well as their coordination with all services provided within primary care, mental health care, and other aspects of the health care delivery system, are now taking place. Speaking about substance abuse treatment programmatic trends, Becker (1995) describes developments that are similar to those taking place elsewhere within the social and human services. There is movement toward bringing other aspects of health care to the level of full partnership with primary care. In fact, the Senate has recently voted to require that insurance coverage for mental illness be provided at the same level it is provided for "physical illness" (*The New York Times*, 5/1/1995). This was accomplished despite severe objections of employers, insurers, and health maintenance organizations which feared that implementing such congressional mandates would lead to loss of financial viability for these institutions. (They also saw this as a precedent for Congress to dictate other health benefits.) This notion was challenged—and the Senate apparently paid heed—by companies that formed specifically to provide mental health services at predictable costs. This issue of parity for mental health services is very important. Currently, managed care companies provide mental health services, often coupled with alcohol and substance abuse services, for any given group of employees, through a contract with the employer in which a set monthly fee is charged per employee for all services that might be needed. Outcome studies support the idea that mental health services diminish the utilization of other medical services in the managed care environment. Therefore, parity is desirable. There is a debate currently going on regarding the wisdom of establishing this parity. Arguments appear on both sides of the issue, but it seems wise to implement the Senate's decision.

Becker goes on to say that state alcohol and drug abuse agencies, providers, and educators are seriously working together to make the case for alcohol and drug abuse treatment with state and federal policy makers. Also, nearly all proposals by states, and the Federal plan, include behavioral health benefits.

Still, there are difficulties and obstacles imposed by the proposed cure for the American Health Care System that must be addressed and overcome.

First, it is necessary that we recognize that at this stage of health care reform—and in the foreseeable future—the duality of a private and some public system remains. The latter handles the poor, who have little political clout, but unfortunately has a depth of entrenched problems not encountered in the former (Becker, 1995).

Second, managed care is designed to cover acute care, which accounts for only one of the possible realities: some people have chronic illnesses which require constant, long-term management. This is an important issue when one considers treatment for behavioral disorders in foster care, or needed long-term substance abuse treatments elsewhere. Experience and research suggests that many of these patients run out of allowed treatment visits before recovery takes place.

Third, the need for introduction, maintenance, and availability of comprehensive services is undisputable, especially for poor and minority urban populations that have been chronically underserved. At times, comprehensiveness seems to be at odds with cost effectiveness. For example, the chronically underserved may need many services that are not covered or understood as needed by managed care organizations. These needs include, for instance, long-term retraining for foster-care children who have developmental delays due to social deprivation; AIDS and sexually transmitted disease prevention efforts for substance abusers and poor urban teenagers, psychosocial educational support for patients and families, and other "wraparound" services. Some sort of arrangement that includes such imperatives will need to be made (Becker, 1995).

Fourth, it is necessary that services provided under managed care transcend arbitrary caps which are often imposed on the length of treatment. Therapists and advocates for those who are subjected to such caps must determine the level at which such caps are antithetical to sound treatment. Also, it will be necessary to lower copayments that are too steep for the unemployed and the working poor to pay. It has been shown that these imposed limits are unnecessary for effective cost control. An interesting trend that has been gaining increasing acceptance is the notion that effective treatment of mental illness provides corporations with a net gain, beyond the cost of treatment, as healthier employees increase their productivity and reliability (Becker, 1995).

Fifth, when needed, longer term care than that provided by acute care services must be delivered and reimbursed. Since this is a public health imperative, Becker (1995) suggests that reinsurance pools and cost-sharing initiatives will be needed for those to whom chronic care and support are essential.

Sixth, it is imperative that policy makers understand the importance of maintaining a measure of cultural sensitivity and cultural competence in the delivery of health services. In the rush motivated by the instinct for survival amid the competitive enrollment frenzy pursued by managed care companies, New York City neighborhood agencies that provide psychosocial and mental health care are being decimated. They are becoming endangered species, despite providing invaluable culturally competent delivery of services. Instead, managed care organizations would lure people out of their familiar neighborhoods to clinics where they receive impersonal care. Many do not return. Though this may seem ideal in terms of cost savings, this urban population is already seriously underserved. Therefore, its members may potentially become sicker rather than healthier, which defeats the purpose of well-planned care. Managed care organizations must attempt to aid these neighborhood clinics toward viability in the present climate. This makes sense from clinical, cultural, and not least, economic viewpoints.

Seventh, payment systems for child welfare ought to change from current practice to be geographically based on coverage. Also, they should reimburse for the full range of services that families need to stay together, avoid foster care, or achieve successful reunification, shortening the time they need to utilize public services (Siberio, 1995)

Last, but equally important, in a time of crisis all concerned need to rise to the occasion. The more efficient way of doing this is by uniting effort and purpose. After all, as life soon teaches people, there is strength in numbers. A crisis is a trying time which can lead to defeat and destruction or, alternatively, to growth beyond that previously achieved. So, we practitioners must do what we can to prevent the danger of limiting and compromising the care of those who both need it the most and have the least influence on the forces that could help them secure it.

References

Becker, S.L. (1995, Spring). *Managed care: Meeting the challenge to substance abuse treatment.* Communique (special issue). Washington, DC: Substance Abuse and Mental Health Services Administration, Public Health Services, United States Department of Health and Human Services.

Bixler, J.B., Gartner, C., & Lindeman, B. (1994). *Managed health care's organizational readiness guides and checklist* (special report). Washington, DC: Substance Abuse and Mental Health Services Administration, Public Health Service, United States Department of Health and Human Services.

Davis, K., & Rowland, G. (1983). Uninsured and under served: Inequities in health care in the United States. *Milbank Men Fund Quarterly 61,* 149–176.

Health Insurance Association of America. (1991). *Source books of health insurance data.* Washington, DC: Author.

Holahan, J., Rowland, D., Feder, J., & Heslan, D. (1993). Explaining the recent growth in Medicaid spending. *Health Affairs, 12*(3).

Jonas, S. (1990). Population data for health and health care. In A. Kovner (Ed.), *Health care delivery in the United States.* (4th ed.). New York: Springer.

Lazenby, H.C., & Letsch, S.W. (1990). National health expenditures, 1989. *Health Care Finance Review, 12*(2), 1–26.

Letsch, S.W. (1993). National health care spending in 1991. *Health Affairs, 1*(1).

Levit, K.R., Letsch, S.W., & Cowan, C.A. (1991). National health care spending, 1989. *Health Affairs, 10*(1), 117–130.

Oss, M.E. (1993). Industry statistics: Managed behavioral health programs widespread among insured Americans. *Open Minds: The Behavioral Health Industry Analyst, 8*(3).

Pear, R. (1996, May 1). Wide mental care insurance is now feasible, experts say. *The New York Times* (Vol. CXLV, No. 50), p. 415.

Siberio, M. (1995, November). *Considerations for implementing managed care in the New York City child's welfare system.* A working draft report of the New York City Task Force on Managed Care in Child Welfare.

Sonnenfeld, S.T., Waldo, D.R., Lemieux, J.A., & McKusick, D.R. (1991). Projections of national health expenditures through the year 2000. *Health Care Finance Review, 13*(1), 1–27.

United States Department of Health and Human Services, Health Care Financing Administration. (1990). *Program statistics: Medicare and Medicaid data book.* Baltimore, MD: Author.

United States Department of Labor. (1988, April). *Occupational outlook handbook.* Washington, DC: Bureau of Labor Statistics.

CHAPTER 8

Cultural Competency and Leadership Issues

The twenty-first century will provide us with many opportunities for forging a new horizon, and a new vision which will encompass a diverse society and rapidly changing technology. The leaders of tomorrow must provide the leadership and understanding to lead and work within a changing cultural environment. It will be those culturally sensitive human and professional leaders who will provide leadership for the opportunities in tomorrow's world.

As other chapters in this book have discussed, the world has become smaller in our necessity to communicate with each other and work cooperatively. Our vision must be inclusive and multicultural in working with clients and patients. The leadership skills may have to be restructured in order to accommodate new groups who need our care and support. A major change or transformation must occur to gain acceptance by multicultural groups.

The literature is filled with concepts, theories, and models to be used to reach and lead people. However, we must utilize all of them within a conceptual cultural framework. As the world continues to shrink, and we are able to cross oceans and continents within hours, it behooves us to adapt to the cultures that are participating with us in this global economy. CEOs, managers, supervisors, and other human service leaders must begin to provide the leadership if we are to improve the delivery and utilization of human services.

The need for multicultural managers in the human services fields is great. Every day these individuals encounter people of various minority and ethnic groups at the work place. Whether it is as employees or as patients, these leaders must deal with multicultural individuals. When cultural differences are not effectively dealt with, the results are cultural destructiveness and cultural incapacity (Cross, Bazron, Dennis, & Isaacs, 1989). Cultural destructiveness and incapacity are caused by forming policies, management techniques, and treatment modules, whether intentional or unintentional, that do not acknowledge differences between individuals of various ethnicities. When programs are designed to accommodate the dominant culture and are not flexible enough to also accommodate minority individuals, then the attitudes and policies and practices of such an agency are very destructive to minority groups. These agencies lack the capacity to help minority clients. Such agencies are most likely to discriminate and to have very negative views of individuals who are of different ethnic or cultural backgrounds. Furthermore, when leaders are not equipped to work with multicultural individuals, then mistrust and frustration will follow.

How Individuals Can Become Multicultural as Leaders and Practitioners

When working with multicultural individuals, whether at a patient-practitioner level or at a manager-employee level, efforts should be taken to ensure that these individuals are treated with the respect and care they deserve. The main essential ingredient for such respect is for the practitioner to adjust his own attitude.

"Attitudes are psychological states that predispose us to behave in certain ways" (Harris & Moran, 1991, p. 40). One such common attitude which must be adjusted is ethnocentrism (Harris & Moran, 1991, p. 40). When working in a field in which multiculturalism is so great, it is of utmost importance that human service professionals refrain from constantly comparing their own way of life to those of individuals from different cultures. When they do so, they are establishing stereotypes about other cultures and preventing effective interaction. Researchers have used the term "culturally encapsulated" to refer to therapists who stereotype ethnic minority groups in such a manner, rather than taking into account their individual differences (Mokuaa & Matucka, 1992). By culturally encapsulating individuals, practitioners tend to categorize any differences they view between their ethnically diverse employees and patients as a form of resistance. Instead, they should "seek to understand other people in the context of their unique . . . cultural backgrounds" (Harris & Moran, 1991, p. 40).

Besides changing their attitudes there are some other common techniques which practitioners can utilize to become both good therapists and good managers.

Acceptance

Practitioners should acknowledge the existence of cultural differences between them and their employees/patients. They should accept "that each culture finds some behaviors, interactions, or values more important or desirable than others." By understanding this concept, they will be able to interact more effectively with members of different cultures (Cross, Bazron, Dennis, & Isaacs, 1989). Only by accepting the uniqueness of different cultures can one really effectively communicate with individuals of various ethnic and cultural backgrounds. Not only should they learn to accept diversity, they should also value it. "To value diversity is to see and respect its worth" (Cross, Bazron, Dennis, & Isaacs, 1989).

Communication

Communication is the next vital step to ensure that patients and workers are dealt with effectively. By carefully thinking about what he or she is saying before he or she says it, the practitioner will be able to communicate effectively with individuals who are ethnically and/or culturally unique.

The following are some pointers which should allow for effective communication.

1. Practitioners must try to use words that are more common English words, such as using the word "effective" rather than "efficacious" (Harris & Moran, 1991, p. 40). Since most immigrants learn English from daily interactions, they are more likely to know such common words.
2. Use words that have only one meaning. For example, verbs such as "get" have many meanings. Phrases such as "I'll get a car" can

have many meanings for individuals whose common language is
not English (e.g., I'll steal/borrow/buy/take . . . a car). Therefore,
statements should be more specific, such as, "I'll rent a car." This
will be more understandable to the listener.

3. Try to talk slower, pausing between statements. This will allow the
patient an opportunity to translate mentally what you are saying
into his or her own language as you speak.

4. Ask the same questions in different ways. Sometimes individuals
are reluctant to admit that they do not understand. Rewording
the same questions and asking them two or three times allows the
individual to understand the question without having to admit
his or her own weakness in the language.

5. It might also help if diagrams are drawn to clarify your instruction. Sometimes what is not understood verbally can be made
clearer with the use of pictures. However, be sure that the dia-
gram is legible and carefully drawn.

"A busy surgeon once drew a stick figure to illustrate to his patient
what he would be doing in the upcoming surgical procedure. To indicate
quickly where he could cut into the abdomen, he ripped the page in half,
leaving the stick figure in two parts. The patient fled the room and never
returned." (Desmond, 1994)

How Managers Can Become Multicultural Leaders

Although the techniques indicated above are effective in both providing
therapy and leadership to minority individuals, there are still many
more qualities that one must incorporate into practice that are just as
important. However, these additional qualities are more specific in the
sense that some are geared more toward patients and others are geared
toward employees. Therefore, let us examine what additional techniques must be utilized in order to become an effective multicultural
manager.

Recent studies have found that "employers are worried about their
ability to motivate diverse groups of employees, their ability to effectively
communicate with employees for whom English is a second language,

and the impact of differences in values and cultural norms on employee performance and work satisfaction and commitment" (Rubaii-Barett & Beck, 1993). Whether individuals hold positive or negative opinions about the growing diversity in the workforce, diversity is an inevitable part of our future. In relation to health services, such a diverse workforce is growing at an even faster rate.

The managers of today as well as tomorrow must understand the cultures and values of their employees in order to be successful and productive leaders (Rubaii-Barett & Beck, 1993). Previous leadership training, which many of these leaders have participated in, often consisted of manager-training courses which focused upon leadership techniques for the dominant culture. Such lessons are now impractical, since it is not only the dominant culture that is in the workforce. Therefore, new strategies and attitudes must be applied by the managers themselves to ensure that they are effective leaders.

To effectively manage diversity, managers must be culturally sensitive to the values and biases of their conventional management techniques and be able and willing to use strategies which are more employee focused to affirm the employees' differences while still maintaining job productivity (Muller & Haase, 1994). There are some very basic ideas that can be incorporated into managerial techniques that will assist managers in their attempt to create a multicultural organization.

Managers must make sure that they are committed to working with a diverse workforce; they must ask themselves if they genuinely want to work with individuals who are of various ethnic groups. If they do not wish to work with individuals of different ethnic groups, then they are not going to be effective managers either today or in the future. In fact, such individuals will be effective only in inhibiting the success and productivity of the human or health service they are managing. By accepting diversity in the workforce, health practitioners are also allowing themselves to recognize and deal with many types of resistance that they or the minority employees may encounter at work (Cunningham, 1992). Once they have decided to work with minority groups, the human service leaders must try not to lose their focus and must be positive in their interactions with the workforce. Since stereotypes are the most harmful things to foster when leading a diverse workforce, managers must try not to judge employees too quickly and too harshly. By forming judgments about their employees, they are forming stereotypes which are all too often unwarranted and unjust.

Problems will be an inevitable part of any workforce. How a manager deals with such problems is an important aspect of becoming a good leader. The managers of today and tomorrow in the human service agencies now must deal not only with disagreements between employees, but also disagreements among employees who are ethnically diverse. Research has found that there are two common methods used by ill-equipped managers when dealing with such problems (Kavanagh & Kennedy, 1992, p. 10).

Managers have a tendency to minimize or ignore the problems or differences they encounter in their ethnically diverse employees. Such avoidance ". . . involves remaining unaware, overlooking, and/or not acknowledging characteristics of a situation, including similarities or differences between or among individuals" (Kavanagh & Kennedy, 1992, p. 13). By ignoring the issue, they are maintaining the resentment and are not clearing up the differences (Kavanagh & Kennedy, 1992, p. 13).

Coercion is another method used by managers to ensure that their employees behave a certain way. By using their power and forcing their employees to behave as they wish, they are creating resentment in the workplace. When individuals are of different cultural or ethnic backgrounds, there will be some issues that they will view differently than their managers. It is the job of the manager to respect those wishes and not attempt to force them to behave in a manner that goes against their beliefs (Kavanagh & Kennedy, 1992, p. 13). Both coercion and avoidance create negative undertones; neither solves the problem, but rather punishes the individual who is suffering from the inequality due to the fact that he or she is different (Kavanagh & Kennedy, 1992, pp. 15)

Instead of relying upon avoidance or coercion to solve the problems, managers should respect and appreciate the differing opinions of their employees. They should encourage opponents to openly discuss the situation, listen to all sides of the story, determine the true cause of the problem, engage the employees in the task of finding a solution, and look for a common ground upon which to settle the issue (Hank, 1992). Only by carefully thinking about and listening to the employees will the managers be able effectively to solve the problems caused by diversity in the agency.

There are some behaviors which managers can infuse into their jobs which will help build trust between them and their diverse workforce. Philip Harris and Robert Moran (1991) list some of these behaviors in their book *Managing Cultural Differences*. Some of those elements, in addition to others which should be of interest to a manager in the human or health service agencies, are listed below.

Behaviors That Managers Can Utilize to Help Build a Trust Climate in a Diverse Agency

1. Promote a feeling of acceptance in your agency among employees.

2. Be honest and open with your employees and demand the same from them.

3. Respect the values, beliefs, rights, and practices of your employees, although they may not always agree with your own.

4. Understand and anticipate diversity, and avoid stereotypes. Make sure that your directions are clear when you are assigning work or eliciting opinions.

5. Wherever possible, explain your reasons behind requests and directions.

6. Be culturally sensitive to the values and biases of your conventional management techniques.

7. When your employees express their doubts, concerns, and feelings, demonstrate acceptance and understanding of the problems by identifying clearly the employee's concerns and discussing them thoroughly.

8. Encourage and create proactive policies.

9. Encourage the hiring and promotion of minority employees.

10. Show respect to all employees regardless of race or gender or creed.

Managers as Policy Makers

It is the duty of the leaders in the human services fields to alter their own qualities not only to better manage individuals of different ethnic and cultural backgrounds, but also to facilitate the same type of change in their organization and employees. Managers can solve the challenges of an increasingly diverse workforce not only by altering their own techniques, but also by altering the policies and views of their organization and employees. As long as the old paradigms are still in effect in their organizational departments, no amount of increased diversity awareness on the manager's part will solve the problems incorporated with a multicultural workforce (Betters-Reed & Moore, 1995). Therefore, managers in

the human care service agencies must "facilitate an appreciation of behavioral norms and values not typically represented by white males and
then adopt policies and personnel practices that demonstrate responsiveness to the differing backgrounds and needs of employees" (Muller &
Haase, 1994). For example, a flexible holiday policy which lets employees
pick and choose from an allotted number of days will be more culturally
sensitive than to have only set company holidays (Jenner, 1994). By offering such a culturally accommodating holiday policy, employees of various religions and cultures can accommodate their own religious and cultural needs. Training courses for employees on cultural sensitivity would
be another policy that could be implemented in the human service agencies. Such training should generate sensitivity to cultural differences, en-
able employees and managers to value differences, focus on models of behaviors for improved interactions, and provide employees with an
understanding about various ethnicities (Farr, 1992; Jenner, 1994).

> The bottom line is to create a friendly environment that allows people
> to do their jobs with the least amount of resistance. Diversity must be
> managed as a vital resource not only because it's the right thing to do,
> but also because it's the best thing to do. (Hanke, 1992)

Managers should encourage and create policies and programs, such as the
ones mentioned, that value diversity by addressing employee interaction,
development, and performance (proactive strategies) (Muller & Haase,
1994). Proactive policies that require the organization to make a written
commitment regarding employee diversity, ensuring and valuing a diverse workforce representation, should be encouraged by the manager
(Muller & Haase, 1994). By creating proactive policies, managers are
working to ease the tension between ethnic and cultural groups by encouraging communication and helping employees relate to each other
and find common ground (Ossolinski, 1992). A very successful proactive
approach to management is known as Total Quality Management (TQM)
(Brocka & Brocka, 1992). TQM emphasizes self-improvement, learning,
and flexible innovative management styles. It relies upon teamwork between employees and encourages cooperation. TQM will assist employees
of diverse ethnic backgrounds to work together. It will allow individuals
to learn about each other through group involvement and help ease cultural tensions.

To ease cultural tensions, managers should also recommend that
qualified employees who are representative of the cultures to which the

organization provides health care services are hired (Muller & Haase, 1994). They should also encourage the employment of minority individuals in all aspects of human services, including managerial positions. These employees should be representative of the ethnic and gender diversity that exists in the agency clientele. By having minorities in higher position jobs in the organization, the manager is encouraging the absence of prejudice and discrimination and decreasing the chance of interring group conflict (Muller & Haase, 1994). Basically, the core theme of all these policy changes should be that it is not enough for the agencies to focus on similarities, but also on differences. By focusing upon cultural and ethnic differences within the organization, employees and managers alike will be able to treat both citizens and fellow staff members with greater respect and understanding.

How Individuals Can Become Multicultural Practitioners

Care means different things to different individuals. For some, such as the American Indian, it would be a form of treatment which would most probably incorporate their own tribal healers as well as the health professional. Hence, appropriate caring behaviors depend upon social categories and cultural expectations (Kavanagh & Kennedy, 1992, p. 21). By taking account of the cultural beliefs of the individual and incorporating them into therapy, the therapist is making the treatment more familiar to the minority patient and enhancing its chances of success.

Therapy

Communication is an essential part of all treatment programs in human service agencies. When English is not the patient's first language, such communication can become hindered. Translators are effective for such language barriers. However, since translators are not always easily accessible, leaders must attempt to communicate with their patients on their own. The communication techniques which were previously discussed will be of great assistance in such a situation. Let us review those techniques. Practitioners should try to use common words in the English language, since those words are what immigrants are more likely to understand. Practitioners should speak slowly and clearly to allow the client to translate mentally their words into the client's own language. Since minorities are all too often reluctant to admit that they do not understand what is being said, ask the same questions in different ways. Use diagrams when instructing patients who are not fluent in English. This will assist them in understanding your directions.

Another fact which leaders should take into consideration when communicating with their patients is that the way individuals express themselves varies according to race and ethnicity. In a study by Isaacs and Benjamin in which they compared the values of Anglo-Americans with those of other ethnocultural groups, they found that other cultures valued more restrained modes of expression, unlike Anglo-Americans who valued openness, directness, and individuality (Isaacs & Benjamin, 1991).

> In many Asian societies an ideal person is expected to remain calm and to control his or her emotions even when upset. Serenity and stoicism are cherished, and expression of any strong emotion, especially a negative one like anger, is strongly discouraged and hence suppressed. (Nilchaikovit, Hill, & Holland, 1993)

If practitioners treated such ethnic groups using the skills they learned from the dominant culture, then regardless of whether it was a health or human service agency, inaccurate diagnosis, assessment, and treatment would be inevitable (Sue & Sue, 1990). The results of therapy in which leaders relied upon techniques more geared toward the dominant culture are obvious. Multicultural individuals have been more reluctant to seek assistance from human or health service agencies (Sue, 1977). Additionally, almost half of the minority patients who do seek help do not return after their first session. For cultural reasons some patients may be passive and quiet during therapy. Since in human services therapy involves open communication and self-expression, such passivity may hinder therapy. In health services, such behavior could cause the misdiagnosis of symptoms. Practitioners should repeat important questions pertaining to the client's mental or physical health in different ways and pay attention to the responses they receive from the client. They should also try to examine closely the expressions and hand gestures used by the clients in order to find out more information. Because many cultures value discretion of expression rather than openness, the observation of nonverbal communication will be very beneficial to the therapist. Emotions which the patient is sometimes reluctant to express may be evident throughout the physical posture and expressions of the patient (Marsella, 1993).

Besides these techniques for better communication, there is another aspect involved in therapy which is important—trust. If there is no trust in the client-therapist relationship, then it is less likely that the therapy will be successfully completed. Trust is especially difficult to achieve when the two individuals involved are of different ethnic or cultural backgrounds. Therefore, the practitioner must work carefully to gain the confidence of his or her client. Admitting their ignorance of the other culture is one way to form such a trust. By admitting his own ignorance, the therapist is sending a message to the patient that he wants to learn about his or her culture, thereby establishing a middle ground between himself and the patient (McGill, 1992). Furthermore, through the patients' own self-identification and self-description, therapists will gain some important information about the patients' expectations from therapy. By doing so, the therapist will be able to provide a form of treatment that will be both beneficial and acceptable to the patient.

Practitioners should also try to establish a good relationship with the patient by appearing calm and confident. They should convey an impression of maturity and a high degree of expertise (Nilchaikovit, Hill, & Holland, 1993). They must understand that as practitioners they are viewed as authority figures by many minority patients. By fulfilling their patients' expectations of them, practitioners are building a sense of security and trust within their practitioner-client relationship. Furthermore, confidentiality is very important when working with minority patients. Practitioners must understand that minority patients may be uncomfortable discussing their problems. Any betrayal of the patient's trust in the therapist may make him or her reluctant to proceed with the treatment (Dean, 1979).

Leaders should also accept the fact that each culture will find ". . . some behaviors, interactions, or values more important or desirable than others . . ." (Cross, Brazon, Dennis, & Isaacs, 1989). In order to be successful, practitioners should be aware of and accept these differences. This understanding is accomplished through learning. Therapists should try to learn about the diverse cultures and beliefs that are predominent in their health or human service agency. Information regarding family, values, history, and even etiquette is important. Only by investigating and reading can any attempt at understanding become possible. Practitioners should take the initiative in informing themselves about their clients so that they may be able to understand them.

Although the practitioner should try to understand the patient and his or her circumstances, he should also remain objective during therapy. Furthermore, therapists should be careful not to overidentify with the patient. Instead, they should work toward a moderate level in which they can maintain both distance and closeness with the patient (Dean, 1979).

As cultures vary, so do individuals' opinions about certain aspects of life. As health or human services practitioners, you will be faced with individuals who have varying opinions about such topics as death, illness, and family. These topics contain different meanings, especially for individuals who are ethnically or culturally different from yourself. For example, minority patients may have their own opinions of what is wrong with them. They may diagnose themselves with conditions of which the practitioners may have never even heard. Leaders must understand that these diagnoses are the result of cultural and personal experiences (Simenson, 1995). Instead of attacking the client's beliefs, sometimes it may be better to confirm the patient's concerns and be reassuring. By understanding that meanings for these aspects of life are culturally shaped, and that culture affects how individuals perceive, experience, and cope with these aspects, therapists will be able to understand better their multicultural client's behaviors and opinions (Klienman, Eisenberg, & Good, 1978).

For many minorities the family is the primary system of support. Such individuals usually have strong ties with their family members. For them the ideas of self are more 'we' and 'us' than 'me' and 'I'. Therefore, therapists may sometimes find it beneficial either to have the family come to some of the therapy sessions or to go to the patient's home for some of the sessions. Then the patient will still feel as though the family played an important role in his or her cure, and the therapist will be able to gain some important insight into the patient's life. This insight may prove beneficial when deciding upon a form of treatment for the client. It is only through understanding and trust that an efficient form of treatment can be implemented.

If translators are required, try not to use individuals who are related to the patient to translate information. Since certain topics, such as reproductive organs, are considered taboo in particular cultures, relatives may not transmit to the patient or the therapist any information they feel falls into a category of inappropriateness (Desmond, 1994). Hence, the information that will be translated may be incomplete because of their mutual embarrassment. Furthermore, if the diagnosis is bad, such as a terminal illness, it is less likely that a relative will convey this information to the patient. In fact, the family member may "plead with [the therapist] not to tell the patient the bad news" (Desmond, 1994). Therefore, using an interpreter rather than a relative would probably be most beneficial for the therapy and treatment.

Treatment

Since leaders in the health services usually play an important role in treatment of patients, it is very important that they alter their treatment programs in order to provide effective and efficient treatment. There are many techniques that can be utilized to assist the human service leaders in treating minority clients.

Since many minority patients do not speak English as their first language, therapists must make sure that patients understand their treatment. Write down key points to the treatment in large and simple English and draw diagrams when possible (Desmond, 1994). Have patients repeat your directions and have them show you how they will be adhering to the treatment. In other words, have them physically show you how they will be following your directions.

Noncompliance with treatment programs is a frustrating but common outcome which practitioners must face when treating minority clients. The cause of such failures is usually because the treatment programs may not accommodate the client's own beliefs or values. Therefore, the practitioners should try to accommodate the treatment to incorporate the client's views. Patient self-determination, therefore, is an important part of the treatment program. By patient self-determination it is meant that the therapist respects the rights of the patient and allows him or her the freedom to make some of the decisions in the treatment process. In other words, the establishment of goals and treatment should be performed together, otherwise unnecessary problems may arise if they are beyond the wishes of the patient (Biestek, 1970).

Therefore, the type of treatment that is provided for one client will probably be different from the treatment provided for another client of a different ethnicity. In fact, such differences are necessary. By engineering the treatment to incorporate the client's own beliefs and practices as well as the form of treatment the human service leader feels is necessary, the patient-therapist relationship is more likely to be productive.

When treating culturally diverse clients, caring leaders must become culturally sensitive. For example, some countries in the Orient feel that herbal tea helps cure many problems. Therefore continuing "the traditional use of herbal teas . . . may encourage acceptance of fewer familiar aspects of care or treatment plans" (Kavanagh & Kennedy, 1992, p. 36).

Try to accommodate the patients' requests as sensibly as possible when they pertain to traditional beliefs. "For example, an elderly hospitalized Japanese man became upset and uncooperative because his bed was situated in the direction used to lay out the deceased in traditional Japan" (Kavanagh & Kennedy, 1992, p. 37). By not disregarding the patients' own beliefs, the practitioners are not only making the treatment easier for the patient, but are also helping to ensure that the treatment is successful.

Do's and Don'ts of Multicultural Therapy

1. Do communicate with the patient. Use the communication techniques listed in the section under "Communication." Observe body language.
2. Do gain the trust of the patient.
3. Do admit your ignorance of their culture and ask questions about their culture.
4. Do preserve confidentiality whenever possible.
5. Do try to learn about the patient's culture.
6. Do understand that patients may have differing views about various aspects of life.
7. Do utilize both family and individual therapy when possible.
8. Do not use individuals who are related to the patient as translators.
9. Do not overidentify with the patient.

Sometimes human service leaders are faced with a quite different type of situation. Practitioners may come into contact with minority patients who are physically and mentally in good condition. However, they complain of illnesses which are unfounded. In those situations sometimes it may be wise to agree with the patient and prescribe a harmless but effective treatment. For example, a young Jamaican girl came into the hospital complaining that she was dying. Doctors could not find anything physically or mentally wrong with the child, but she refused to leave the hospital. Under further questioning, it was discovered that an old lady in Jamaica had put a curse on her and said that she would be haunted by the old woman's spirit. The child claimed the spirit was trying to kill her. Therefore, a treatment consisting of garlic cloves and flowers was prescribed to keep her and her home protected from the spirit. The child was able to go home and never complained of any more spirits (Johnson, 1995). Sometimes such placebos are the most effective cures.

Diversity is an increasing and irreversible trend in America. Although it requires a rethinking and reprogramming of therapy and management, diversity is something for which human service leaders must prepare. If leaders in the human services are not prepared for the cultural differences they will encounter, they will be destructive and dangerous not only to their patients and employees, but also to society. By failing to become culturally competent they will be destroying the morals and beliefs that are at the core of all human agencies across the world. They will fail to help individuals who come to them in need.

This chapter examined how a leader in the human professions can become culturally competent. It pinpointed techniques which will assist leaders not only in managing employees, but also in the client-therapist setting. We discussed the importance of communication and acceptance, regardless of whether the minority individual is an employee or a patient. These techniques, when combined with respect for the employees and the patients that these leaders will encounter, will assure a successful and positive environment.

It is time that our professional leaders ask themselves if they are competent and skilled to care adequately for their patients and manage their employees. Furthermore, they must ask themselves if such management and care will be enough for the future. Our world is shrinking at a very fast pace. Therefore, it is the responsibility of our leaders to grow in knowledge at an even faster rate. However, it is not only their responsibility, but also our own. Before we can expect others to understand us, we must attempt to understand them. True, leaders in the health and human services professions must learn to understand different groups regardless of their ethnicity or beliefs. However, is it fair for us to expect from human service professionals what we ourselves are unable to give? It is not the task of just one individual group to grow in cultural competency; it is the task of all who are affected by cultural diversity.

References

Betters-Reed, B., & Moore, L.L. (1995). Shifting the management development paradigm for women. *Journal of Management Development, 14.*

Biestek, F.P. (1970). *The casework relationship* (p. 57). Chicago: Loyola University Press.

Brocka, K. B., & Brocka, M.S. (1992). *Quality management: Implementing the ideas of the masters.* Homewood, IL: Richard D. Irwin.

Cross, T.L., Bazron, B.J., Dennis, K.W., & Isaacs, M.R. (1989). *Toward a culturally competent system of care* (Vol. 1). Washington, DC: CASSP Georgetown University.

Cunningham, P. (1992). Fostering advancement for women and minorities. *Public Management, 74.*

Dean, R.G. (1979). Understanding health beliefs and behavior: Some theoretical principles of practice. In *Removing cultural and ethnic barriers to health care* (pp. 49–67). Chapel Hill: University of North Carolina Press.

Desmond, J. (1994). Communicating with multicultural patients. *Life in Medicine, 7–25.*

Farr, C. (1992). Cultural diversity in the 1990s: Building and supporting a multicultural workforce. *Public Management, 74,* 20–26.

Hanke, E. (1992). Diving into diversity. *Credit Union Management, 17,* 50–52.

Harris, P.R., & Moran, R.T. (1991). *Managing cultural differences.* (3rd ed.). Houston, TX: Gulf Publishing Company

Isaacs, M.R., & Benjamin, M.P. (1991). Toward a culturally competent system of care. *Monographs or programs which utilize culturally competent principles.* Georgetown University Child Development center, CASSP, Technical Assistance Center.

Jenner, L. (1994). *Diversity management: What does it mean?* Oakland, CA: HRfocus, Harrison Associates.

Johnson, T.M. (1995). Behavioral science teaching rounds. In *Culture and medical education action plan round table symposium.* New York: New York Medical College.

Kavanagh, K.H., & Kennedy, P.H. (1992). *Promoting cultural diversity: Strategies for health care professionals.* Beverly Hills, CA: Sage.

Klienman, A., Eisenberg, L., & Good, B. (1978). Culture, illness, and care: Clinical lessons from anthropologic and cross cultural research. *Annals of Internal Medicine, 88,* 251–258.

Marsella, A.J. (1993). Counseling and psychotherapy with Japanese Americans: *Cross cultural considerations. American Journal of Orthopsychiatry, 63*(2), 200–207.

McGill, David, W. (1992). The cultural story in multicultural family therapy. *The Journal of Contemporary Human Service.* Family service America, Inc. Vol. 73, no. 6.

Mokuaa, S., & Matucka, R. (1992). The appropriateness of personality theories for social work with Asian Americans. In S.M. Furuto, R. Biswas, D. Chung, D. Murase, & F. Ross-Sheriff (Eds.), *Social work practice with Asian Americans* (pp. 67–85). Newbury, CA: Sage.

Muller, H. J., & Haase, B. E. (1994). Managing diversity in health services organizations. *Hospital & Health Services Administration, 39*(4), 415–434.

Nilchaikovit, T., Hill, J., & Holland, J. (1993). The effects of culture on illness behavior and medical care: Asian and American differences. *General Hospital Psychiatry, 15,* 41–50.

Ossolinski, R. S. (1992). Celebrating workplace diversity. *Public Management, 74,* 18–21.

Pachter, L. M., & Weller, S. C. *Acculturation and compliance with medical therapy* (pp. 163–168). Washington, DC: Ambulatory Pediatrics Association

Rubaii-Barret, N., & Beck, A.C. (1993). Minorities in the majority: Implications for managing cultural diversity. *Public Personnel Management, 22.*

Simenson, D. (1995). Cross-cultural medicine: My first year as a doctor. In *Culture and Medical Education Action Plan Round Table Symposium.* New York: New York Medical College.

Sue, D.W., & Sue, D. (1990). *Counseling the culturally different.* New York: Independent Publishers Group-David White.

CHAPTER 9

Cultural Competency and Human Resources

We have been stressing the need for cultural competency as the appropriate means to address health and human services to minorities. We would, however, like to stress that cultural competency may be interpreted as just another fashionable method to market and reach certain ethnic populations and groups. Some of us may even debate what "competency" in a culture really is. We also have questions about what makes someone culturally competent, who decides what competency is, and who decides when someone is culturally competent. These are very important questions that many minorities, especially Latinos, are asking and need answered. If we are to provide true education, disease prevention, and social, health, and human services, issues on culturally based services must be decided with the direct input of minorities.

Many of us feel that there is a distinction between culturally competent and culturally based services. For minorities, competency includes those values that are actually rooted in the client group's customs, language, idiosyncrasies, religion, politics, and family structure. It is not enough just to be bilingual and bicultural, one must also take into account the local customs, the alterations brought on by assimilation, the local dialect, and the communication methods of the overarching culture. In this chapter we will try to address culturally based services as a means to cultural competency through the eyes of the various public, social, and human service programs, and what they mean to disadvantaged populations and minorities.

Affirmative Action and Its Relation to Cultural Competency

During the 1960s, civil rights activists and proactive equal rights proponents took to the streets and questioned our educational system and our schools. They evaluated the system, demanded changes in employment policies, regulations, and procedures, and then challenged our legal system to protect and uphold these rights and privileges for all citizens. This was the period when new and different paradigms of doing business and providing human and social services were evaluated. Although Congress enacted the Civil Rights Act in 1957 to protect persons against discrimination in employment practices, school admissions, and financial aid guidelines that were based on sex, color, religion, or ethnic origin, it was not until the 60s that institutions were challenged to uphold the Act's intent. This opened the doors for many disadvantaged communities and minorities, but unfortunately was not enough. Although advances have been made, unemployment today remains high for minorities, and dropout rates are soaring, especially in urban inner city minority populations (for example, in Texas, the dropout rate for Mexican Americans is higher than the state level).

In academic institutions, universities, colleges, and other professional centers of higher learning, there has been some advancement in the number of minorities enrolled in schools, although much remains to be done. This is especially true with regard to increasing the pool of minorities in the sciences and health professions. Even more notorious is the fact that there has been little to no increase in minority faculty positions. Minority faculty are important because they help serve as role models, mentors, and teachers for others. More important, minority faculties and researchers are part of the cultural competency equation that will help develop new and better service delivery mechanisms for minorities.

As a consequence, every branch of the government, both state and federal, had to make sweeping changes to adapt to these new directives. This was especially true of social, health, and human services organizations, such as: the Department of Health and Human Services (DHHS) (in those days it was called Health, Education, and Welfare Office [HEW]), and all of its affiliate branch offices and secretariats of the Public Health Service (PHS); the Centers for Disease Control and Prevention (CDC); the Health Resources and Services Administration (HRSA); the Health Care Finance Administration (HCFA); the Federal Employment Commission; the Department of Education; the Department of Agriculture; and the National Institutes of Health, to name a few of the major agencies and secretariats. Also created were new "acts," mandates, and offices such as the Office on Aging (OoA), Office of Civil Rights (OCRs), and the now defunct Equal Employment Opportunity Commission (EEOC). In addition, states through their own sister/comparable agencies also were charged with the implementation of these guiding mandates and principles. In Texas, some of these agencies are the Texas Department of Human Services (TDHS), Texas Employment Commission (TEC), Texas Rehabilitation Commission (TRC), Texas Department of Health (TDH), Texas Commission for Alcohol and Drug Abuse (TCADA), and the Texas Department of Mental Health and Mental Retardation.

These agencies were charged with the execution of the different anti-discrimination acts and equal opportunity mandates. Their efforts were meant to help minorities reach the pathway into better living conditions. The problem was that very few agencies knew how to work with minorities without being either racist or paternalistic, so implementing culturally competent services was even more difficult. A new term, "affirmative action," was coined and was to become the guiding principle for these new directives and opportunities. It altered the way in which federal, state, and publicly funded programs would have to function regarding hiring and firing practices, and social, health, and human service delivery mechanisms. This mandate was also carried into our colleges, universities, and other institutions of higher learning with regard to admission practices and policies and the manner of financial aid distribution. The directives were to provide alternative avenues that would help minorities and other disadvantaged populations and groups to reach parity in the current social, educational, and economic status.

Affirmative action became a systematic form not only of facilitating opportunities in employment and schools, but it also forced people to re-evaluate their health and human service delivery mechanisms, many of which focused on education, communication, and awareness methodologies. Agencies and programs that received federal and/or state funding needed to uphold these mandates. They also had to define, educate, and implement services, employment practices and policies, and education requirements, all of which were protected under the Civil Rights Act, the Disabilities Act, Human Rights disclaimers, and Anti-Discrimination mandates which were based on sex, color, religion, ethnic origin, and later age. Furthermore, these needed to be done in a culturally sensitive and appropriate fashion so that disadvantaged groups and minorities would understand, access, use the services, and consequently benefit from them.

Subsequently, programs, agencies, government services, employers, and educational institutions needed to provide better and more appropriate means of communication for many minorities, especially Latinos. Bilingual and later bilingual/bicultural service, were initiated through every means of production: print, audio, and language. Services were provided through various forms of communication, and information distribution, such as interpreters, bilingual information, and the hiring of minorities themselves. In this fashion, services could become more accessible to disadvantaged communities and minorities. Until this change, many social, health, and human service agencies and programs continued to acknowledge that minorities did not access their programs and services, and they wondered why. What is even more startling is that some of these services were literally next door to minority neighborhoods, barrios, and low-income housing (projects). These agencies needed to change their service delivery methodologies to reach and service minorities; incorporating culturally competent service was the beginning of the change. Human services programs, such as Aid to Families with Dependent Children (AFDC); Women, Infants, and Children (WIC); Early Periodic Screening, Diagnosis, and Treatment Program (EPSDT); family planning programs; food stamps services; food commodities programs; Meals on Wheels, and other food distribution services for the elderly are just some examples of human and social service programs that needed to implement culturally based practices to enhance their services and outreach practices to minorities and other disadvantaged groups.

We would like to note that when discussing services for minorities, especially Latinos, we include not only social service delivery, but also comprehensive health care delivery services which include mental health, rehabilitation, long-term care, and prevention. These services needed to be evaluated. The country is also changing, with an ever-growing elderly population that is increasingly ethnic and that requires that the service paradigm be reevaluated. It is no wonder that the health care and human services programs had an enormous challenge in including these new mandates. This was especially true for primary and urgent care services, prevention, family planning, rehabilitation, and mental health.

Our educational institutions and programs also took a hard look at the way they provided education. A new system including bilingual education, English as a second language programs, alternative education services, and free lunch was instituted. As more minorities became involved in decision making both at the policy and political levels, additional culturally competent methods of facilitating services were studied and reviewed, and recommendations for the implementation of these methods were provided. In addition, methods currently in use were also reviewed, revised, and changed to provide better and more competent and relevant services. Some changes included the reevaluation of the language practices in service delivery. Not only were services to be provided in the minority's primary language, but the customs, local environment, literacy level, and the means of communication also were considered.

For example, it was not enough to speak Spanish to reach Latinos. It was necessary for the agency or program to use the correct local Spanish, and/or other means of communication, such as visual aids and other nonverbal communication methods. Other nontraditional methods were recommended, such as using a family member as an interpreter, communicating in mixed English and Spanish (Tex-Mex, Tejano, Barrio), using international signs of communication, or using bilingual and bicultural printed materials and information. In this fashion, the information produced and used was written or communicated in the local language or dialect and not in the directly translated format, which might as well have been written in English, or for that matter, Martian.

This form of better understanding through culturally based services sometimes just meant allowing more time to exchange information in a more natural and friendly atmosphere. For many Latinos, especially Mexican Americans and elderly people, taking time to explain and exchange information in a casual format and speaking directly to a person is the accepted cultural means of communication; it is more satisfactory and much more meaningful. In Spanish there is a saying, "Hablando se entiende la gente, y si es de cara a cara, es mejor." What this very important "refran" (saying) means, is that open communication is a better means of understanding, and if you do it in person, it is much better. Other considerations that are also part of the service delivery equation need to be included. Some of these considerations are to make services more accessible, affordable, assessable, adaptable, useful, and useable. These elements were to be incorporated into appropriate culturally based (competent) services that could make a difference in the way minorities access, use, and maximize the service they were obtaining. Putting it very simply, culturally based services make minorities more comfortable by building "confianza" (trust).

As an example, if someone were going to the employment office and were only spoken to in English, if the client/customer/student/patient only spoke Spanish, communication was never going to occur. Services might be accepted more readily and better understood if they were provided in the client's own language, preferably in a known and friendly environment (an office with designs, pictures, and ambiance that was culturally Latino, for example), and if they were provided by someone who was a member of the client's own race or ethnic group. If minorities and other disadvantaged groups understand the rules, regulations, appointment system, and so forth, it will definitely improve the use of the agency services. Imagine what it would mean for prevention, education, wellness, and productivity if we provided health, human, and social services in this manner. It would also mean long-term savings for the economy. Most social scientist and human service experts agree that if our community is more educated, better trained, and healthier, productivity is an inevitable result.

Some agencies have already made inroads in this area and have even tested culturally based methods and services with some success. Programs such as WIC, EPSDT, Federal and State Immunization Programs, and more recently AIDS services are some examples of programs using culturally based services. In fact, public health service programs in tuberculosis control were the first to recognize the need for culturally based and community oriented services. Housing projects and alternative community training employment and educational services have also incorporated culturally based (competency) service and methodologies with some success.

Great efforts were made in housing and urban development programs to facilitate affordable housing. However, culturally competent services did not go far enough. For example, even with bilingual services and culturally appropriate information, caregivers do not consider that many minorities did not read or write in their native tongue, so that traditional mainstream communication methods were not reaching them. Some considerations that were not included were: hours of service were not accessible, information was not provided in a nonverbal and simple communication method, and information was not clear and no consideration given to local dialects. (Just consider insurance and the new Medicaid managed-care requirements.) More importantly, there were still not enough minority providers and caregivers. There were additional differences between programs who just provided services in a more sensitive fashion rather than providing them in a culturally-based, bilingual and bicultural, community-oriented way. Today, many Latinos (and other minorities as well) have begun to promote culturally based and community oriented services, as an appropriate service delivery methodology that naturally purports a change in the current social, health, and human service delivery paradigm.

Cultural Competency Implementation

What are culturally based services? Before discussing the planning, establishment, and implementation of culturally based services, we must recognize what they are and when we need to apply them. Part of the definition has already been discussed in the previous paragraphs. We now want to present some guiding principles, concepts, recommendations, and models that noted Latinos such as Dr. Sally Andrade, Dr. David Hayes Bautista, Dr. Carmen Carrillo, and Dr. Catalina Herrerias have developed and proposed. These experts, as well others such as Drs. Manuel Miranda, David Espino, Maria Guajardo, and agencies such as the Center for Health Policy Development, Inc. (CHPD), the National Coalition of Hispanic Health and Human Services Organization (COSSMH0), and the National Council of La Raza (NCLR), all have extensive experience in planning, developing, implementing, and providing culturally based services in their respective areas of expertise. There is no doubt that other minorities and ethnic groups also have noted culturally based service experts, especially Native Americans and African Americans. However, for this discussion we will center on Latino and Mexican American culturally based, bilingual/bicultural models that serve as a path toward cultural competency.

First, when providing any social, health, and human service to minorities, one must consider the following general principles: (1) Consider and involve the whole family. This is very true for Latinos, especially Mexican Americans. Do not provide services exclusively to children; whenever possible, include the extended family, no matter how many they are. (2) Be sensitive to the cultural values, mores, and traditions of the specific group and do not lump all minorities together. For example, not all Latinos, not all Native or African Americans, are the same. In considering Latinos, although there are very many cultural and language similarities, there is quite a difference between a newly arrived immigrant and a first or second generation U.S. born, or between different subgroups of Latinos. (3) Be able to communicate in their native language, and whenever possible use providers and caregivers from the same ethnic group or race.

According to Dr. Sally Andrade, from the Center for Institutional Evaluation, Research and Planning at the University of Texas at El Paso; Charlene Doria-Ortiz, Executive Director of the Center for Health Policy Development, Inc. (CHPD), from San Antonio, Texas; and Dr. Maria Guajardo from the Latin American Research and Service Agency

(LARASA), from Denver, Colorado, when writing and developing culturally relevant prevention program objectives, one must have certain guiding parameters and principles that are quite different from the traditional and mainstream model/paradigm. Dr. Guajardo and Charlene Doria-Ortiz have both used unique models of culturally based/competent training programs for social, health, and human service providers and caregivers. Both provide training and technical assistance to both minority and nonminority service providers. Both experts center their training around the family, family values, community, and the customs of Latinos. However, no progress can be made without the service provider first recognizing the patient/client's cultural identity, values, customs, and determining how these factors affect their lives. This is an important understanding and realization that helps the provider in better understanding the patient/client. These questions need to be addressed before minorities and other disadvantaged groups can even begin to see how they fit into the larger society. Some minorities, among these many Latinos, believe that they should accept the dominant society and learn from it, but not give up their cultural identity. On the contrary, allowing minorities to retain their culture, and to mix and coexist with the dominant society allows people to understand each other better.

Cultural competency training programs such as those conducted by Dr. Maria Guajardo and Charlene Doria-Ortiz ascertain that there are various levels of competency that need to be understood when agencies, programs, and individuals begin to implement them. In her training session, Dr. Guajardo proposes the following levels of competence that were developed at the Georgetown University Child Development Center: "Toward a Culturally Competent System of Care." These are, starting at the lowest level: (1) cultural destructiveness, (2) cultural incapacity, (3) cultural blindness, (4) cultural pre-competence, (5) cultural competence, and (6) cultural proficiency.

1. Cultural destructiveness: Each of these levels needs to be understood by everyone who is going to conduct culturally based services, especially since it is the current fashion. Cultural destructiveness, for example, is the most negative level and is represented by attitudes, policies, and practices that are destructive to cultures and, consequently, to the individuals within the culture. A system that adheres to this extreme assumes that one race is superior and should eradicate "lesser" cultures, because of their perceived inferiority.

2. Cultural incapacity: A system or agency does not intentionally seek to be culturally destructive, but rather lacks the capacity to help minority clients or communities. The system remains extremely biased, believes in the racial superiority of the dominant group, and assumes a paternal posture toward "lesser" races. The characteristics of cultural incapacity include: discriminatory hiring practices, subtle messages to people of color that they are not valued or welcomed, and generally lower expectations of minority clients.

3. Cultural blindness: These agencies propose unbiased philosophies and practices. They function with the belief that color or culture makes no difference and everyone is the same. The belief is that all helping approaches traditionally used by the dominant culture are universally applicable; if the system worked as it should, all people would be served with equal effectiveness. This is the common view of many liberals. However, the consequences of such a belief are to make services so bound to the cultural mainstream as to render them virtually useless to all but the most assimilated people of color.

4. Cultural pre-competence: As more programs and agencies try to implement culturally competent services, many reach a level of almost competent. The agency realizes its weaknesses in serving minorities and attempts to improve some aspect of its services to a specific population. Such agencies try experiments, hire minority staff, explore how to reach people of color in their service area, initiate training on cultural sensitivity, enter into needs assessments concerning minority communities, and recruit minority individuals for their boards of directors, commissions, or advisory committees. One danger at this level is a false sense of accomplishment (or of failure) that prevents the agency from moving into true culturally based, and ultimately, culturally competent services.

5. Cultural competence: These are agencies and programs characterized by the acceptance of and respect for the differences among certain populations. They continue to perform self-assessments regarding culture, provide careful attention to the dynamics of difference, promote continuous expansion of cultural knowledge, resources, and adaptation of service models to better meet the needs of minority populations. These agencies and programs provide support for staff to become comfortable working in cross-cultural situations. Furthermore, these culturally competent

agencies and programs, understand the interplay between policy
and practice, and are committed to policies that enhance services to
a diverse clientele.

6. Cultural proficiency: This is the most positive level, characterized
   by holding culture in high esteem. Culturally proficient programs,
   agencies, and services seek to add to the knowledge base of culturally competent practices by conducting research, developing new
   therapeutic approaches based on culture, publishing, and distribut-
   ing the results of any of these demonstration projects. Attitudes,
   policies, and practices are three major arenas in which development can and must occur if we are to move toward cultural
   competence.

To implement any culturally based service, there are certain considerations that need to be considered and followed. They make a distinction
between how we currently provide services that are not reaching many
minorities and other disadvantaged groups and what needs to be improved and implemented. The following table is an adaptation by Dr.
Sally Andrade from Writing Culturally Relevant Prevention and Program
Objectives (1981) that draws a comparison between different implementation models. This table is also an excellent example of comparison between current mainstream considerations and cultural considerations.
These are very important and thought-provoking ideas that should be
considered when implementing culturally based services. Rethinking in
this fashion is certainly challenging; however, the benefits for any human
service agency or program could be quite positive.

Dr. Catalina Herrerias, Assistant Professor of Sociology at the University of Pennsylvania, has also developed "Guidelines for Working with
Hispanics" and states that these are to be used to help facilitate more effective, ethnically competent work with Hispanics. She does caution us
that the relevance of the information she provides will depend on the
level of acculturation. As already briefly mentioned, among minorities
and especially Latinos, there are large debates on the issue of acculturation and what that means to culturally based services and cultural competency. Some Latino experts, for example, say that acculturation im-
poses adverse pyschosocial and developmental effects, while others (in
the minority) say the opposite, that acculturation is desirable. While there
is no doubt that some acculturation into the dominant mainstream society is inevitable, there are also negative psychosocial repercussions and

TABLE 9.1

Program Objectives and Cultural Considerations

Existing Model	Cultural Considerations
Identify results or conditions to be achieved rather than activities to be performed.	How is achievement viewed and valued in this group or setting?
Use time limits to provide milestones of achievement.	Are the project time lines realistic and attainable?
Make statements in terms of what is to be done rather than in terms of what is to be avoided.	Is there a history of having planned activities imposed on the community through negatively stated sanctions (educational, political, etc.)?
Design program to achieve a single result.	Is there universal agreement among the cultural group on the individual result desired?
Readily indicate a data baseline.	Is there a realistic data baseline? How can one be developed?
State the program in quantifiable terms that are measurable in terms of established standards.	Are there cultural standards? How can established standards be more inclusive?
Indicate the minimum achievement or "standard" that is acceptable.	Are the standards achievable and relevant to the culture? Has there been an acknowledgment of those standards by formal and informal leaders?
Fit within the framework of the overall goal and and policies of the program.	Are the overall goals and policies in line with the culture?
Have realistic and attainable goals and policies.	Are the goals and policies realistic within the cultural constraints? Are they attainable with respect to cultural needs and desires?
Be consistent with available resources.	What resources are available within the culture? Are they being ignored due to a focus solely on needs and problems? How can these resources be accessed?

the underdevelopment of some minorities' natural resources (their people) as a result of acculturation.

Yet the impact and influence of the minority cultural influence on the dominant culture is a prominent and curious one. For example, when many Mexican-American children attended grade school, it wasn't fashionable to bring tacos from home and eat them in the school cafeteria. Today, however, tacos have become a lucrative business throughout the United States, and Latinos have come to replace their exquisite homemade tacos with commercially made Anglo products: what a paradox.

There is no doubt in the minds of many that culturally based services fill a major need in the delivery of all social, health, and human services, no matter what the acculturation level is. Among Mexican Americans, taking care of cousins, and in some instances brothers, sisters, or parents who have recently migrated from Mexico, as well as taking care of our elderly population, in a culturally based manner that promotes understanding of our customs and language is crucial. Moreover, there is sufficient evidence to support the concept that providing culturally based services promotes better-educated persons and consequently healthier and more productive persons.

We have now discussed what cultural competency is and changes in the current service delivery paradigm, and now we will discuss culturally based implementation guidelines and strategies. First, however, we need to discuss barriers that impede the path toward culturally based services and cultural competency. To do this we will provide information to help dispel myths and perceptions that serve as barriers to the implementation of culturally based services. We will center most of the examples on the Mexican American community. These myths and perceptions, and the accompanying statistics, were compiled by LARASA (Denver, Colorado) and presented in their cultural competency training. Note that most examples are related to undocumented residents, which is appropriate because there is a fanatical and sometimes paranoid belief that the United States is being taken over by undocumented groups that are depleting the country's natural resources. This paranoia is linked to minorities, especially Latinos. Please note the following examples.

Myth 1. New and undocumented immigrants are taking away jobs from "legal" Americans

Without getting into the complex political debates stemming from the present undercurrent that blames economic problems on the new kid on the block, we must face the facts that apply to this population. They are not here to take away jobs from anyone; on the contrary, most are here legally. In fact, according to the United States Immigration and Naturalization Service, only less than 7 percent of minority workers are illegal. In addition, according to a survey of amnesty applicants, 34 percent were employed as menial labor, and another 30 percent were employed in service occupations. Most jobs held by minority workers are in manufacturing and farm labor–related occupations paid at or below the poverty level, making it unlikely that most mainstream or legal United States residents would take or even want these jobs.

On the contrary, minorities, despite legal status, continue to serve as a primary and important work force. Minorities continue to comprise the largest work force, with an extremely committed ethic to work, and yet they continue to work at minimal-pay jobs. These jobs keep minorities at or below the poverty level and do not allow them to reap any of the benefits that many Americans have—retirement, health insurance, life insurance, paid vacations, and holidays. Just look at the clerks at your neighborhood convenience store, the people in the kitchen of any chain restaurant, the grocery baggers at the supermarket—they are a new group made up of minorities. In addition to these low-paying jobs, we can add the thousands of seasonal and migrant farm workers, who, through the sweat of their brows, provide food for our tables. Yet these persons are the ones who continue to be disenfranchised from social, health, and human services. Even worse, because the services are not culturally based, when they do try to access these services, they may try only once.

Myth 2. Minorities and undocumented groups take away services from Americans

Fewer than 1 percent of undocumented minority groups receive federal assistance through social security, supplemental income, worker's compensation, unemployment, or other insurance benefits. Fewer than 0.5 percent are eligible for food stamps and other AFDC benefits, unemployment is at 3.5 percent versus 5.5 percent for the general population, and 83 percent are part of the labor force, in comparison to 77 percent of the general population. In addition, legal minorities are less likely to turn to public assistance programs because of a strong work ethic and cultural pride. Undocumented workers do not qualify for these services. As stated above, because more minorities consist of working-class members who are below, at, or slightly above the poverty level, they do not qualify for public assistance programs. In addition, even if they did, they would not access these services.

Myth 3. Educating minorities and undocumented aliens adds to the problems of meeting the educational need of taxpaying citizens; providing free nonemergency medical and health care services increases the costs to the general population and takes away services from them

A study conducted by the Urban Institute concluded that immigrants and other minorities contributed more than $70.3 billion in taxes in 1992, while using only $41.6 billion in government services. In addition, denying services to immigrants and/or minorities will not solve the problem of immigration. Illegal immigrants will continue to come and stay. They will not return to the motherland, instead becoming productive workers who will contribute to the United States economy and to their motherland's economy as well. If minorities are not allowed to receive social, health, and human services, they will only add to the demand in acute care, social services, and other public assistance programs. The denial of educational services to both legal and illegal populations will only add to an ill-prepared society in subsequent generations. In a time when high technology and other technological, academic, and scientific advances require a well-educated population, we continue to deny our best resources—our people. Health care costs will also escalate because of the possible increase in acute and emergency care services. The possibility of new and larger epidemics can also add to health care concerns and their additional associated costs. Those in public health and prevention, as well as in human service programs, know that paying some now is more economical and desirable than paying more later. If only we could convince people to access services, cultural competency could be part of the solution.

As we stated earlier, we think that these three myths clearly indicate the paranoia that mainstream America has regarding minorities and recent immigrants. The attitude that many Americans have toward minorities and undocumented workers is a major and disastrous problem.

The following are the principal guidelines Dr. Herrerias has developed for working with Latinos; however, many of these will also assist any provider with culturally based services for other minority groups:

1. A client's name is an important part of both his or her culture and identity. Every attempt should be made to spell and pro-

nounce it correctly. Do not Anglicize a Spanish name.

2. Formality is viewed as a sign of respect. Address all clients except minors by their surnames, unless a client initially requests that his or her first name be used. With time, a client may ask that you address him or her on a more familiar basis; however, first names should not be used without the client's permission.

3. With an older client, adding "Don" or "Dona" before the first name is a sign of respect, particularly if the worker is younger than the client. A client should be addressed in such a manner first.

4. The term "Hispanic" is an umbrella term that refers to any individual with Spanish ancestry. It is a generic term similar to "Hispano" or "Latino." It is not a true ethnic identification.

5. Avoid asking an Hispanic individual if he or she speaks Puerto Rican, Mexican, Cuban, etc. With the exception of slang, idiomatic expressions, regionalisms, and some sections of Spain (e.g., Catalan, Galicia), Spanish is Spanish.

6. Most Hispanics are bilingual, but at least half of the United States Latino population prefers to speak in Spanish.

7. Speaking in Spanish enables Hispanics with Spanish-dominant language fluency to more honestly express their feelings and emotions and allows for a significantly greater level of comfort in self-disclosure.

8. Under most circumstances an Hispanic client will likely feel more comfortable interacting with Hispanics than with non-Hispanic staff members.

9. If an Hispanic client's caseworker is not bilingual, a qualified/competent interpreter with a background in the particular human/social service setting should be used. This may even exclude other Spanish bilingual and/or bicultural staff members employed by the same agency who are not familiar with a given subject area or the pertinent terminology used in that field.

10. When the use of an interpreter is required, she or he should be an integral part of the therapeutic alliance or service delivery system for the sake of clarity, continuity, and confidentiality.

11. Hispanics tend to be physically expressive, gesturing with their hands and face (e.g., eyes, eyebrows, and mouth) while they talk.

12. Many Hispanics may feel uncomfortable with giving a person in authority much direct eye contact, as this is perceived to be disrespectful.

13. Physical distances between Hispanics are approximately half that required by Anglo-Americans in face-to-face interactions. Thus, a client may perceive the added distance between him- or herself and a non-Hispanic worker as alienating or rejecting.

14. The Hispanic family is the individual's primary source of social support and extends beyond a nuclear family configuration.

15. The Hispanic definition of family extends to nonblood relatives, and includes *compadre, comadre, padrino,* and *madrina*—a ritualistic kinship system.

16. Hispanic relationships are hierarchical in nature. Status and authority are accorded by virtue of age and experience, with males holding the highest status.

17. If the husband (or common-law mate) does not accompany the wife to the initial intake session, the worker should attempt to contact the male figure, even to the extent of meeting with the husband at his place of work. Whether or not the husband chooses to participate in the therapeutic process, obtaining his cooperation and/or approval is important as a mark of respect for his position within the family.

18. In worker-client contact when both husband and wife are seen together, most of the communication should be channeled through the male as a sign of respect for his position of authority in the family.

19. Non-Hispanics have defined *machismo* in terms of physical aggression, sexual promiscuity, dominance of women, and the excessive use of alcohol. In reality, to be *macho* means to love and have affection for and to protect the family, and to have dignity, honor, and respect for others.

20. Historically, Hispanic women have tended toward more somatic complaints, which is consistent with their cultural value of doing for children, husband, and other family members before doing for themselves. Therefore, Hispanic women often suppress their needs, and sometimes become ill as a result.

21. Parents foster a great sense of interdependence and responsibility in children which often extends throughout a person's lifetime.

22. Many Hispanic mothers do not experience the "empty-nest syndrome" because even when their children leave home, mother-child interactions continue. Once grandchildren are born, they tend to spend quite a bit of time with the grandmother, especially if they reside in the same or nearby community/city.

23. Hispanic mothers tend to be very tolerant of their children's behavior, more often preferring that the children's father (or household male authority figure) provide the discipline. However, this is changing as more women become single heads of households.

24. Children are traditionally taught to respect their elders, and to be polite.

25. Hispanic children are not usually included in adult conversations. They are expected to act quiet, reserved, and well behaved in front of strangers.

26. Due to the hierarchical nature of Hispanic societies, young children should not be utilized as interpreters. Inappropriate use of a child as an interpreter elevates that child to a position of authority in the family and disrupts the roles within the family.

27. The first place the Hispanic turns to for help is her or his family.

28. Hispanics, in seeking support outside of the family, may turn to their physician, priest, or schoolteacher, particularly in instances of a case of *nervios* (nerves) or *ataques* (fits).

29. To seek the services of a therapist would stigmatize the Hispanic as loco (crazy); thus the services of a physician, priest/minister, folk healer, and/or spirit are sought first.

30. Although a predominant number of Hispanics are Roman Catholic, many attend Spanish-speaking churches such as Pentecostal, Jehovah's Witnesses, Seventh Day Adventist, Baptist, and Nazarene.

31. If an Hispanic client says he/she is feeling guilt and/or shame over something he/she perceives to be an unfilled cultural expectation, ask about the extent of religious affiliation. Many times a priest or other clergy can help to substantially reduce feelings of guilt and anxiety.

32. While metaphysical beliefs cut across socioeconomic lines, most

people relying on folk healers and spiritists are generally lower-income Hispanics.

33. Middle- and upper-income Hispanics who utilize folk healers rationalize their use as being for "scientific" reasons.

34. A session with a spiritist generally parallels that with a therapist, in that the spiritist diagnoses the problem, aligns with the client, and attempts to identify ego strengths, but the spiritist also touches the good protecting spirits.

35. It is not unusual in some Hispanic homes to find a small altar in a closet or corner of a room with statues of saints and candles burning for various reasons. Some candles are lit for the saints and others for protective spirits.

36. When an Hispanic does not immediately agree to comply with a specific treatment or service, it does not mean that the individual lacks motivation, interest, or understanding. Rather, the client is probably going to discuss it with other family members first to get their advice or opinion.

37. Once *confianza* (trust) has been established, Hispanics will be more informal, and the relationship will be characterized by warm, intense interactions (*personalismo*).

38. Hispanics frequently use humor, which may be misunderstood as not accepting a serious situation. Humor provides a viable coping mechanism.

39. An Hispanic may make an offer of food or drink to a caseworker on a home visit. To reject this offer signifies rejection of the person.

40. It is not unusual for a client to present a caseworker with a small gift over the course of treatment. Nonacceptance is taken as a rejection.

41. Hispanics have a different orientation to time than Anglo-Americans. For Hispanics, it seems that the clock does not run but walks instead. Arriving late for scheduled appointments should not be taken personally by caseworkers. If an Hispanic client arrives late for an initial appointment, the subsequent appointment might be set 15 to 30 minutes earlier than the expected time of arrival as a way of working within this orientation to time.

42. *Fatalismo* (fatalism) is a cultural value expressed by the belief that
    if something were meant to be—if it were destined—it would
    come about. This belief has been reinforced by the strong adher-
    ence to religion. Often Hispanics will add the phrase *si Dios quiere*
    (if God wills) to the end of any statement referring to expecta-
    tions or desires. Another fatalistic expression is *que sera sera*
    (what will be will be). Taken to the extreme, this encourages
    relinquishment of responsibility. Taking the approach that "God
    helps those who help themselves" helps bring this cultural value
    in line with active self-participation.

43. If all else fails, the Hispanic client will be the worker's best source
    of information concerning where he or she falls along a con-
    tinuum of cultural values.

The aforementioned list, has served as excellent guidelines and recommendations in consideration of a culturally based program. Furthermore, there are various entities and models for those social, health, and
human service agencies that need training and technical assistance. We
would now like to further expound on different agency services that need
to evaluate the current use of culturally competent services and methodologies, as well as how to implement training.

Human services programs have made strides as they become more
decentralized, through the establishment of bilingual and bicultural materials, and the hiring of more minorities. Yet much remains to be done in
the area of training, staff development, and hiring more minorities. Especially at the decision-making level, the development of new and creative
ways of communication that are sensitive and appropriate to the targeted
group, and the development of new ways to serve minorities as an agency
are needed. Who knows what will happen with current policies and mandates that are trying to reverse culturally competent services. The serious
concern, especially in education and health care, is that we will be creating a second-class citizenry that could continue to burden our already
overburdened society. With regard to health and human resources, there
is also the potential to introduce new diseases and epidemics at a time
when there is very good communicable disease control and prevention.
Some examples of valuable human service programs are support for assistance in public housing, nutrition programs, aid to dependent children, and assistance and aid to our elderly.

Housing must continue to provide an adequate support system to allow families to obtain and maintain housing. Both public and private housing groups need to provide information, financial and otherwise, to minorities in a fashion that they will understand. For many this is the first time they have ever made a financial investment, the first time they are away from home, and the first time they have made a major decision. Although much has been said about disadvantaged and minorities living in public housing, little has been said about the neighborhood groups and housing resident groups that have been formed to help each other through many different situations. These groups are vital, because the families themselves discuss their own problems and their own solutions. Federal and state authorities, such as local housing and urban development, need to work more closely with these groups, as well as with other community-based groups which may provide an insight into special concerns. Advisory groups can be formed that require community input. In addition, training programs relevant to minorities must be created to help them with housing problems.

An example of culturally competent services facilitating needed services is the case of providing fire alarms to public housing residents and the elderly, mostly Mexican American. As a mandate to new federal and local housing regulations, fire alarms are required to be installed in public housing. Insufficient financial assistance was offered, and ultimately the residents needed to purchase them. Authorities strategized and strategized over the implementation of this program. An important boost was the allocation of funds through various sources to pay for the alarms and their installation. The problem now was how to get people to accept them. A well-organized education program using media and other forms of communication frequently used by the Mexican-American community was started. Spanish and English radio stations and print media were used to promote the message, and local community-based newspapers were also enlisted. Family members of the residents were contacted to assist with the educational campaign; Mexican-American students, health and fire officials, as well federal and local housing authorities were also used. By the time the alarms were installed, residents were waiting and willing.

Health care is presently undergoing several changes, many of which do not include culturally competent services. It is essential that health care programs either initiate culturally based services or enhance their current culturally based services toward their goal of cultural competency. This is especially true of outpatient care, prevention and health promotion services, long-term care, rehabilitation, chronic care services, and especially managed care. Here, too, many of the initial programs were simply carbon copies of the services and materials that were being used for mainstream patients and clients.

Another crisis that exists today is the extreme shortage of minority providers and the continued existence of medically underserved areas, many of which are in rural minority communities or inner-city minority communities. These are also disproportionately uninsured and rely heavily on public assistance programs. Here again, the implementation of culturally based services will make a significant difference. These services must ensure that they fill the needs of the minority population by providing services when clients can access them and can understand the need and urgency for them. Location, costs, transportation, communication, and hours of service must be included in the service delivery mechanism.

Also, one must remember to include community members in the decision-making process. They will be the best ones to tell you if the services are accessible. In addition as already stated, outreach services and prevention education need to be presented in nontraditional ways. For minorities many times this means through radio; for Latinos, through Spanish language radio and print. Health information should be presented through community-accepted means of information, like schools, churches, and families. Those who are involved in the promotion of cultural competency and who provide culturally based training and services need to assure appropriate communication methods. For Latinos and especially Mexican Americans, this is very important. The following are methods to overcome language barriers (*interpreters are staff members who will have the primary responsibility of communication*):

1. Service providers must overcome language barriers by training interpreters in bilingual (and bicultural) proficiency, interpreting style, mental health, and nontraditional health care terminology through ongoing supervisory and peer feedback, role playing, "teatro" (theater), and viewing patient/provider interactions.

2. Service providers should also build teamwork by meeting regularly with the agency/program interpreters. You can learn much from them about your patients/clients/users, about yourself, and about cultural and language issues that affect yourself, the agency work, the service delivery system, and the organization.

3. Service providers should implement effective interview skills. Start by introducing the interpreter, then look directly at the patient/client/user, not at the interpreter.

4. Service providers must also determine whether the patient is most comfortable with Spanish or English, and whether written materials will also be useful. Remember that the language of communication, even if it is Spanish, must reflect the local dialect and not necessarily Castilian.

5. Service providers need to ensure that written materials are linguistically and culturally appropriate for the target population, local ethnic group, or special population. Direct translations will almost never be appropriate. Always include cultural euphemisms and customs of communication.

6. Service providers should always convey a warm "saludo" (welcome). Make sure that your waiting room, general area, or reception room facilitates a warm welcome to the clients/users/patients and that it is large enough to accommodate other family members. This will show great respect and courtesy, especially to Latinos. Try also to communicate the culture through the physical decorations, announcements, bulletin boards, signs, and other messages.

Managed care is another social, health, and human service delivery system that needs to apply cultural competency in all of its services. With the new reform in managed care health care delivery this is even more important to poor, minorities, and other disadvantaged populations. Traditionally the Medicaid population has been seen by only a few health care providers in certain parts of town (mostly in the heavily minority populated sector) and by the human service offices that authorized these services. These were mostly insensitive personnel who didn't provide culturally competent services and therefore distanced minorities even further. Because managed care programs were historically built on low-cost operations, they concentrated on wellness, prevention, and nonemergency care. Chronic diseases, rehabilitation, and long-term care were not considered primary care access services, as they were too costly. Managed care programs initially categorized minorities as "high risk," associating them with illness and consequently high costs. As Medicaid reform ensued, in states such as California, New York, and Texas, policies and procedures changed. All of sudden managed care programs were vying for state contracts to provide services for the Medicaid population, which in many cases consist mostly of minorities.

In fairness to managed care programs and traditional health maintenance organizations (HMOs), both have for quite some time tried to cater to minorities, and have initiated some innovative partnerships and services to the community. In many cases HMOs were the first to initiate continuity, prevention, and limited outreach health education to minorities in a culturally competent manner. They realized that if for no other reason, it was economically desirable to provide culturally based prevention and wellness services so that patients and clients would take advantage of the HMO, and thus reduce heath care costs. However, as we move into larger managed care services for the Medicaid, poor, and minority populations, we must remain vigilant to ensure that HMO services continue to provide the highest quality care. This quality care must have a check and balance system that promotes the best care and does not lower its standards nor create a double standard of care. It must provide culturally competent services so that minorities access these services correctly, promptly, and efficiently. All of the culturally competent implementation service delivery recommendations, strategies, methodologies, and communication methods that assure culturally based bilingual/bicultural services must be incorporated in the managed care system. If even the smallest procedure, such as the enrollment process, is not provided in a culturally competent fashion, minorities will not use this new opportunity of health care delivery.

In many states, the managed care regulatory agency has advised Medicaid recipients that they had a time limit within which to choose a managed care program and provider. While some programs made an extra effort to provide culturally based information, it was not enough, because they usually fell into the lower levels of competency. The lamentable consequence is that many minorities and poor will have a provider chosen for them, thereby losing the one sensitive and caring provider that has cared for them for many, many years—all because of a lack of communication. We hope that the regulatory agencies and managed care programs provide their services to this great population in need in a culturally competent manner.

Nutritional programs also need to become more culturally competent. Whether through the free or reduced-price lunch services in the schools, elderly programs, elderly and homeless meal programs, health care nutritional diets for diabetics or hypertensives, or during prenatal care, nutritional programs have not done enough to reach out to minority populations, especially Latinos. As children, some remember accompanying their grandmother to the food distribution service. They believed it was most dehumanizing: standing in line and having powdered milk, cheese, butter, and/or peanut butter literally thrown at you was not their idea of "human service." Yet many of our parents and grandparents did this every week for many years. They had no idea what these food stuffs were for, because they were not part of their staple diet. If these foods were given along with an educational program that related them to our cultural diets, the program might have been more useful.

Today many of our elderly continue to use the Meals on Wheels programs; however, not until this system changed to a more culturally appropriate one were the foods appreciated and the centers used as more than a place to eat, but also as a place to come together, share, and support each other. Many people remember asking relatives that ate in the nutrition programs what they ate; often the response was, "No se, algunos ejotes sin sal no habian frijoles ni tortillas, y ni me los acabe" [I'm not sure what I ate; I think they were unseasoned string beans. I wish they would have had beans and tortillas. I didn't even finish the food.] In addition, the location and hours of service also played a role in utilization of the services.

Some health care programs have made a great effort at least in translating the diets. However, they have not gone the extra step of making sure the information was culturally based and more importantly—that it was understood. Diets for diabetics and hypertensives, as well as for pregnant women, were simply a mirror of mainstream diets translated into Spanish. Not until caregivers and others paid attention to culturally based eating patterns did anyone realize what needed to be done. For example, when traditional foods and cooking methods were incorporated into the diets, better results were obtained.

Providers who treat diabetics or hypertensives, for example, might have been prescribing a low-salt diet that required certain intake of proteins and carbohydrates; a culturally appropriate diet would have allowed the family to eat their customary foods cooked as they liked as long as no salt was included. (For Mexican Americans, recommending corn tortillas instead of flour would have been appropriate.) Currently there are a few Latino researchers who are working with these type of diseases and whose therapies include culturally based diets. Some of this work is being done at the South Texas Research Institute, the UTHSC-SA, and many community-based local groups as well that serve to provide culturally competent services, information, and training to some of our established caregivers and providers.

Employment services have already been mentioned, but we would like to stress again that the advances made since the 1960s could be overturned by the minority-bashing paranoia that is beginning to creep through the American people. If this happens, the doors that were opened to many minorities will again shut, and this time they will be more difficult to open. Employers are urged to utilize culturally competent services in their hiring and employment practices. If they do this, the employees will become more productive. After all, we are in an era of very strict competition, not only within our own continental borders, but within the entire world. Don't culturally competent services make sense?

Education may also take a turn backward, especially in the state of Texas where a fifth circuit court of appeals overturned a Supreme Court affirmative action decision and has everyone running from anything that is labeled minority and culturally competent. If this continues, then the great strides in bilingual/bicultural educational mandates and services may disappear, and if so, the chances are that whole generations of minorities, especially Latinos, will remain stagnant, undeveloped, and underdeveloped educationally and socially. This would be a great tragedy for the future of our society. We will await the new policies and procedures and hope that our educational system and our institutions of higher learning make a stand for what is morally and ethically correct.

Conclusion

We end this chapter on culturally competent services in social, health, and human service programs and agencies by saying that the thrust of this whole issue is access, mobility, and equal opportunities for everyone, while recognizing and accepting differences. If we all do this, and learn to respect the good and great that every culture brings to the human society, then maybe we can learn to live in harmony and peace. Then maybe our children and our children's children will have an opportunity to thrive, and produce a better tomorrow for mankind; a better tomorrow built on respect and tolerance, learning, sharing, and understanding. Culturally based services as a means to a more culturally competent society is part of the answer.

Reference

Andrade, S.J. (1990).*Writing culturally relevant prevention program objectives.* Adapted from *A guide to multi-cultural drug abuse prevention: Evaluation* (1981).Washington, DC: National Institute on Drug Abuse.
Andrade, S.J., Balcorta, S., Carrillo, C., Doria-Ortiz, C., Flores, J., Gasco, L., & Guerra,

S. (1993). *Mexican American and other Latinos in the United States, unique families in need of a quality health care delivery system.* Testimony to the National Task Force on Health Care Reform, prepared by the Center for Health Policy Development, Inc., San Antonio, TX.

Carillo, C. (1993). *Principals for paradigm shift: Towards a human services policy for Latinos.* Testimony to the National Task Force on Health Reform, Washington, DC.

Center for Health Policy Development, Inc. (CHPD). (1984). *Razalogia: A culturally-based training model.* San Antonio, TX: Roberto Vargas & Samuel C. Martinez.

Hayes-Bautista, D. (1989, December). *Latino adolescents, families, work, and the economy: Building upon strength or creating a weakness?* Los Angeles, CA: UCLA Medical School.

Herrias, C. (1991). *Guidelines for working with Hispanics.* Pittsburg, PA: University of Pennsylvania.

Latin American Research and Service Agency (LARASA). (1996). *Culturally competent training model.* Denver, CO: Maria Guajardo.

Levine, J. (1994). *White like me, when privilege is written on your skin.* New York: Prisms.

McKinney, M. (1996). *Medicaid, managed care and cultural competency training.* Presentation for the National Hispanic Medical Association, San Antonio, TX.

National Coalition of Hispanic Health and Human Services Organization (COSSMHO). (1994). Meeting the health promotion needs of Hispanic communities. *American Journal of Health Promotion.* Washington, DC: Jane Delgado.

Obregon, B.O. (1996). *National Latino conference on aging, ancianos in the twenty-first century.* Denver, CO.

Randall-David, E. (1989). *Strategies for working with culturally diverse communities and clients.* Washington DC: Association for Care of Children's Health.

Texas Department of Health. (1996). *Medicaid—Managed care standards and policies.* Austin, TX: Author.

Texas Health and Human Services Coordinating Council. (1991, January). *Health and human services in Texas: Reference guide.* Austin, TX: Author.

United States Department of Health and Human Services. (1990, September). Reaching Hispanic/Latino audiences requires cultural sensitivity. *The Fact Is.* Rockville, MD: National Clearinghouse for Alcohol and Drug Information.

Vega, W.A., & Murphy, J.W. (1984). *Culture and the restructuring of community mental health.* New York: Greenwood Press.

Zate, M. (1995). *Bicultural bedside manners. Hispanic Business,* Vol. #2.

PART III
Policy Imperatives

CHAPTER 10

Future Policy Directions for Cultural Competency

Although health care reform has been discussed for many years, it was not until the last presidential election that the health care delivery system of this country was a major issue of concern. Today the concern for health care influences the current national, state, and local health care delivery system policy debate. Although universal health care has never enjoyed the prominence it merits, changes in the language, direction, and administration of many health and human service programs have occurred.

This is especially true with regard to entitlement programs and services for the poor, minorities, and other disadvantaged populations. Since no real and substantial agreement on health care reform was reached, policy makers then concentrated on welfare reform. The implications this debate has had on our current policies for Social Security; Aid to Families with Dependent Children (AFDC); food stamps; Women, Infants and Children (WIC) Program; Headstart; Medicare and Medicaid; health insurance; managed care; and educational programs have been astronomical.

Today, our policy makers have the opportunity to reevaluate the current health and human services programs and organizations and how they deliver their services to their clients, patients, and other consumers (users). Certain changes have already been made that include using community input and/or incorporating community advisory groups as part of the decision-making process in the administration of the programs that will service the community. Many people are calling for the development of partnerships between community-based organizations and public and private entities. These partnerships are to work together toward solving the problems of the current health care delivery system.

Another administration procedure has been to establish a service delivery model that incorporates more diversity in its programs and implementation policies. This creates another opportunity for service providers and caregivers to reflect on their current service delivery model. It adds a greater responsibility to the agencies and organizations who deliver these services by challenging them to make their services more accessible, assessable, acceptable, and affordable for all of their clients, patients, and users.

As the face of America changes, so should its service delivery processes, policies, and methodologies. If these services are to be used by the great majority of the population entitled to use these programs, then the service delivery paradigm must change and must adopt more diversification in the service delivery methodologies. For these methodologies to be a success, they must include culturally based services that serve as a stepping stone to cultural competency and therefore facilitate use of their services. This, however, has not happened to a great extent. Although state and national policy mandates these changes, our current policy makers have continued to debate this issue and have now implemented drastic changes under the caveat of balancing the budget. Very recently, Congress approved a new welfare system that puts limitations on services and incorporates a "phase-in work-training plan" that will wean the participant from the entitlement program to become a "productive citizen."

While all of us agree on the need to balance the budget, our policy makers may have gone too far. As already discussed in several earlier chapters, social, health, and human services programs that assist disadvantaged populations, the poor, and minorities are being used as a scapegoat to balance the budget. In reality, however, many of these groups are contributing and constructive work force members, who fill many of the nation's important jobs. Furthermore, even though many work for very low wages, they do not access many of the entitlement services, primarily because the services are not presented in a relevant, culturally based fashion that facilitates the use and access of these services. In addition, for many minorities, it is also a matter of pride, duty, and responsibility to be able to take care of their own.

What is of even more concern is that our policy makers may have not realized that by limiting services to welfare recipients and not adjusting for education, health, and future technology, they may be causing and promoting negative long-term effects, such as increasing the pool of low-wage earners. This, in turn, could possibly cause even more serious competition and displacement of today's current workforce, adding to the social responsibility of human services and care programs. Throughout this chapter, different social, health, and human services directives and policies will be discussed that may need to be replaced, further evaluated, implemented, and changed, as well as new ones that are more diverse and that better reflect today's population makeup. This ultimately will provide better services.

Blaming the poor and minorities for the public debt and justifying this blame by saying they do not want to work, they don't have high aspirations, aren't high achievers, and thus prefer to rely on welfare, has been the excuse given for too long by many of our policy makers. In reality, they failed to evaluate and analyze productivity statistics and entitlement program services used by this population. Minorities, especially Latinos remain a very hard-working, highly conscientious, and ethical workforce that does not like to rely on welfare.

General Comments on Entitlement Services

When new changes go into effect, current welfare recipients, such as those enrolled in AFDC, WIC, Medicaid, and other entitlement programs will all be quickly ushered into an alternative system of doing business. This new policy will have a five-year limitation for program participation. Within those five years, it is expected that the recipients will have had enough time to obtain sufficient education and/or training to wean themselves from public assistance. After five years, they should be able to fully sustain themselves and their family.

While in theory this may sound good, provisions for counseling, training, educational attainment, and the implementation of culturally based bilingual/bicultural services that will assist in the transition must also be taken into account. These support mechanisms must be incorporated to assist long-term users of public assistance entitlement services, new persons receiving these services, and to help minorities fully understand their use and long-term alternatives. It is also very important that time and consideration be given to special populations who receive these services, such as the elderly, the handicapped, and the mentally challenged.

Children, single parents, and teenagers who are pregnant are additional groups that need to be given special attention. Programs such as

Head Start, that provide not only a nourishing atmosphere conducive to learning, but also meals, must be kept intact until the overriding circumstances of poverty, diseases, unemployment, and insufficient education and training are overcome.

Economic circumstances, however, may continue to be so bleak that further assistance to enhance the learning and development of our children will still be needed. Programs such as Head Start need additional support, not less. This cannot be accomplished if we set very specific term limitations, especially given the years of inadequate services, lack of preparation and training, and an educational system that did not provide appropriate culturally based services.

These factors also need attention before reducing and/or taking away someone's entitlement. High costs associated with other social problems such as the incarceration system must also be evaluated. Factors affecting identity and self-esteem play a large role in propagating the cycle of poverty and dependency of a welfare system. More cultural competency in every area of the support mechanism might contribute to better understanding between people, thus promoting a more productive population. In the long term this is less costly because the need for public assistance programs could be greatly reduced.

An example of an alternative effort is the Nahuatl (Aztec) tradition of requiring the maladjusted in society to work. This effort contributes and produces for the good of the community. If someone robbed the community/society of any common good, he was put to work for the community, providing a needed social service. While there is some semblance of this happening in various communities, especially with our youth, these efforts do not incorporate long-term remedial projects for the maladjusted social offender, channeling them into actual programs that could assist families and communities.

Occasionally offenses are handled effectively. For example, a chemical company was illegally and inappropriately discharging its toxic waste into a primarily minority community, endangering not only lives and the environment, but the future of the environment and the livelihood of the children and the children's children. The company was cited by the Environmental Protection Agency (EPA), made to clean up the toxic waste, and was also made to contribute to the community in two ways—to improve the physical community and to assist the families affected.

Together with other businesses and community-based groups, the company built a new system of parks, additional streets, drainage projects, and it promoted ecology programs. It also developed a tutoring program with its own professional staff of chemists, engineers, and mathematicians, who tutored and mentored local disadvantaged youth through volunteer school programs and other student activities.

This was an exceptional effort that exemplifies what I meant when I stated that persons who are being sent to prisons, increasing the society's costs in caring for them, could instead be made to contribute to society. The work then becomes an entire community's responsibility, and not just that of the government. The effort in the example involved the original company; affected families; local, state, and federal authorities; the judicial system; and other private businesses. This kind of model is a community-oriented and culturally based alternative. During the implementation phase of the community development and tutoring it took into account the diversity of the population, and also considered the needs and customs of disadvantaged groups and minorities. While this may not be the answer in every situation, it is an alternative that merits consideration. This effort/model could reduce costs and allow for additional resources that could be directed toward entitlement programs, training, and other educational efforts.

Another concern with the current entitlement limitation decision, is that long-term recipients, many of whom have been institutionalized in the past service delivery system, will need assistance to make the changes. Some may be too old, some too unskilled, and the majority too young to function without assistance. In addition, the AFDC programs must also adjust for the change in the service paradigm. For years, many persons on public assistance programs wanted to work and many times needed to work, because the assistance was not enough. These, however, were cited on several occasions by case workers and AFDC officials and lost needed benefits because they made the effort to try to work and become independent. Others on AFDC, felt, very astutely, that if you worked for less money than what the public assistance program provided (even though that was not enough), you might as well stay home and raise the children.

This system did not promote or provide an incentive for training, educational advancement, or getting off welfare. On the contrary, it punished those who made the effort to go outside the system and seek additional support and/or additional employment. It would be interesting to evaluate the numbers of persons on public assistance entitlement programs who left the assistance as soon as their children went to school, became old enough to seek their own jobs, or found something better. There are many critics of the present welfare system who would agree that the system promoted more welfare instead of independence.

For new persons entering the welfare system, getting caught in this new limited-access implementation mechanism could also prove to be a nightmare. If our schools have failed our poor, minorities, and other disadvantaged communities, and there is no other training or educational alternative (especially for a young mother, father, or pregnant teenager), what other system is in place for health and human assistance? Although a few private, religious, or community action services are available to help these persons, the majority will rely on welfare.

Again, although the intent is good, the current limitation policies may also not allow for all of the developmental challenges that a young, pregnant teenager and her partner face. Moreover, many are already being challenged with a new responsibility of independence or should we say interdependence . . . a family/children. What mechanisms are in place that will allow for flexibility in training, finishing high school, entering college, or seeking a vocational trade? If these factors are not taken into account, we might just further the negative psychosocial development of these young people, making the transition to adulthood even harder. This may be a case of two wrongs not making a right.

Daycare for children is another issue that must not be overlooked when we discuss entitlement limitation and welfare reform. If these programs are meant to assist our dependent families to allow their children to have a chance at full participation in society, then daycare/child care services must also be available while the parent returns to school, furthers his or her training, and/or begins to seek employment. Lack of daycare services for children is not only a problem for people trying to get off welfare, it a national problem that has afflicted working-class families as well as many middle-class families throughout this country for years.

We are a country without any significant daycare assistance policy to aid families with the development and care of their children while parents continue with their training, further their education, or go back to work. For years many wealthy and developed countries, and now many underdeveloped countries and countries poorer than the United States have understood this concern. They have made great efforts to create a national policy to help families with daycare. These countries have felt that it was in the national interest to invest in both their current children and their children's children. This is an issue that was lost in the great health care and welfare reform debate.

If our working-class parents cannot find adequate and decent child care services while they continue to seek additional economic and professional growth, in many instances this growth becomes impossible. For example, we know of many couples who started working right after high school or after college, and after many years of hard work and dedication, they wanted to have children and raise a family. To do this both husband and wife had to work. When the children were born both parents had to continue working, so they chose daycare to help raise their children. For many, especially minorities, the decision to leave one's own children with total strangers is very painful and difficult.

Many young, two-parent-working families were faced with difficult decisions about daycare costs. For many it became an impossibility to pay for daycare services, and in many instances, this forced one parent to quit his (or more commonly, her) job. This was done because many couples were working simply to pay for the daycare service. It became financially necessary for one parent to stay home, but many soon realized the second wage earner's income was sorely needed. Today, this is the dilemma that many working-class and poor families continue to face. Can you imagine people on welfare seeking daycare services for their children while they go out and find work, or continue their education and/or training? This could literally become a nightmare. Yet it should be a national priority, if we are to compete with other developed nations, to provide comprehensive child care while parents become productive citizens.

While we have many good child care facilities and programs, ranging from simple "nanny" care, to the most advanced learning and developmental care programs, to after-school programs that care for our children even up to high school age, there is no national policy that prioritizes this issue of care for every person who may need it. As I have said, other countries have made child care a national priority with adequate policies and programs. Resources are provided by the country's policy makers to ensure that the child care is provided in a quality fashion that promotes appropriate child care development and is affordable to everyone that needs it. Some of these countries have had a national policy and provided some form of child care service for decades.

Policies in the United States should include community-oriented efforts with curriculums, staff, and services that are reflective of the populations and groups being served, and should be provided in a culturally based fashion. There are models of many successful programs, such as those affiliated with Head Start funding, among them the Parent Child Incorporated Program in San Antonio, Texas, and the "AVANCE" (advance) program headed by Dr. Gloria Rodriguez, who has been recognized by the White House. When working to develop the parenting skills of the disadvantaged, working poor, and minorities, access to child care has always been part of the solution. It would behoove our policy makers to study and learn from the experience of these programs and to evaluate the nation's current policies to address this serious problem.

Education, Employment, and Staffing

Along with the need for better policies in entitlement program practices and in providing child care, there is also a need for employment training and education to assist in the development of our community resources. Most important is the reevaluation of our current educational system. For many poor, minorities, and other disadvantaged groups, the system has in many instances failed. Just look at the current drop-out rates of minorities and other disadvantaged populations from high school, undergraduate, and higher education programs. Look also at the number of minority faculty in our institutions of higher learning, our research programs, and in the management and administration of both private and public entities . . . the numbers are dismal.

To further aid in the reduction of costs associated with current publicly funded programs and the overburdening of many of our society's present systems, policies should be created to meet our present and future employment and economic needs—that means training and educational programs. Unfortunately, our educational system continues to fail us, especially if you are minority and/or disadvantaged. Many of the reasons have already been discussed in the chapter about the need for cultural competency. These culturally based services will help make the present services and programs more accessible. Thus, the services and educational system will better prepare our youth and future workforce to meet the challenges of tomorrow's high-tech, fast-paced society.

Along with adequate support for child care, current policies in job training, educational curricula, and higher education need to be assessed and reevaluated. Are these programs and services truly reaching our minority and disadvantaged populations? If not, what do we need to do to adjust them, because as the face of America becomes more diverse, we need to ensure that these programs meet the needs of everyone. However, with the current trend of blaming all of the nation's woes on the poor and minorities, it is even more important that policy makers develop training and education programs that will assist this population to become more productive citizens. We can no longer turn our backs on minorities and disadvantaged groups, because, as we know, in many cases, they truly are the backbone of the nation. Yet our educational and employment practices many times seem to implement practices that are detrimental to the progress of these communities and that may actually hinder the progress of the nation.

Our policy makers must also consider staffing patterns in programs that serve minorities and other disadvantaged groups, for they must reflect the population whom they serve. Persons who provide any kind of social, health, and human services programs must do so in a culturally competent fashion, which may require additional training. If this is done, human services may become more appropriate and used more. The long-term benefits may be quite surprising!

It has already been mentioned that there are excellent programs that already provide culturally appropriate community-oriented services. Existing models of cultural competency have already proven their worth and should be considered by our policy makers. It is apparent that many of our public authorities are already considering different paradigms of providing social, health, and human services, which include cultural competency training, to address adequately the needs of minority populations.

We only hope that these efforts are not just a trend or fashion statement, but that they are truly incorporated in standard operating procedures. Furthermore, as these programs are implemented, we hope that our policy makers allow for flexibility in testing and implementation of these models. The recognition of diversity and cultural competency will only strengthen any effort to streamline our welfare system. Lastly, we hope that community-based organizations, both private and public, are included as part of the solution. These partnerships are essential in the decision-making equation.

Managed Care Services/Health Maintenance Organizations

Culturally based operating procedures and policies in some managed care programs have already improved health care services in a managed care setting. Policy makers must evaluate these results and continue to implement them in all of their services. Managed care services in the form of health maintenance organizations have already introduced and provided health care services in a new fashion. Most of the apparent changes were in the philosophy of promoting preventive care. While this sounds good in theory, HMOs were founded to provide services, for the most part, to "well persons." By so doing, associated health care costs would be lowered. The proponents of managed care assert that the cost savings would be passed on to the client/patient/consumer. All of the protocols, policies, and procedures were based on this wellness and prevention theory.

As patients became high risk for whatever medical reason, many disadvantaged persons were abandoned; we must guard against this result. On the business side, by dealing with well patients, profits were substantial. As health care costs continued to escalate and competition grew, so did the costs of managed care. Some employers could no longer afford this service to its employees in its present form and increased the premium portion of the employee. Even so, in many instances, it was more economical and often more beneficial to belong to a managed care/HMO program. But clients began to pay higher co-payments, and as HMOs became more cautious in their services and benefits, people became more uneasy.

Along with various public health initiatives, some large HMOs realized that offering culturally based services seemed to provide more positive results. This was accomplished by providing health education to assist patients in understanding their own health care, thus ensuring better use of health care services, and by lowering health care costs. Another important managed care action was to hire a more diverse group of minority workers who provided more appropriate, culturally based health care services. Outreach and marketing also targeted minorities; this effort helped increase the use of health care preventive services. It also promoted increased and better relations between employers and insurance companies, by selling them on the idea that if their workers were healthier, they would also be much happier, and consequently more productive.

To support this theory, various wellness programs were incorporated into managed care programs, some of which are health education, weight reduction, nutritional counseling, and wellness exams. Although this was not an entirely new form of health care delivery, it did promote a change in patients' attitudes toward health care delivery, and the concept began to grow. As more managed care programs are developed, and as the states take a more active part in this effort, there are certain requirements to keep in mind:

1. Ensure that these services include care for teenagers and the elderly.
2. Safeguard the benefits to poor and disadvantaged groups.

3. Provide appropriate health care services for the disabled.

4. Include nursing home health care, long term care, and rehabilitation care services.

5. Ensure the quality of health care with sound and adequate health care standards.

6. Ensure that the premiums of managed care services for the poor and other disadvantaged groups and minorities are fair and affordable.

7. Establish a system of arbitration and complaints that incorporates the consumer, especially disadvantaged groups and minorities.

8. Require that states provide special, dedicated resources to ensure that these services continue, even after the end of every fiscal year.

9. Ensure that these services incorporate consumer protection benefits and practices.

When the health care needs of minorities and other disadvantaged groups are addressed, we must also ensure that patients and/or clients understand what these services mean to them. The system must be fully explained to them in a way that they will understand and believe. This is especially true concerning enrollment, user, and benefits information. Cultural competency will be of great assistance when addressing these issues.

As the health care reform effort unraveled, policy makers began to evaluate and promote managed health care services for disadvantaged communities, the poor, and minorities. Some of these services were initiated through prenatal, newborn, pediatric, and elderly care programs. In an effort to better serve, minorities continued to be hired, and limited, culturally based bilingual programs were initiated and implemented. Because of this track record, states were directed to initiate managed care health programs for their publicly assisted entitlement health care program services.

Thus, every state began to evaluate its Medicaid and other publicly assisted health programs and determine how it was to initiate managed care services. Although well-intended services were planned, proposed, implemented, and accepted, states should still be careful in the development of their implementation strategies.

For example, policies should not be instituted that promote health care delivery systems different and separate from the present quality care services. It would not be ethical that managed care state and/or private programs and services change their quality of care standards because they are providing health care to minorities and the Medicaid population. On the contrary, if health care costs are the driving force, it makes more sense to develop comprehensive health care and prevention policies that incorporate culturally based services. This culturally based service must be provided through qualified training programs that support the hiring of a more diverse staff, one that more adequately reflects the population that is being served.

Some suggest that a two-tier private health care system already exists. This is what we need to avoid when managed health care programs for disadvantaged population and minorities are implemented. It would be a shame if this new service delivery mechanism also provided health care through a two-tier managed care system.

Policies should be instituted that safeguard those standards of quality care and at the same time promote culturally-based educational and prevention services. In addition, they should also increase their outreach and community-based efforts, if they are to make a sincere effort to assist in providing services to minority and poor populations. This is so important, because if the poor are asked to choose between a known service that they already trust and use, in many instances they may choose not to use the new system, especially if it is too foreign, not accessible, and not acceptable. Outreach policies must be included, as well as educational efforts that promote culturally based messages for both health care services and enrollment procedures.

Another very sensitive issue is the assignment of providers. Within poor communities, and especially within minority populations, traditional and historical providers and caregivers must be given a grace period to work with their patients and inform them of this new system called managed care. For many years and in many communities, there was only a handful of providers who served minorities and poor. These were both private and public caregivers, and community/migrant health centers as well. In many instances these are now, if not phased out completely, certainly being limited. Patients are confused, and are being asked to choose a new provider when they were used to the one in their neighborhood. These community and traditional health care providers must be incorporated into the policy decision making of how health care is going to be provided in this new world of managed care.

Another factor that needs to be included in the new world of managed care is the adequate provision of health care services to chronically ill patients, mental health patients, those with long-term disabilities, the elderly, and those with other special problems that may require additional secondary and tertiary health care services that managed care may not have traditionally covered.

A chapter has already been dedicated to the concerns of culturally based health care efforts for the elderly, especially minority elderly. If this is done, social, health, and human services in all aspects of care for the elderly will improve. As with the national tendency not to give the necessary attention to child care, so it is with care and attention to the elderly. For example, it was not until the Post-National White House Conference on Aging that the United States truly created a national policy on aging that addresses the special needs of our elderly. It is also recommended that additional policies in health care, social, and human services for the elderly be evaluated, new ones planned, recommended, and implemented. This is an important issue, since the United States population as a whole is aging. This factor alone obligates us to look at our present focus and emphasis, which primarily targets the young. Certainly as we live longer, more productive lives, the elderly become a crucial segment of our population.

Health Care Services

There are many issues in the health care policy arena that need attention; some of these may have briefly been discussed in the previous chapters, and others have not yet been mentioned at all. It is a shame that universal health care did not materialize; even though it was not the answer to every health care ill, it was a beginning. There are health care policy issues that merit further attention and decision making, especially in the area of minority health care services and standards. Some of these issues are health care concerns of many years' standing: adequate maternal and child health services, communicable disease control, infrastructure for these services, a weak public health service in many communities, and continued severely medically underserved areas, especially in the southwestern United States, rural America, and many inner city communities, to name a few.

Add to this the new and emerging public health care concerns and medical problems such as HIV/AIDS, Respiratory Syncytial Virus (RSV),

Hanta Virus, and other viral and bacterial diseases. Chemical and other toxin exposures such as lead exposure, and the more common occupational pesticide exposure, are also a major concern.

And what about other health care problems in many areas of South Texas and all along the United States–Mexico border? Conditions that are basic public health concerns, both old and new, such as the lack of basic sanitation; poor nutrition; communicable diseases such as tuberculosis and simple enteric (dysentery) diseases; as well as other occupational and environmental contaminant exposures are a serious concern. Many of these issues lack appropriate health care and prevention policies to address them at the local, state, and federal levels. These must be considered and put on the table as priority health care concerns.

For example, basic social and human needs as appropriate nutrition continue to plague us. Some of these health care concerns affected by inadequate nutritional intake should also cause our policy health makers to reevaluate current programs. Other direct or indirect exposures to developmental and nutritional factors should also be considered. Some of these nutrition-related issues that continue to affect proper growth and development, both in utero and after birth, include neural tube defects, slow psychosocial development, pica, and diarrhea. Many of these are related to poverty and social and economic conditions. This is especially true in certain populations, such as minorities and other disadvantaged populations, making this an important health care issue that merits additional policies and safeguards to protect our future children.

It seems that because of all of the modern technology available, we are able to keep our very premature neonates alive. The basic necessities of prenatal care (and therefore, use of procedures and technology to diagnose and prevent prematurity) may not be as accessible to our nation's poor, minority and other disadvantaged groups. If appropriate, timely, and culturally based services were made available as part of nationally mandated prenatal program policies, the use of these services might increase.

Even if these services were provided at an initially higher cost to the state health systems, they would probably be more cost effective in the long term, as they would greatly reduce costs and expenditures for later illness. Yet, we need to be reminded that all of the preventive health care services may not accomplish anything significant if the services are not used. Policies, therefore, should be established that require community action–based services. These should promote culturally based awareness methodologies, including nontraditional methodologies and procedures that facilitate the use of these health care services by the poor, minorities, and other disadvantaged groups.

Policies that promote the attachment of health care services to other services may need to be studied as alternative implementation procedures. However, incentives as reinforcement mechanisms and procedures should be cautiously avoided. Instead, other culturally based and community-oriented models should be explored, such as those that build on a person's pride, identity, and cultural awareness. This method may also require changing the service delivery paradigm. As mentioned before, minorities, especially Latinos, may be more inclined to use health care services that are provided in an atmosphere that respects the person's own language, customs, and traditions.

Although minorities and other disadvantaged groups recognize the importance of these health care services, many still do not use mainstream health care and preventive services. Part of the reason this happens is because they are too cumbersome to access, primarily as a result of a disassociated and fragmented health care delivery system. Policies that promote smaller outreach services, provided by local neighborhood clinics that support comprehensive health care instead of fragmented services, may also need to be explored. It makes no sense, and on the contrary could present barriers to health care delivery, to separate services. For example, a mother who takes her child for a wellness exam should be able to obtain not just the physical exam but also the appropriate immunizations, WIC/nutritional counseling, and other needed entitlement screening services. If possible and appropriate, exams should also be provided for other family members as well. These health care services should not pose a hardship or an added barrier to the families of disadvantaged populations. If there is to be continuity and use of the health care system, especially when we consider minorities, services should be provided in a pleasant manner, leaving a positive experience for the patient and family members.

Any time a disadvantaged person or minority receives health care, health educational information should always be offered in conjunction with the health care service received. Often the information will help the person better understand the examination or preventive health care recommendation. This effort allows for more interactive participation in the patient's health. In fact, the more a person learns about his or her health status, the healthier he or she could be on the long term. Other care components that need to be included are dental and vision screening exams. These, too, should be part of wellness and preventive health care policies.

Serious dental and visual conditions have been overlooked too often and should always be included in health care policies for disadvantaged populations. Although there will be opponents to this proposal of "one stop health care" delivery, it could be proposed as an option to the patient/client. For many publicly assisted clients, this could be a desirable means of health care delivery. Furthermore, the object of this type of service delivery is to remove barriers to access and if this is an acceptable means for some, then it should be provided.

Another form of delivery for maternal and child health services is to establish programs in frequently visited places away from home such as schools. Data support school-based clinics and health care services as an efficient and cost-effective method of providing health care services, especially to minorities and disadvantaged populations. Both parents and children are a prime and captive patient population. There are already various types of school-based efforts throughout the United States. Some have been in existence since the late 1970s and have a proven track record in providing health care services to students and disadvantaged populations.

The increased use of preventive health care services, the creation of better health awareness, and in many cases, quicker and more efficient medical and health interventions when needed, underscore their success. Occasionally, serious health care problems have been detected at an early stage through screening and other school-based preventive health care services. Some of these conditions have been hearing and visual problems, upper respiratory conditions, chronic urinary tract infections, osteomuscular problems, and some congenital defects.

Other social, mental, and crucial and acute health care services such as immunizations, teen pregnancy care, and other needed health care counseling have been provided quite successfully through these school-based clinics and services. With minorities and other disadvantaged populations, school-based health care services could also provide care for other family members, especially younger siblings, the student's parents, the faculty, and the faculty's children. This is an example of true community-based health care services. A policy that supports the establishment of community/school-based efforts should also be explored to support this effort. Another aspect of this effort for many disadvantaged populations and underserved communities could be the promotion of health professions. These clinics could involve the student's participation and expose them to health careers. For many this could be an opportunity to learn from close role models and friendly faces what health professions are all about. With the continued current crisis of medically underserved areas and the need for minority health professionals, this may be another educational pipeline strategy.

Other policies that need to be evaluated are those that provide basic health care services to populations such as those that live on the United States–Mexico border. Although there have been great improvements in the health care status of border residents, many continue to face the same adverse health conditions that affected many communities at the turn of the century, such as a lack of sanitation that many times promotes dysenteric gastroenteritis. These unsanitary conditions could prove to be very serious, especially for small children, the elderly, and the frail

Other diseases, such as rabies and hepatitis A, may not be unique to the border area; however, in states such as Texas, the rates for these health conditions have always been higher along the border. One main cause for these health conditions is because an adequate infrastructure supporting a good system of health care delivery and prevention does not exist. Furthermore, the preventive public health services and health education that are so urgently needed in these communities is often not inadequate to respond in an efficient and timely manner.

When the North American Free Trade Agreement (NAFTA) was approved, many who were skeptical of the trade agreement at least felt that it could be an opportunity to provide additional resources to enhance the current infrastructure, or to build new and better ones for this very forgotten and ignored area. Many had high hopes that the side agreements by the three countries would provide some relief. Some policies, procedures, and proposed legislative mandates were very promising. This was especially true between Mexico and the United States, as federal and state agencies of both countries were obligated to evaluate current health and environmental conditions in partnership.

Preventive health and public health policies that promote epidemiological surveillance, disease investigation, and applied research; health education; and the implementation of sanitation services and practices are a few of the health care services that were proposed and whose progress needs to be followed. In addition, the implementation of such basic services as water chlorination, waste water treatment, and the construction of proper drainage and sewer systems, are equally important policy health issues. Other air, land, and soil contamination prevention methodologies were also explored, recommended, and proposed as implementation strategies for prevention and good public health measures.

More important were the partnerships that border states developed with Mexico to stop the spread of communicable diseases and possible environmental contaminants. There is no better example than the efforts of local communities, sister cities, and official organizations such as the United States–Mexico Border Health Association. Both entities have for years tried to promote better social, health, and human conditions along the United States–Mexico border through various joint efforts in prevention, surveillance, and communicable disease control.

As an example of cooperative endeavors toward prevention and health care services, the following recommendations were proposed at a joint binational meeting of health and environmental care local and state officials in San Antonio, Texas, on January 1995.

1. Establish official communication links between state officials and, even more importantly, between state, local, and health authorities. Such links are vital in ensuring cooperation and coordination.

2. Establish a rapid and efficient system for the exchange of health information and epidemiological data, especially for the purpose of disease control and for the exchange of immunizations records.

3. Coordinate joint activities that share promotional and human services and resources.

4. Update and exchange a binational list of local health authorities along the United States–Mexico border.

5. Formal agreements between the states should be explored.

6. Allow the exchange of information about infectious diseases, toxic exposures, and other emergencies within forty-eight hours to the proper health authorities on both sides of the border.

7. Install a border health and environmental laboratory that would share epidemiological information, training, and the evaluation and study of hazardous and toxic substances.

8. Develop a joint plan of action to address toxic substances emergencies and hazardous material management training, education, and prevention.

Other issues in health care delivery, emergency care, poison control, and enhanced immunizations and surveillance were always part of the policy discussion.

However, a very important and innovative educational and community effort was to train and teach local grassroot persons to provide and promote preventive health care services. This was especially true for these seriously medically underserved areas. Learning from the Mexican public health system of training "Promotores De Salud" (promoters of health), an effort was made to help communities by building self-determination.

These efforts consisted of training a small group of community lay persons in various health care preventive measures, such as prenatal care, sanitation, immunization, hygiene, communicable diseases, and pesticide and toxin exposure prevention. These were just a few of the services that would be taught. These persons in turn would then be charged with training and teaching other community groups. Although this is highly practiced not just in Mexico, but in many underdeveloped and poor countries, this is not so in the United States.

We would, however, recommend it as an alternative throughout many of the underserved areas in many other parts of the United States. High rates of disease, lack of health care, and high rates of mortality and morbidity among disadvantaged populations and minorities could be strikingly reduced. In addition, the health care costs for primary care emergencies and tertiary care could be drastically less.

Our policy makers, federal, state, and local health and human services authorities should be encouraged to reexamine the current system of health care delivery for this forgotten area, and to study the current recommendations made from several organizations such as: Environmental Protection Agency (EPA), Border Initiative, National Institute of Environmental Health Services (NIEHS), Centers for Disease Control and Prevention (CDC), State Departments of Health, Health Resources, and Services Administration (HRSA), Border Health Task Force, and many other governmental agencies and task forces.

Although there is already a movement to better coordinate and communicate between these organizations so they can enhance and maximize services, more needs to be done, especially as relates to funding and programs. There are many occasions when both federal and state agencies and programs duplicate efforts and examine, compete, and implement the same services or address the same concern. As communities, community-based organizations, and other local health care services that receive public funding are asked to maximize, avoid duplication, become innovative and creative, and develop partnerships with different private and public providers, so should our governmental authorities.

Mental Health and Substance Use/Abuse Programs

Much of what has already been discussed has significant policy implications for the mental health care delivery system. When we consider health care for disadvantaged populations and minorities, we should always consider the basic public health philosophy of care for the total self: the well-being of the psycho-social-mental-physical being. If this concept of what many call "bienestar" were promoted and practiced, preventive health and educational services would always include mental and psychosocial care. It is these services that many times provide the added support needed for many of our disadvantaged populations.

We have already discussed our elderly health and human care services, which also need this total comprehensive approach. Although there are services already in place that provide some mental health and social services along with routine health care, they are the exception and not the rule. Policy makers must ensure that a system of health care exists that looks at a different paradigm of health care services.

The current mental health delivery system for disadvantaged populations has not been too sensitive or accessible to these groups. Mental health should be regarded as another part of routine family health care that merits culturally based approaches which reflect the local community's characteristics, customs, culture, and language. It should also be understood that to many minorities and disadvantaged, mental health care services are not a priority; however, mental health services may be just the support system that they need.

In addition, when one views mental health services for disadvantaged populations, minorities, and the poor, one must also consider those additional factors that may contribute to the actual mental health problem or concern. Some of these may involve the family; for instance, substance use/abuse and unemployment. If we choose to treat only the disease and not consider the other social and environmental factors, we may provide only minimal, "Band-Aid" services. Therefore, the mental health concern, problem, and/or disease may continue, until the underlying cause of the problem is discovered and treated. This can also apply to physical causes of mental and neuro-psychosocial health problems. What health care policies of the future must consider is that man is totally connected to his surroundings, and anything that affects them may affect his health. This, for many, is a totally new concept, and could certainly cause a great deal of discussion and thought-provoking methodologies of care for the future.

Whatever the concern in health care delivery for disadvantaged populations, the poor, and minorities, policies should be established that take into account the diversity and uniqueness of our present and future population. Policy makers should also consider incorporating prevention and early intervention, along with strong community-oriented programs. Cultural competency and acceptance of differences should be recognized and accepted. Training and educational models that provide cultural competency services and technical assistance should become part of routine social, health, and human services delivery, especially as society demographics change. Historical and routine care service, such as outreach and home health care, and more community-action services that include consumers and providers alike in the decision making, could provide innovative, cost effective, and efficient services in the long term.

References

Arizona–Mexican Border Foundation. *Policy planning for substance abuse prevention at the U.S.–Mexican border.* (1993, October 22).

Bautista, D. H. (1990, September 27–28). *Defining the Mexican American population: Changing demographics.* Los Angeles: Chicano Studies Research Center, UCLA.

Border Substance Abuse Policy Workshop. (1993, October 22,). CHPD, San Antonio, TX.

Center for Health Policy Development. (1994, November 18). *Hispanics in the Southwest and migrant health issues.* National Advisory Council on Migrant Health at the Fourth Annual Midwest Migrant Stream Forum. San Antonio, TX.

Center for Health Policy and Development. *Hispanics in the Southwest and substance abuse prevention.* San Antonio, TX.

Congress of the United States Subcommittee on Legislation and National Security of the House of Representatives Committee on Government Operations. (1990, April 3).

Consumer Union of the United States. (1995, November). *Waiver request pending on Medicaid vote.* Austin, Texas.

Department of Health and Human Services. (1993, March). *The Surgeon General's Regional Meeting on Hispanic/Latino Health: Public Health Regions VI & VIII Final Meeting Proceedings.* San Antonio, TX.

House offers broad Medicaid plan. (1995, May 17). *Austin American Statesman.* Austin, TX.

Innovations. (1995). *The Hopkins Managed Care Program.* Baltimore: John Hopkins University.

Innovations. (1995). *HMOs and HIV: The Managed Care Revolution.* Baltimore: John Hopkins University.

Mahoney, E. & Critlender, R.A. (1995, November). *Helping states increase primary care that is affordable, available, and appropriate.* National Academy for State Health Policy.

Moy, E. & Bartman, B.A. (1995, May 17). Physician race and care of minority and medically indigent patients. *JAMA,* 273(19).

Muller, C. *A window on the past:* The position of the client in twentieth-century public health thought and practice. *American Journal of Public Health,* vol. II.

National Coalition of Hispanic Health and Human Services Organizations (COSSMHO). (1984). *Meeting the health promotion needs of Hispanic communities.* Washington, D.C., COSSMHO Publications.

National Institute of Medicine. (1988). *The future of public health.* Washington, D.C.: National Academy Press.

National Task Force on Health Care Reform, UCLA. (1993, April 6). *Mexican American and other Latinos in the United States: Unique families in need of a quality health care delivery system.* San Antonio, TX. Center for Health Policy Development.

The Pew Health Professions Commission. (1995, December). *The critical challenges: Revitalizing the health professions for the twenty-first century.* San Francisco, CA.

Samuel T. O. (1984.) *Annual Session of the American Association of Dental Schools, Dental Education in the Future.* New Orleans.

Star health plan. (1996). Austin, TX. Texas Department of Health.

The Texas Health Promotion Planning Committee. (1991, June). *The context of health care in Texas.* San Antonio, TX: Center for Health Policy Development.

TXMHMR. (1996). *Managed care in texas mental health and mental retardation.* Austin, TX: Author.

Underrepresented minorities in the health professions. (1990, March). The seventh report to the President and Congress on the status of health personnel.

White House Conference on Aging Policy Committee. (1995, May 2–5). *Official 1995 White House Conference on Aging: Adopted Resolutions.* Washington D.C.

CHAPTER 11

Twenty-First–Century Perspectives on Cultural Competency

Aliki Coudroglou (1995), in a book review titled "The Elusive Human Rights," makes several important points regarding the ways American society handles social problems. Some of these points are quite useful as contextual background for this piece. Coudroglou informs us that:

1. Despite decades of social policy revisions, our society remains unable to deal effectively with social problems;

2. Even as the era of the "global village"—to use a phrase that has become commonplace—dawns, the United States has embarked on yet another internal confrontation;

3. This society espouses social contracts while dismantling social institutions;

4. Despite new understanding of the need to "eradicate" human suffering, social policies in this country, paradoxically, have not changed to fit such need.

These points are well taken and must be seriously considered, especially when one deals with notions of efficiency and cost-containment in health, social, and human services. Although an effort to contain costs and increase efficiency is warranted, it must be attempted with the above points in mind so as not to further victimize those who have chronically been denied the life amenities shared by the more fortunate. Our society must develop a new understanding of what constitutes efficiency and how to balance cost containment against need. Solely using economic definitions is cynical and cuts spending by destroying the safety net for those who have no other protection. These measures are often couched in sociopolitical ideologies that, although beautiful in theory, cause real suffering when applied to real people. One must also be alert to the fact that all too often cost containment and efficiency are done so that resources will change hands, benefiting the few and causing hardships to the many. Instead, one must think of cost containment and efficiency that will save resources, which will revert to the system and be translated into better services and greater well-being for those who must rely on it.

As we delve into the task of offering insights into the subject matter of this chapter, we will refrain from breaking up the flow of ideas with frequent citations. The subject matter tends to be somewhat dense, but needs to be understood by those who provide services to the chronically underserved. Maintaining the flow of ideas unbroken by frequent citations can be useful. So, unless absolutely necessary to cite sources in the body of this chapter, the citations will be found in the References.

Current Climate in the Health, Social, and Human Services

Contemporary dominant political ideology, coupled with economic and social imperatives, signals preference for certain budgetary measures at federal, state, and local levels. Thus, hearing of proposed cuts in Medicaid is now common; as well as proposed reductions in spending for higher education; reduction in public assistance benefits; proposed cuts in emergency food assistance, family planning services, youth services, adult protective services, domestic violence programs, family preservation programs (Federation of Protestant Welfare Agencies, 1996), and more. Analogous to a domino-type effect, federal spending cuts in entitlement programs trigger states' proportional cuts in matching funds for the same programs. The same applies to spending at the local level, as it is dependent on state aid. Political passage of personal and business tax cuts produces revenue shortfalls rendering governments cash-poor and unable to support programs at previous levels, which further compounds the problem. (Public opinion has not corroborated the ideological position that government should have a small role in the lives of the citizenry. Public opinion has consistently come out for government involvement. Since in a democracy public opinion prevails, the political establishment should start to reflect such opinion more truthfully.) Often protected in the past, social and human services have become prime candidates for the chopping block.

Federal government cutbacks in health and social service programs are all too real. States contribute their share of cutbacks, provide block grants for social services, and enroll their Medicaid recipients wholesale in managed care. Block grants and managed care are examples of the exercise of fiscal efficiency. In block grants, a certain amount of money, arrived at somewhat arbitrarily, is earmarked to be spent in a general area of care, for example, foster care. However, the specific way funds are to be allocated to the various types of services within foster care is left to the discretion of those managing the funds. Allocating funding in this manner often means that such funds are below the level estimated as necessary to maintain previous levels of service. Therefore, painful choices must be made by giving services differential priorities according to subjectively or, less often, objectively assigned value. Such economic efforts, to succeed, require standardization and depersonification (Bauer & Koenigsberg, 1996) of both patient and health care professional. This transforms the roles of both. (We are aware that referring to health care professionals, social care professionals, human services professionals, etc., as "providers" is part of the current trend toward depersonification and standardization of the professions. We continue the practice because the term is used in technical parlance, a better term does not occur to me, and identifying each specific profession at every opportunity would be too cumbersome in a piece directed to a broad audience.)

Managed care strives for fiscal efficiency through shifting financial risks to providers and through use of the concept of capitation as opposed to fee-for-service. Since the range and number of services to be provided is limited and subject to approval, the theory goes, money will be saved while sparing people the waste of unnecessary services. On the other hand, in a continued effort to further cut costs and remain profitable, managed cares, by fiat, cut services their administrators do not understand or that they deem unnecessary and, therefore, wasteful, but that providers consider essential and cost effective.

"Etiological" Discussion

How did it get to be this way? Jack Schoenholtz (1996), in an excellent article titled "Reversing Managed Denial," gives useful directions toward answering this question. I base my efforts here on his enlightened discussion. In the early 1970s the government mistakenly placed emphasis on cost containment, rather than illness containment. The prevailing but flawed idea was that people's health could be maintained and disease could be prevented without an action plan to end poverty, poor education, and unemployment (and obviously, their consequences). This fundamental turn of events opened the way to just the health and social policies that are so en vogue today.

In 1972, in an effort to change the impact of President Lyndon Johnson's social policies legacy, President Richard Nixon signed the HMO Act. He also made cost containment the heart of public health policy.

Health insurance coverage was allocated in a faulty manner; many geographical locations were underserved. Tens of millions of young, healthy employees, who would have otherwise shunned coverage, flocked to the new opportunities offered by HMOs. The concept of health maintenance, worked out without plans for illness containment, was the vehicle for maintaining and enlarging the risk population without spreading the cost of the illnesses detected. This result is the opposite of what traditional insurance strives for. In 1974, during President Gerald Ford's tenure and over his veto, congress passed the ERISA (Employee Retirement Income Security Act) to bring under federal control pension, health, and welfare benefit plans, organizing under this system state laws that offered minimal protection to beneficiaries. ERISA defined self-insured welfare benefits as noninsurance and exempted them from state regulation. In 1981, investment-grade interest rates for insurers took a downward turn, making it too risky for large insurance companies to stay in the indemnity/risk business. The companies abandoned such business but accepted providing risk-free administrative management for ERISA plans. The new arrangements made it possible for insurance companies to manage not only their gross premium income but also their losses, through manipulating the amount of health care expended. This double-edged management made the issue of speculative risk for managed care a nonstarter. In a climate like this, the result was the now all-too-familiar move away from a socially relevant system of health care funding—insurance indemnified risk—to a business model, which encourages speculation and has as its highest goal the production of income and profit. Enter managed care, which offers insurance based on price negotiations, relying on what managed care defines as medical necessity.

During the Reagan-Bush years insurance companies went into the HMO business, founding some managed care organizations still currently in evidence on the national scene. The same benefits and risk exemption discussed earlier also applied to these organizations. Naturally, such organizations are interested—and do succeed to some degree—in influencing government to make national health care policies modeled after their own way of doing business.

Despite all its business sense, managed care has been subjected of late to serious criticism. It has restricted services according to arbitrary rules that appeared contemptuous of patients' well-being to the point of causing public anxiety, such as discharging women from the maternity ward within one day of delivery; making and enforcing "gag rules" on doctors who are ordered not to inform patients about expensive tests and procedures; making enormous profits bound to keep shareholders happy, but not returning some profits to the pot to benefit clients; and giving their CEOs extremely high salaries. The question arises: Will managed care eventually reduce society's costs? The question remains to be answered.

Nevertheless, to be fair, one must acknowledge that expenses in the health and human services have been growing at alarming rates, coming dangerously close to the brink of unaffordability. The current changes, perhaps transitional, are tailored to replace a system most people have been critical of. So there are no tried and true models that can be put up, against which to measure current changes and judge the wisdom of making them. Providers are thus reduced to reacting, feeling alarmed by real threats to their ability to render services for those who need them, especially the poor. Providers have a strong sense of what is likely not to work. (Some current changes are likely not to work, since their premise is flawed, as discussed above.) Still, providers accept the need to curb excesses and control costs. In other words, safety net providers (*Opening Doors*, Winter, 1996) see the need for change, but are concerned with the direction current changes are taking our society as they threaten, in the long run, the well-being of the needy through emphasizing short-term savings, and profit through limiting service rather than through illness control. Safety net providers can foresee higher future expenditures to provide services for said populations if their members are allowed to deteriorate because of short-sighted underserving.

More on the Meaning of Current Policy Changes

Safety net providers are concerned about such a profound change in social policy in America today. Caring for the poor, they see a definite threat to the scope of care they can continue to provide in the future. Many essential services currently provided do not figure as part of the vocabulary of managed care. Managed care determines what constitutes appropriate care by controlling the purse strings.

Psychosocial support, patient and community outreach, patient education, family planning counseling, and help that are culturally sensitive as well as cross-culturally competent, are among essential, efficient services not particularly understood as such by managed care. These services, complementary to standard medical care, are provided as an addition to such care. Safety net care providers are concerned that such services are going to be the first casualties of the managed care war on waste. After all, managed care is a system built to limit services as a means of controlling costs. Thus, services that cannot be directly justified as essential tend to be discouraged and denied outright. Given that managed care shifts risk to providers, the latter will tend to be, perhaps, too cautious to offer services that almost certainly won't be paid for. Safety net providers, who see these services as essential and cost efficient, fear serious and costly long-term repercussions, although recognizing that there will be short-term, short-sighted savings.

At this point we come back to the suggestion that current changes in health and human services are part of a transitional period. It is imperative that we do this within the context of being realistic: Health and human services have been targeted for the chopping block. It is quite possible that other developments will temper the current changes; some may be abandoned all together. The attempt to be realistic, however, requires consideration of some ideas. First, it must be reiterated that there is no turning back to the way things used to be. That way has been rejected and replaced to some degree. Second, since the model that replaced it is still being sorted out and smoothed over, a transitional period is upon us. Far from inspiring nihilism, a defeatist attitude, this transition signals opportunities for safety net providers to design and deliver effective, cost-efficient, necessary services to those who need them. They should resist being told which services are necessary and must be convincing through persuasive arguments. They must also reach needed consensus on which services are important and why. All of this—and more—demands that safety net providers adapt to the new climate and be prepared to overcome adversity. Every indication exists that the future is far from certain. The best one can do is develop a high level of adaptability, never losing sight of one's individual mission and the mission of the collective, the profession to which one belongs. This is a reasonable response to a system that may be in flux for a long time to come. This proactive stance stresses one's preparedness to make sound decisions at difficult crossroads. Safety net providers are liable to travel many such crossroads as the sweeping changes in the health and human services continue.

About Efficiency

Efficiency, in the context of the social and human services, is currently defined in economic terms as ways of saving money. After all, shareholders, employers, the state, or any other person or organization that has a stake in the process, has interest in savings. Society as a whole is also expected to want savings, as suggested by the principle of scarce resources. This principle says that resources are finite and therefore, expenditures on something will drain resources, detracting from the ability to spend on something else. Thus, spending on "safety net" services will detract from other expenditures. However, as stated before, safety net services can be highly efficient and cost effective through providing the means for the chronically underserved to acquire long-term viability. An illustrative example of what adopting a longer view can help accomplish is provided below in the subsection on preserving culturally relevant neighborhood clinics. It is also very important to note that safety net services have a human value that cannot be given a material price. This ought never to be forgotten.

Adopting a broader definition of efficiency to go beyond economics and to include other social parameters is a good starting point in reviving a social conscience in policy making in the area. Being realistic and working with the changes to soften their harsh edges is also imperative, rather than fighting a losing battle while failing to adapt and overcome difficulties. Since the system is in transition, opportunities exist to influence outcomes and the direction of change itself.

For the twenty-first century, efficiency should be conceptually revisited to encompass the inclusion and maintainance of a sense of human and social usefulness and social conscience.

Efficiency and Cost Containment

What about embarking on the treacherous terrain of making predictions for the twenty-first century? Unfortunately, we are not blessed with the ability to predict the future; nor do we have a crystal ball that works reliably. So we will refrain from making clairvoyant pronouncements, focusing on providers humanely shaping a possible future by being action-oriented now.

Analyses made thus far suggest that current changes will have great impact on the future. Therefore it is necessary that those with a social conscience do their best to influence the process. That is, those who provide services and therefore know what is needed should participate in steering the process of change in a direction that makes sense; not only economic sense, but social sense. Promoting fiscal responsibility is socially useful only in the context of preserving essential services for those who need them. The notion of what is essential should come from consensus achieved by professionals, rather than from uninformed actions of gatekeepers. Essential services should be: (1) addressed to meet specific individual needs, (2) culturally relevant, (3) community based, and (4) aimed at nurturing and supporting sound development of individuals and families. Rather than something to be achieved through underserving—rationing or denying essential services for short-term profits—efficiency ought to be defined as what works best for the lowest cost for a given condition, factoring in consumer choice and satisfaction. To achieve this in a stable way capable of surviving into the next century, safety net providers need to be active in several fronts, exercising their leadership, creativity, and persistence. In what follows, we detail only some of them, leaving to the reader the task of bringing the list closer to completion.

Educate Consumers and Do Community Outreach

People who use the system are entitled to know what their rights are. A community's perception of its health needs and its actual health status ought to be known by safety net providers working with such communities. Care provided can then be tailored to specific needs. Consumers of care will thus be helped in a tangible fashion and will tend to have increased loyalty to community care providing organizations.

Be Politically Active

Many decisions that affect providers and the people they care for are political. Therefore, providers must be politically alert and active to the maximum extent of their ability. Keeping pace with political activity in one's professional area and working for or against political actions in the area according to what one's conscience dictates, is often good preventive strategy. A provider who does this is also a powerful community advocate. He or she knows the needs of the community and will have those in mind when doing battle in the political arena. Naturally, this stance is potentially quite efficient as it supports care for those who need it; and cost effective as it comes out on the side of needy community members without cost-inflating political ulterior motives.

Educate Managed Care Companies

To consistently provide care to those who need it is quite a difficult task that requires the involvement of complex organizational structures. Logically, given that managed care is a newcomer in this arena but a de facto player, it needs to be brought in and appropriately educated. Safety net care providers should be the educators. They understand the needs of the community and know how to meet them in a cost-effective manner. To play this role, providers need to adapt to significant changes in the playing field so that their responses can meet expectations while opening new grounds. One example is to convince managed care organizations that certain services which such organizations are likely to ignore are essential and cost effective and therefore must be provided. Having technical expertise is no longer sufficient; one must also identify problems and continue to correct or remedy them. It is also important to establish that services provided are necessary, valid, reliable, and cost effective. Solid community orientation coupled with outcome research and consensus building among providers is essential to accomplish this task. Information gathered at the community level, experience, consensually validated interventions, results of outcome studies, and the like, have the potential to be powerful tools in convincing managed care to financially support the treatments and programs providers consider essential. This support will tend to endure, freeing providers to concentrate in pushing the envelope further on behalf of the care-receiving population.

Providers ought to participate in regional and national workshops and work toward the development of valid, generalizable practice guidelines, within the purview of each profession.

Preserve Culturally Relevant Neighborhood Clinics

Cultural relevance and appropriateness in the delivery of social and health services are important enough to warrant making them a running theme in this book. Let us amplify the concept of culture to encompass the typical ways that smaller communities think, feel, and behave. For example, East Harlem, New York, is an ethnic neighborhood which, though not monolithic by any means, has codes of behavior that, though unspoken, are quite predictable. Certain communities react predictably, vote predictably, and handle social matters consistently over time. These cultural dimensions should be paid attention to, if professional work done in these communities is to be successful.

Neighborhood community agencies have been providing culturally relevant, sensitive, and appropriate services for many years. Some of these agencies are the sole care providers for a sizable portion of the surrounding population. If these culturally adept neighborhood clinics are allowed to die in the name of "efficiency," and neighborhood people are shifted to where rationed care will be centrally provided to save money in the short run, there will likely be an ominous side effect. People will be liable to wait longer to seek care they need or forfeit care all together. Naturally, this will produce deceptive short-term savings, since people will underutilize resources. On the other hand, the population in question, already distressed and chronically displaced, will tend to become sicker, and therefore bound to use overwhelmingly more resources in the long run. Factor into the equation the attendant human suffering; the development of chronic, intractable problems; and the demoralization of the population thus manipulated, and the wisdom of those short-sighted, short-term savings becomes seriously questionable. So preserving culturally proficient neighborhood clinics is the truly cost-efficient way to go.

Promote Diversity in Health Care Management

The premise here is simple. It is highly desirable, socially wise, technically and cost efficient, and culturally sensitive to recruit more ethnically and racially diverse health care managers and administrators. This is especially true when consideration is given to increasing the number of traditionally underrepresented minorities in such positions.

Programs should be set up that identify early, qualified members of underrepresented minorities entering the field, provide them with the appropriate education, including leadership-skills training in the area, and mentoring opportunities. The goal is to produce professionals who can be empathic to users of the system, providing for their needs, and can work efficiently with insurers, policy makers, businesses, and government. Graduates should then be teamed up with employment through professional placement programs. For furthering their careers, comprehensive but focused continuing education should also be available.

Diminish Barriers to Care

There should be no barriers between people and needed care. In the United States the health and human services are so advanced that, conceivably, one can get whatever care one needs, but unfortunately, many people are left wanting for care, particularly those chronically left at society's margins, like the poor and underserved. Clearly, lack of access to needed care worsens the conditions care should resolve or mitigate, which will later require dire, costlier measures for their management. This is analogous to dying of thirst a few feet from the river. These few feet are barriers to care. At other times these barriers are more like an abyss; like looking from above at the flowing, life-giving river in the unreachable depths of a canyon.

Barriers to care are cost inefficient and come with serious social costs and demoralization of community members and, sometimes, the demoralization of whole deprived communities. So, providers must spare no effort in breaking down barriers to care. The first step is identifying such barriers. Next comes classification (economic, geographic, psychologic, or socio-cultural); how far do they reach? do they single out a specific sector of the community like women or children? and so forth.

Research

Needs-assessment studies and treatment-outcome research must be done, with results being compared across regional and state lines. The prime emphasis of such studies ought to be on what helps most, where it is indicated, and how cost efficient it is, and only secondarily on cost containment per se. Thus, length of treatment has to be variable, since different people respond differently to similar interventions.

In this context, cost efficiency must not be reckless cost containment, which leads to underserving. Cost efficiency must be measured against the societal costs, economic and otherwise, of the condition and the long-term costs of potential chronicity, which has a social price tag.

Build Demonstration Projects

Demonstration projects are useful in that they are a microcosm which can be controlled and fine-tuned before being generalized. They need to be organized so that cookie-cutter approaches are rejected; so that individuals are given timely access to specific services and are matched to the best intervention tailored to their needs; and so that the intervention program will produce enduring results. They must be carefully planned so as never to cut corners and compromise quality of care for the bottom line.

As mentioned above, we refrain from making pronouncements about the future, usually a risky business and riskier still as we consider something that is in so much flux as are health and human services. Suffice it to say that these services have been targeted for the chopping block, which suggests difficult times ahead. Rather than rolling over and playing dead—an attitude dictated by hopelessness and helplessness—safety net providers should take action now to fashion and secure a role for themselves in providing necessary services for the population, especially for those who need such services the most and have chronically had limited access to them. Safety net providers are the experts and should have a major say on what services are necessary. Action now will preserve this role in the future. Action must be focused, authoritative, and based on consensus at local, state, regional, and national levels. Also, safety net providers must take a multidimensional approach in their quest to retain and provide the relevant services desperately needed in the communities they serve. To this end, we offer a short, incomplete list of action points, mere suggestions of what to do, as they occurred to us. Safety net providers should expand on the list, tailoring it to what is most relevant in their specific area of endeavor.

References

Bollas, C., & Sundelson, D. (1995). *The new informants: The betrayal of confidentiality in psychoanalysis and psychotherapy.* Northvale, NJ: Aronson.

Center for Substance Abuse Treatment, Substance Abuse and Mental Health Services Administration. Washington, DC: U.S. Department of Health and Human Services (1995, Spring). Memo to the field from CSAT's treatment improvement exchange, T.I.E. communique.

Coudroglou, A. (1996, March). The elusive human rights. *Readings, 11*(1), 18–22.

Johnson, L.D. (1995). *Psychotherapy in the age of accountability.* New York: Norton.

Mechanic, D., Schlesinger, M., & McAlpine, D.D. (1995). Management of mental health and substance abuse services: State of the art and early results. *Milbank Quarterly, 73*(1), 19–55.

Poynter, W.L. (1995). *The preferred providers handbook: Building a successful private therapy practice in the managed care marketplace.* New York: Brunner/Mazel.

The Robert Wood Johnson Foundation and The Henry J. Kaiser Family Foundation. *Opening doors. Reducing sociocultural barriers to health care.*

Schoenholtz, J.C. (1995). Reversing managed denial. *Academy Forum, 40*(1, 2), 4–6.

Siberio, M. (1995, November 17). *Considerations for implementing managed care in the New York City children's welfare system.* A working draft report of the New York City Task Force on Managed Care in Child Welfare. Cosponsored by Federation of Protestant Welfare Agencies, and Children's Defense Fund, New York.

CHAPTER 12

Conclusion

The challenge, as the twenty-first century is within arm's reach, is for all people to understand that the world we once knew is rapidly changing and that we must decide how to get along and help one another. Cooperation is essential for the preservation of humanity and of the life-sustaining environment, whether one considers fairly homogeneous societies or diverse ones. Nevertheless, to be useful, analyses and recommendations must address specific societies or characteristic aspects of a given society. To that end this book addresses American pluralistic society and its cultural components.

Projections exist that in the United States by the year 2,000, currently underrepresented minorities will make up more than 40 percent of the work force in the health, social, and human services. Consequently, human service professionals and health care practitioners are urged to endeavor in some pertinent broad areas: (1) To ensure that services provided are relevant to and needed by the community; (2) To manage ethnic diversity to provide majority and bicultural workers in the health, social, and human services organizations with a measure of balance; (3) To ensure training of a multiculturally competent and sensitive staff, at ease with each other and with ethno-culturally diverse patients. Furthermore, particular attention should be paid to the specific ethnic makeup and evolving nature of specific communities when programs are designed and implemented, so as to ensure a good fit.

The four ethnic minority groups highlighted in this book share one dominant characteristic: a very strong family orientation. So, when working with migrant families, for example, practitioners must address any erosion of family structure while assessing effects of migration and levels of cultural assimilation that individual members and the family unit exhibit.

Health care professionals should understand culture-bound syndromes; individual and community reliance on indigenous practitioners; and effects of traditional treatments and their ethno-cultural relevance for the community. They should also ascertain the prevalence of mental illness.

Why Cultural Competency?

People see and understand the world through their culture. It follows that people can best be reached through their culture. *Healthy People 2000: National Health Promotion and Disease Prevention Objectives* (U.S. Dept. of Health and Human Services, 1991) calls for significant improvements in the health status of the entire American population by the turn of the century. It outlines three goals: (1) to increase the span of a healthy life for all Americans; (2) to reduce health disparities among Americans; and (3) to achieve access to preventive services for all Americans. Achievement of these goals is especially important for ethnic-racial minorities and other underserved populations.

In a report to the seventy-fourth Texas Legislature, the Office of Minority Health of the Texas Department of Health shows that racial and ethnic health perceptions and health behaviors are often unconventional when compared with what modern medicine has led one to expect. Not taking this into account may hinder practitioners' efforts at health promotion and healing.

It is essential for good outcome that professionals understand the culturally based preferences of the people they serve. For instance, what alternative treatments are patients receiving or inclined to seek? what services are culturally acceptable? Key areas that merit professionals' attention include:

1. Often, African-American communities' views of health and illness differ from those of the general American population. These differences are related to their cultural African heritage and are not a deliberate ploy to confound the professional.

2. The same holds true for Hispanic Americans, whose culturally based beliefs and practices impact on the health and help-seeking behaviors and social needs of this population. Largely, illness is believed to be caused by a variety of factors, including the body's "hot/cold" imbalance, dislocation of parts of the body, magic or supernatural causes, strong emotional states, and envy. While seemingly at odds with materialistic scientific thinking favored in Western culture, these beliefs should not be ignored as irrelevant, but rather pursued actively, since they may be hidden to avoid ridicule. Whatever else practitioners do to remedy the situation, they must accept that prayer, religious rituals, use of amulets, use of herbs and spices, curanderismo, etc., will be employed as parallel treatment for the current problems and prevention of future ills.

3. Native Americans represent less than one percent of the United States population. Native Americans are culturally quite diverse. Their 507 federally recognized nations vary widely socioculturally with regard to economic resources and lifestyles. Traditionally, Native Americans cooperate with one another and share property. They emphasize living for the moment as opposed to future commitments or punctuality, which, by Western standards, impacts on their health and illness behaviors. Professionals working with this population will be successful and effective as they master these cultural points.

4. Although often grouped together, Asians and Pacific Islanders come from distinct countries with distinct societies and cultures. Nevertheless, most share the idea that the world is a vast entity and that each being within the world has a specific function. This reciprocal relationship with nature and a marked sense of an a priori dualism, like that represented by the yin and yang, form the base for very powerfully adhered-to traditional healing and social support systems. Traditional medical and healing practices, such as use of medicinal herbs, are widely used in the Asian-American community for the prevention and treatment of illness.

It is easy to see from these examples that American society is diverse, a trend that will continue. Therefore, it is not only professionals working primarily with an ethnic group different from their own who should be mindful of becoming culturally competent. Chances are one might have such professional encounters wherever one happens to be. An open mind on the subject is desirable. Also, chances are good that professionals will encounter colleagues from different cultures in the work place: the same considerations apply to such encounters.

References

National Center for Health Statistics. (1994). *Healthy people 2000 review, 1993.* Hyattsville, MD: Public Health Service.

Spector, R.E. (1991). *Cultural diversity in health and illness.* Norwalk, CT: Appleton and Lange.

U.S. Department of Health and Human Services. (1991). *Healthy people 2000: National health presentation and disease presentation objective.* Washington, DC: Public Health Service.

INDEX

Italics indicate illustrative or tabular material.

ABOUT THE AUTHORS

Pedro J. Lecca, Ph.D., R.Ph., LMSW, ACE Fellow, is the sixth Dean and Professor of the College of Pharmacy and Allied Health Professions at Texas Southern University in Houston. He held an appointment as Professor and Director of Health Care Specialization at the University of Texas at Arlington. He has also held an appointment as Assistant Commissioner of Mental Health/Mental Retardation and Alcoholism for the City of New York. He has received many honors, including a National Health Service Research Fellowship and an ACE Fellowship, and has been an Examiner on the 1997 Board of Examiners of the Malcolm Baldridge National Quality Award. Dr. Lecca has written more than twenty books on health, culture and interdisciplinary team practice, mental health, transcultural perceptions, minority health manpower, and preschoolers and substance abuse.

Ivan Quervalú, Ph.D., M.S.W., is Co-Director for Academic and New York City Programs for the Multicultural Education, Research, and Training Institute, Department of Psychiatry at Metropolitan Hospital Center. He is an Assistant Professor in Clinical Psychiatry for New York Medical College, where he teaches psychiatry to medical residents. He has written numerous manuscripts and produced videos on minority issues in health and mental health and has coordinated many cultural competency conferences, workshops, and seminars.

João V. Nunes, M.D., is Associate Medical Professor and Acting Chairman, Department of Behavorial Medicine, and Course Director of Behavorial Science at the City University of New York University Medical School/Sophie Davis School of Biomedical Education. He is also Medical Director of the Sleep Disorders Center at City College (CUNY) and Co-Principal Investigator of MERTI. He trained in Psychiatry and Child Psychiatry at Albert Einstein College of Medicine and in psychoanalysis at a New York University affiliate. He has received many honors during his tenure at New York Medical College and has published widely.

Hector F. Gonzalez, M.D., M.P.H., provides administrative and program support as well as health careers development services for the Center for Health Policy Development (CHPD) Inc. in San Antonio, Texas. He has also served as the first Director for the Texas Department of Health Border Health Office, as the interim director for the Communicable Diseases Section, and is Vaccine Preventable Disease Epidemiologist for the San Antonio Metropolitan Health District. He has provided extensive health care services and health care clinic management for migrant/community health centers in various South Texas rural communities, such as Crystal City. Lastly, he has also published, co-authored, and helped produce various manuscripts, papers, and a variety of grants.